THE POLITICAL IDENTITY OF
ANDREW MARVELL

The Political Identity of Andrew Marvell

edited by
Conal Condren and
A.D. Cousins

Scolar Press

Published by
SCOLAR PRESS
Gower Publishing Company Limited
Gower House
Croft Road
Aldershot
Hants GU11 3HR
England

Gower Publishing Company
Old Post Road
Brookfield
Vermont 05036
USA

British Library Cataloguing in Publication Data
The political identity of Andrew Marvell.
  1. Poetry in English. Marvell, Andrew, 1621–1678
  I. Condren, Conal II. Cousins, A.D.
  821.4

Library of Congress Cataloging-in-Publication Data
The Political identity of Andrew Marvell/edited by Conal Condren and A.D. Cousins.
    p. cm.
  Includes bibliographical references and index.
  ISBN 0–85967–818–0
  1. Marvell, Andrew, 1621–1678—Political and social views.
  2. Politics and literature—Great Britain—History—17th century.
  3. Political poetry, English—History and criticism. 4. Great
Britain—Politics and government—1660–1688. I. Condren, Conal.
II. Cousins, A. D.
PR3546.P65 1990
821′.4—dc20   90–38602
              CIP

ISBN 0–85967–818–0

Printed in Great Britain by
Billing & Sons Ltd, Worcester

Contents

Notes on contributors

Conal Condren is Associate Professor in Political Science at the University of New South Wales. He has published widely on the political thought of the Renaissance and early modern period and the theory of its interpretation. His most recent books are *The Status and Appraisal of Classic Texts*, Princeton University Press, 1985; and *George Lawson's Politica and the English Revolution*, Cambridge University Press, 1989.

A.D. Cousins is a Senior Lecturer in English at Macquarie University, New South Wales. He has published a number of articles on sixteenth and seventeenth-century English literature and is the author of *The Catholic Religious Poets from Southwell to Crashaw: A Critical History*, Sheed and Ward, London, 1990.

N.H. Keeble is Reader in English at the University of Stirling, Scotland, UK and has worked extensively on the political and religious contexts of seventeenth-century English literature. He is currently preparing a Calendar of the correspondence of Richard Baxter and is author of *Richard Baxter: Puritan Man of Letters*, Clarendon Press, 1982, and *The Literary Culture of Nonconformity* *in Later Seventeenth-Century England*, Leicester University Press, 1987. Dr. Keeble is a Fellow of the Royal Historical Society.

William Lamont has a personal chair at The University of Sussex. He has written prolifically on seventeenth-century religious and political history, most notably his trilogy of studies, *Marginal Prynne*, London, 1963; *Godly Rule*, London, 1969; and *Richard Baxter and the Millennium*, London, 1979.

Annabel Patterson is Professor of English and Literature, Duke University, North Carolina. She is one of the most distinguished of scholars working on the interface of literature and history in the early modern period. Her works include *Marvell and the Civic Crown*, Princeton University Press, 1978; *Censorship and Interpretation: The Conditions of Writing and Reading in Early Modern England*, University of Wisconsin Press, 1984; *Pastoral and Ideology: Virgil to Valéry*, Oxford University Press and University of California Press, 1987; and *Shakespeare and the Popular Voice*, Basil Blackwell, 1989.

Christopher Wortham is a Senior Lecturer in English at the University of Western Australia. He has worked extensively on early modern English literature, editing *Everyman* with Geoffrey Cooper, and, with David Ormerod, *A Text of Dr. Faustus*, University of West Australia Press, 1985. He is at present editing a volume of Marvell's poetry.

Steven Zwicker, Professor of English Literature, Washington University at St. Louis, is a scholar of Restoration English literature; his works include *Dryden's Political Poetry*, Brown University Press, 1972; *Politics and Language in Dryden's Poetry: The Arts of Disguise*, Princeton University Press, 1984; and, with Kevin Sharpe, *Politics of Discourse: The Literature and History of Seventeenth-Century England*, University of California Press, 1987.

Preface

The chapters in this volume represent a general confluence of ideas about Marvell rather than a single position. We did not consider constraining the essays into agreement or having them the same length, believing that the natures of the different topics on which contributors were asked to write required flexibility. The contributors were selected because of their expertise within a general field but were not asked to survey it as a whole; rather, they were asked (if they chose) to focus on Marvell's political identity through discussing work they considered representative of, or particularly significant within, a given area of Marvell studies.

We should first and foremost like to thank the contributors for their co-operation and professionalism, which have made the volume far easier to prepare than we had any right to expect. We should also like to thank Brian Last and Ellen Keeling of Scolar Press for their help and support, the University of North Carolina Press for permission to re-print material forming part of Professor Patterson's contribution, originally published in *Poems in Their Places*, ed. Neil Fraistat (1986), and Averil Condren for both invaluable sub-editorial advice and preparing the Index.

C.C.
A.D.C.

Introduction

Conal Condren and A.D. Cousins

A number of studies have recently examined what, in English literary criticism, has now come to be called the 'new historicism'.[1] Particularly valuable have been the studies by those practising a form of that historicism – despite the risk that the theorists of a critical movement may mythologize not only their own aims and methods but also those of preceding, or of other contemporary, movements. One such risk for theorists of the new historicism is that of inventing a conveniently monolithic 'old historicism'. After all, historicism is a porous concept or, to change the metaphor, a labyrinthine one and specific historicisms often share a marked resemblance to each other in practice, whilst of course there is something more substantial than such a resemblance when they share common theoretical postulates.

It is, however, not the purpose of this introduction to provide yet another new historicist manifesto or to consider what postulates might be shared by differing modes of historicist discourse. The first seems no longer necessary; the second is a task far beyond the scope of an introductory essay. What can be said is that a family of historicist forms of interpretative discourse to be found in departments of literature, philosophy, history and

politics, has in recent years encouraged interaction between scholars divided less by discipline than by institutional arrangement
and a division of curricula labours.

The fact that, as a discursive form, the new historicism has an
institutional context, compensates for some of the difficulties in
providing it with a precise theoretical identity. In institutional
terms it is a recognition of a gradual *rapprochement* between
historians, especially historians of ideas, and literary critics. This
has resulted in a pronounced willingness by each to borrow from
the other, causing some erosion of traditional institutional demarcations.

This is not to say that institutional demarcations have begun to
collapse altogether, or that they necessarily should (for if the
demarcations are not considered to be entirely arbitrary, then
crossing them must be seen as causing some degree of incoher-
ence). Neither is it to be unduly sanguine about interdisciplinary
exchange where demarcation seems theoretically unjustified. The
difficulty is that the more it is important for scholars to draw and
rely upon the work in neighbouring fields, the more vulnerable
they are to the consequences of time-lag. Christopher Hill's
important work seems almost to have achieved a foundational
authority for many cultural materialists working on seventeenth-
century English literature – a status distinctly at odds with its
much disputed standing in the seventeenth century historiographi-
cal mainstream, dominated as it has been for nearly two decades
now by 'revisionism'. That sort of discrepancy is likely to engen-
der a degree of prima-facie scepticism amongst historians when
confronted by cultural materialist analyses.[2] In a similar way, a
literary critic would be suspicious of any interdisciplinary-minded
historian who turned to the disputes between Cleanth Brooks and
Douglas Bush for a currently authoritative set of views on
Marvell's 'Horatian Ode'. Such practical difficulties, however, can
hardly be said to negate the great and mutual advantages that can
be gained from interdisciplinary co-operation where there is some
commonality of theoretical approach and where a subject matter
is also shared.

Marvell was one of the first to benefit from the alliance of a
'new' literary criticism and a 'new' historiography, in particular,
from the 'new' historicism which emerged over twenty years ago
within the interpretative community of political theorists. In some

respects, what has been happening over that time within literary criticism forms a counterpart to what has happened in political theory, which had until the late 1960s been strikingly Eliotesque or Leavisian in its attitude to its own canon of great texts. These, assembled into what was sometimes even called a 'great tradition', were treated as if, in dialogue with each other, they were obliged to deal with issues that we consider important. The study of this tradition was called the history of political thought and in most senses of that term, was shown to be strikingly unhistorical. Marvell (being a poet) has no place in that tradition, but in 1973 John Pocock dedicated a volume of his essays to Quentin Skinner, foremost amongst the 'new' historians of political thought, and to the Marvell scholar John Wallace.[3] Pocock, claiming that a revolution in the study of political thought had already taken place, correctly saw that Skinner and Wallace were engaged in very similar activities, albeit from the different institutional environments of intellectual history and of English literary criticism. The names on the dedicatory page symbolized the potential for seeing Marvell as a political thinker.

Since Wallace's *Destiny His Choice*,[4] some of that potential has certainly been fulfilled through attention to the political and intellectual contexts in which Marvell operated. The work has been largely that of historically-minded critics who have seen such contexts as a necessary means to understanding Marvell better as a poet. Although, no doubt, readings of some kinds have therefore been virtually marginalized, the overall result has been to enrich the possibilities of interpretation through the stimulation of questions that the more closed world of the old 'new' criticism would have considered irrelevant. The answers to those questions, nonetheless, have still largely focused on Marvell as a poet. This is understandable but it is also narrowing for he was, of course, much more than a poet – and he would be of interest to historians, especially to historians of political discourse, had he never written any poetry. The problem for the historian is not how to use the intellectual and political contexts to illuminate the poetry, but how to use the poetry, amongst Marvell's varied output, to illuminate seventeenth-century politics. Even if the poetry is left out of consideration, Marvell wrote more about politics than anything else; he had a manifestly political career and has left a remarkable and complex resource in his letters. He was a vigorous and courageous pamphleteer, living and dying on the edges of momentous political events. And there is indeed the poetry which raises the additional problem of how to place all facets of Marvell's work in perspective, a problem exacerbated by the difficulty of establishing a definitive canon. However, that set of problems aside, much of the poetry certainly written by Marvell (and more additionally attributed to him) is of a highly and explicitly political nature; further, much is pervaded by political allusion and/or intriguing political judgement. Appropriately, the very publication of his *Miscellaneous Poems* in 1681 was something of a political act, for by that year his name had become a political emblem for a cause. That, in turn, set a precedent for the subsequent attachment of his name to a range of causes, ideologies and political dispositions, which often had only a tenuous relationship with his own life and work. Establishing a firm political identity for such a protean figure raises a number of difficulties which, if not unique to Marvell, are in his case acute; we shall suggest that the problems, taken together, need to be approached through the intersecting perspectives of historians and literary critics.

Broadly speaking, the following six problems can be identified. The first (and to literary critics the most obvious) lies in what have been perceived since Eliot as the principal characteristics of the poetry: elusiveness, irony, paradoxicality and balance. Such terms pervade twentieth-century Marvell studies, the poetry frequently being seen as a constant challenge to the desire for the coherent and final reading of texts. Marvell studies have shown as well as any how ambiguity and associated phenomena, inherent (by chance or intention) or fabricated (by critical ingenuity or ignorance, by the discontinuities between the author's world and our own) have proved the life-blood of academic interpretation.

Second, a similar elusiveness has come to be perceived in the prose works – performances in public rhetoric, interventions in troublesome circumstances wherein a degree of circumspection, indirection and protective evasiveness might be expected. It has been widely agreed that Marvell's political identity, from the early poetry to the later prose, seems to be obscured by a continuous rhetorical obliquity.

This is related to a third problem, caused by the very diversity of discursive forms employed by Marvell. To some degree, each poetic mode will impose on a writer requirements of its own, perhaps to the point at which what can be expressed in one cannot entirely be conveyed in another. But if one is to deal with Marvell's political identity as a whole, the situation is obviously more difficult, for added to Marvell's variety of poetic modes are the differing modes of the letter and the tract. Insofar as these and the poetic modes cannot be reduced, each to the terms and conventions of the other, then it seems futile to expect in Marvell's writing the revelation of a neatly coherent identity. The principle of decorum, then, tends to compromise one's expectations of such an identity, and Marvell's own sense of decorum was pronounced. An additional complication is the question of the intertextual relationships conditioning Marvell's uses of those diverse modes.

Fourth, if these are problems created by a single figure's shifting among differing forms of discourse, so too do changing circumstances and his perceptions of them bring other complications. Whether or not the period of the English Civil Wars can properly be called that of the first of the great European revolutions (an hypothesis much debated of late) Marvell's times were ones of instability and dramatic change, as he and his contemporaries knew well enough. Just how far we can reasonably expect those who lived through such tumults not to alter their beliefs, attitudes and priorities, is a moot point. Tracing an identity across intellectual space and through time carries with it a temptation to reductionism – to take our priorities as determining *the* authentic voice, (the desire for a fixed identity seems to require such a voice); hence the temptation to abstract selections from the later Marvell to illuminate the earlier.

Yet whether we conclude that we can establish a relatively continuous or only a discontinuous political identity, in terms of what elements do we make such claims? Here there is a fifth problem, that of disentangling the variables suggestive of change or of continuity. We might isolate Marvell's specific affiliation within the political domain: for example, to country opposition to the monarchy, commitment to the Cromwellian commonwealth, civic humanism or to an embryonic Whig party. We might look for a more general pattern of abstract principles which his works seem to affirm, a constitutionalism perhaps, or a loyalism to any status quo. We might try to unearth a disposition independent of or antecedent to an articulated doctrine or principle. We might posit identity in terms of rhetorical posture, as Annabel

Patterson has, or suggest one in terms of a proclivity to use certain rhetorical techniques, as has Hodge.[5] Perceived discontinuity in terms of any one of those variables might not contradict continuity seen under the auspices of another. Unless such variables are kept distinct, however, and the differing analytic status of each is acknowledged (for they may be explicit within the texts or hypothesized by the interpreter) there is ample room for argument at cross-purposes, as the criticism of Marvell's works at times indicates. Indeed, insofar as any of those variables needs to be hypothetically postulated to render Marvell whole or to make his apparent changes explicable, there is always the danger of conjuring a myth of intellectual coherence from the interstices between his words. There is a thin line between interpreting a lacuna and inventing a voice; with a writer so adept at conceptual ellipsis, it is easily crossed.

Sixth, if the variables involved in establishing Marvell's political identity cause problems, so too does the defining concept of the political itself. In seventeenth-century England, the notion of the political domain was fluid, at times even fugitive. It could easily flow into the more firmly established realms of rhetoric, science, law and, above all, religion. Marvell's political identity, whatever else it is, is also in part a religious one. To say that means much more than accepting the idea that religion was a political issue in seventeenth-century England and that as a political animal Marvell held religious opinions. At one level, such an acceptance is trite; but at another, it seems to presuppose the political and the religious domains to have overly rigid identities. In fact, religious categories of argument seem to varying degrees to have permeated and shaped political ones. Thus a political allusion or image in Marvell can often properly be seen to have a religious resonance and a religious one often a political implication. For many of Marvell's contemporaries, it might be nearer the mark if one were to say that politics was a religious problem. Thus we can expect questions of political identity to spill into issues of religious identity, and this does not make the reader's task any easier, for religious discourse was itself various and complex. On some issues subtle nuances of doctrine divided Protestant sects; on others, Protestant and Catholic theology could be much as one. A Marvell seen to be placed in the relatively open context of such a politico-religious domain will be more difficult to define than one seen to be inhabiting a merely secular political context. If it means any-thing to state that Marvell was in part a writer of the 'English Revolution', then there is an intimate relationship between how he and this political context are conceived. If, as was normally the case a generation ago, the Revolution is prototypically under-stood as the first in a sequence of secular political upheavals (to be followed by the American, the French and the Russian Revolutions), then the readings of Marvell are likely to be pulled in a secularizing and neoterically political direction. If conversely, as some are now claiming, the Revolution should be seen more as the last of the European Wars of Religion, an upheaval in which the nature and direction of the Reformation was at issue, then the identity of Marvell is *ipso facto* likely to be recouched – the politics becoming less secular and more fluid, the terms of their specification less familiar.

The conceptual lacunae that have been seen as so characteristic of Marvell's work have always been invitations to forms of contex-tualization. But with so many difficulties in the way of establishing his historical and hence political identity, it is not surprising to find both critics and historians pouring into his works categories of their own time, by-passing some of the intricacies and alien characteristics of his. Attempts to specify Marvell's political identity have been subject to a domesticating drift through the use of what Frank Kermode has called 'strategies of accommodation'.[6] This has been the case even where the interpreter has not placed Marvell in the context of an English Revolution seen as a harbinger of the modern world. Marvell was accommodated to the High Church cultural values of T.S. Eliot; his image gave way to Wallace's rather different 'conservative' loyalist. Wallace's image stood in contrast to that which had been fashioned by a nineteenth-century liberal constitutionalist tradition of historiography which had made Marvell something of a Liberal hero; it stood in counter-point also to an understanding of the English Revolution in the progressive idiom of Tawney and Hill. Writing at the uncertain nexus of liberal and Marxist traditions, writers such as Ashcraft and Chernaik have created a 'radical', or 'liberal' or 'left-wing' Marvell.[7] Each designation in its turn has involved some sacrifice of historicity – which might not have been a problem for new critics and deconstructionists. Such sacrifices may, to an extent be unavoidable, and may involve gains as well as losses. Whether the gains are considered adequate compensation depends on one's understanding of historicity. This returns us to the point that historicism itself remains a porous category, with variable tolerances of anachronism and conceptions of context. Perhaps it is best seen, especially in Marvell studies, as a disposition rather than as the cut and dried doctrine that the suffix – 'ism' might suggest.

The heart of the matter might be described in this way: the less vague the categories in terms of which Marvell might be given a specific political identity (for example, country whig, commonwealthsman, engager) the more of his texts are likely to slip through our fingers – time and intellectual space both playing their subversive parts. The more general and open the categories (puritan, conservative, liberal) the less can be established by relying on them. Discouraging though this may seem, it need not result in silence or in a quiescent acceptance of diversity. We need be stultified only if we assume that a political identity has to be fixed, like Lovelace's grasshopper trapped in the ice, or defined by an essence unaffected by time.

In the face of the problems listed, it is perhaps more appropriate to see Marvell's political identity in terms, as it were, of a family resemblance. After all, Marvell, insofar as we know him, is a shorthand term for a various family of texts from which we customarily hypothesize there to have been a unified informing mind. Wittgenstein developed the notion of a family resemblance as a metaphor to guide our understanding of language.[8] Just as we recognize someone as a member of a family, not by a fixed visible essence but through possession of a contingent though finite range of features, so we understand certain phenomena to be languages. Marvell's texts, then, and those doubtfully attributed to him may be seen as pages in a family album. The only Marvell whose identity we are able to establish is that of a family of texts having a range of features, shifting over time, as it were, from grandparent to grandchild. Such a composite picture would seem to be best described from the intersecting approaches of different scholars. In this way the chances of a myth of coherence are less likely, and texts of the kinds that do not fit the priorities of one interpreter are not, we hope, evaded.

In the essays that follow, issues of context and intertext, of religion's interaction with politics, are variously taken up in relation to Marvell's verse. The essays on the poetry suggest, among other things, Marvell's interest in examining – from a distinctly Protestant perspective, if not from that perspective alone – heroic virtue as a political presence in or absence from English society (Marvell seeming in his poems to associate its presence with social unity and renewal, its absence with their opposites). Christopher Wortham, considering how the three Cromwell poems 'document the beginning, middle and end of Cromwell's ascendancy in the form of an accidental triptych', traces the ways in which those poems 'record the process by which Marvell came first to admire Cromwell, with some hesitation and almost grudgingly; then to revere Cromwell as an elder statesman; and finally to lament his passing as the end of hope for a new order in England.' In reading Marvell's images of Cromwell he focuses on the poet's use of Pindaric as well as of Horatian rhetorical strategies, on his juxtaposition of Hobbesian ideas with chiliasm, on his interplay of scripture with ancient myth – and on the discontinuities no less than on the continuities among poems which emerge from such diverse occasions.

Discussing 'Upon Appleton House', A.D. Cousins argues the poem to be 'at once an appropriation and, theologically as well as politically, a comprehensive rewriting of the country house poem', in which 'Marvell's persona, drawing on or paralleling a main strand of Calvin's theology, represents Fairfax not merely as someone whose active virtue makes the little world of his estate . . . a perfect moral commonwealth, but as someone whose regenerate private life will enable him – through the most immediately consequential product of his regenerate state, his daughter, Mary – to contribute significantly to the renewal of a devastated England that has only recently emerged from [a 'fall' into] civil war'. Steven N. Zwicker, however, when examining 'The Last Instructions' – Marvell's verse satire on the manifest unregeneracy of Restoration politics – relates in particular the poem's unheroic image of Charles II to the intimate 'relations throughout this poem, and in the culture more broadly, between sexual appetite and political corruption.' Zwicker suggests that

> We have come to associate the court of Charles II with bawdry and heartless licence; but there is nothing in the slightest licentious in the high-minded verse that celebrates this sexual restoration. At its centre were lineage and political continuity; from the promise of the royal line issued a series of topics that bound sexual fertility to those very

qualities which the king had pronounced on his return home: liberality, generosity, and forgiveness.

But, he goes on to argue, '[b]y the mid–1660s that bacchic moment in which the king and nation first embraced had long ago disappeared; the failure of the king's legitimate sexual abundance was only too obvious; and the morals of the royal family were searched for explanations of that failure. Licence and fornication had, by the mid 1660s, an urgent moral and political significance.' Within that context, Zwicker proposes, Marvell's verse satire contradicts Waller's effusive 'Instructions to a Painter' primarily by focusing 'on enormity and appetite', on the connection in Restoration politics between 'sexual greed and political corruption.' It is demonstrated that those points of focus are basic to the images of Henry Jermyn, Anne Hyde, and Castlemaine – images that are reinforced by the poem's account of de Ruyter and counterpointed by its celebration of Douglas, which emphasizes his sexual as well as heroic virtue. It is shown that those portraits point directly toward the satire's portrait of Charles II, and Zwicker remarks that Marvell's depiction of the king (prior to the envoy) 'finally argues England herself [to be] matter simply to excite and relieve the king's desires.' He concludes:

> The restoration of Charles II in 1660 had twinned hopes of stability and abundance with the person of the king; that his private pleasures and civic care should have proved fruitless and negligent was a conclusion to which Marvell had come by the summer of 1667, and to which he gave, in *The Last Instructions*, a brilliant, implacable, and damaging form.

The prose works of Marvell's later life reveal some continuity with the earlier poetry. Refracted by the shift from poetry to prose and focused anew by an increasing sense of political disappointment in the restored House of Stuart, this continuity consists principally in Marvell's engaged political protestantism and the adaptation of the discursive techniques of poetry to the requirements of publishing in a dangerous world.

William Lamont addresses explicitly Marvell's little-discussed defence of the non-conformist minister, John Howe, demonstrating it to be a reliable guide to Marvell's precise religious location during his final years. For, although it is accepted that Marvell must clearly be counted as one who became opposed to Restoration orthodoxy and its politics, the opposition of which he was a part was as divided and fluid as it was substantial. Partly taking issue with Hill and Chernaik, and also with all who see Marvell's balance as unqualified, Lamont shows that the simple association of Marvell with the religious views of men such as Milton and Dr. John Owen will not do, despite the former being a friend, the latter a sometime influential chaplain to Cromwell. They were both willing sectarians and independents and Marvell took the trouble to defend Howe quite unequivocally against the sorts of views they held. Marvell can be seen consequently as more closely allied with less willing non-conformists such as Howe, Baxter and Humfrey – a point which on its own makes Marvell's views more consistent with the fact that he was a conforming M.P.[9] Such people on either side of the thin line that separated conformity and non-conformity wanted comprehension for non-conformists, tolerance for sectarians.

As Lamont shows, taking a cue from Margarita Stocker's work, the divisions within English Protestantism were vital enough to make the often cautious Marvell go to print. What was at stake was the reading of the nature of the Restoration and the role of secular authority in religious affairs.

Of particular significance was the image of the early Christian church, through which those contemporary issues were being discussed – which was not merely a matter of tactical evasiveness. Prior to the Reformation, Marsilius of Padua in his *Defensor Pacis* (1324) made the early church and the reign of Constantine central to debate about politico-religious corruption and the rise of episcopacy; and Constantine was to remain a *topos* throughout Reformation discussions of those matters. The question was still important for Marvell and his contemporaries as to whether Constantine (for some a *figura* for Cromwell, for others perhaps for the restored Charles) was, by joining Church and State, responsible for the seeds of corruption which were to germinate into the medieval papacy.

Lamont argues *inter alia* that Marvell, like Baxter and Howe, retained a faith in a magisterially directed Protestantism for considerably longer than separatists such as Owen, who blamed the Emperor directly for corruption of the church. Moreover, in principle, Owen, unlike Howe, believed in the firm separation of Church and State – a disestablishment of a national church, not comprehension within it. Those differences (amongst others) are considerable and, analogically, their occlusion in Marvell studies has resulted in something like calling Trotsky a Stalinist on the grounds that he was a Communist.

Going to print to co-opt the symbolism of early Christianity was not necessary for non-conformists or separatists, sharing much-used channels of communication. Indeed, print was very much an optional consideration for seventeenth-century writers, for it meant the sacrifice of intimacy and relative control over the extent of an audience. *Ipso facto* it required adjusted strategies of argument and suggests a differing range of reasons for the sort of anonymity of which Marvell was fond.

This is a point which all the writers on the late prose works and Annabel Patterson, on the final publication of the preceding manuscript poetry, develop in their own ways. In the context of discursive medium, however, N.H. Keeble is able to show that the constituency letters have a peculiar and central place. On the one hand, they are private manuscripts directed to a specific and small audience with fairly precise requirements of the author. On the other, they were always potentially public. As Keeble argues, the intercepted letter was the most important source of information for the authorities against dissidents, and L'Estrange's network of hunters and gatherers was no less efficient than had been its parent body under Thurloe during the Commonwealth, as Marvell would have known full well. What Archbishop Ussher had referred to in his correspondence as 'slippery times and dangerous days'[10] had become no less slippery or dangerous since Civil War and Restoration. It is the literary consequence of this almost ingrained epistolary reticence which Keeble explores. At one level, Marvell's voice by his very position as a member of Parliament is a political one and some of the subject matter is potentially explosive. At another, the narrative blandness, the flow of what seems to be randomly listed snippets of information and the formal subservience of authorial persona to constituency duty, conspire to distance Marvell from his text and relieve him of responsibility for what he relates. In this way, the letters become as capable a means for the shrewd construction of an authorial self as do the poems.

Similarly, the letters constitute, as it were, a rehearsal for having printed his most famous political tracts, the *Essay on General*

Councils and the *Growth of Popery and Arbitrary Government*, in which Marvell poses as a mere relater of events. Conal Condren concentrates on the latter though noting differences between it and its companion piece of the previous year, which Lamont also discusses. The comparisons reinforce by a different route Lamont's claims about the rhetorical significance of early Christianity and about Marvell's understanding of the Reformation and of the character of English politics.

The *Account of Popery* discusses contemporary history directly rather than at a considerable chronological remove, and in Condren's essay it is claimed that the appeal in the work to Charles as a latter day Constantine is specious and protective. All faith in Godly princes seems to have gone. Not surprisingly, going public required anonymity.

Condren's argument, having one starting point in the recent work of Jonathan Scott, is that the message is clear and deliberately inciting and that it seems to place Marvell finally close to those who feared that the head of the Church of England was undoing what was left of the Reformation. In exploiting anti-Catholic hostility Marvell was invoking Civil War memory; Condren argues that it is particularly misleading to see Marvell as a moderate harbinger of the 1688 Revolution and the Liberal-Whig ethos of the eighteenth century. It is, however, precisely in the context of an extreme and very public message that Marvell exhibits extraordinary mastery of the protective strategies of indirection and symbolic suggestiveness and a (feigned) balance for which his poetry is famous. A second starting point for this essay, then, is provided by Annabel Patterson's emphasis on rhetorical strategy throughout Marvell's career, and by Lamont's work on Baxter's disenchantment with a Godly Prince in Stuart guise after so much Constantinian promise in Cromwellian dress.

The symbolic value of the printed word is taken up in another way in Annabel Patterson's concluding essay. The notoriety of the *Account of Popery* and the heroic potential generated by Marvell's sudden death were at least some aid to a divided, desperate and demoralized opposition to Charles II in 1681. If direct opposition was becoming ever more dangerous and a re-opening of hostilities realistic only for a few, symbolic action could still be undertaken. Patterson suggests that the publication of the *Miscellaneous Poems* must be seen as just such an act; and if it is, both the choice of poems and their ordering constitute a coherent political statement. The elaboration and celebration of values Marvell had taken to be above all Protestant and English, which were displayed through his images of Civil War heroes, are given a new force as a public statement in 1681, especially as they culminate, she argues, in an image of active republicanism. If this was not Marvell's own arrangement, concludes Patterson, it was the work of one who knew the politics and poetry of Marvell extremely well. It is perhaps symptomatic of how much of Marvell has been lost that Margoliouth rearranged it all, not seeing the political wood for the aesthetic trees – a point that Wortham makes also at the outset.

The politics of the *Miscellaneous Poems* captures in miniature the themes and variation of political identity we have sought to explore in these essays, as indeed it must. For the *Poems* not only include the works discussed in the early essays, but Marvell's name upon the title page capitalized on the reputation of the satirist, and the volume appeared in the immediate wake of the last prose and its notoriety. To use Marvell's own favoured theatre imagery, it can be seen as the final act in the fashioning of a political identity and it comes complete with typically Marvellian irony and an author off-stage. The title-page belies a political coherence, the author's death masks another's action in his name. But it also casts Marvell to play a continuing part in the theatre of political heroism. The assessment of posthumous exploitation is a task beyond the scope of these essays but it is one that needs to be predicated on the recapture of the elusive identity to which they have been addressed.

Notes

1. See, for example, Louis Montrose, 'Renaissance Literary Studies and the Subject of History', *English Literary Renaissance*, 16 (1986), pp. 5–12; Jean E. Howard, 'The New Historicism in Renaissance Studies', ibid., pp. 13–43; Kevin Sharpe and Steven Zwicker, 'Politics of Discourse: Introduction', in *idem*, eds., *Politics of Discourse: The Literature and History of Seventeenth-Century England*, Berkeley, Los Angeles, London: University of California Press, 1987, pp. 1–20; Hayden White, 'New Historicism: A Comment', *The New Historicism* ed. H. Aram Veeser, New York and London, 1989, pp.

293–302; Stanley Fish, 'Commentary: The Young and the Restless', ibid., pp. 303–315.

2. As, for example, in Kevin Sharpe's criticism of Margaret Heine-mann's study of Middleton: see his *Criticism and Compliment: the Politics of Literature in the England of Charles I*, Cambridge: Cambridge University Press, 1987, p. 33.

3. J.G.A. Pocock, *Politics, Language and Time*, London: Methuen, 1973.

4. John M. Wallace, *Destiny his Choice: The Loyalism of Andrew Marvell*, Cambridge: Cambridge University Press, 1968.

5. Annabel Patterson, *Marvell and the Civic Crown*, Princeton: Princeton University Press, 1978; R.I.V. Hodge, *Foreshortened Time: Andrew Marvell and Seventeenth Century Revolutions*, Cambridge: D.S. Brewer, 1978.

6. F. Kermode, *The Classic*, London: Faber and Faber, 1975, p. 39ff.

7. Warren Chernaik, *The Poet's Time: Politics and Religion in The Work of Andrew Marvell*, Cambridge: Cambridge University Press, 1983; Richard Ashcraft, *Revolutionary Politics and Locke's Two Treatises of Government*, Princeton: Princeton University Press, 1987.

8. Ludwig Wittgenstein, *The Philosophical Investigations*, trans. G.E.M. Anscombe, Oxford: Blackwell, 1953, 1968 edn., paras. 65–7.

9. Marvell's name does not, for example, appear in the detailed list of occasional or non-conforming Restoration MPs drawn up by Douglas Lacey, *Dissent and Parliamentary Politics in England, 1661–1689*, New Jersey: Rutgers University Press 1969, Appendix II. In a marked number of respects, Marvell's views seem very close to those of George Lawson, (1598–1678) conforming minister of the Church of England, theologian and political theorist, whose arguments were taken up and popularized by John Humfrey, perhaps John Locke and later Daniel Defoe.

10. The expression provides the felicitous title for Amanda Capern's Ph.D. thesis on Ussher, University of New South Wales, 1990, unpublished.

1 Marvell's Cromwell Poems: an Accidental Triptych

Christopher Wortham

Introduction

Marvell's political poems of the Interregnum were written during a period when England lurched from crisis to crisis, when it seemed to many who lived through its upheavals that the world had been turned upside down.[1] To some, the times signalled that chaos was come again; to others, that the second coming was at hand: but, for many, there was only uncertainty and confusion. Whatever political opinions or apprehensions there may have been in England during the 1650s, there was one irreducible fact that confronted all shades of opinion – the ascendancy of Oliver Cromwell.

Marvell's three major poems on the subject of Cromwell – 'An Horatian Ode on Cromwell's Return from Ireland,' 'The First Anniversary of the Government under O{liver} C{romwell}', and 'A Poem on the Death of O{liver} C{romwell}' – give witness to that ascendancy. The 'Horatian Ode' marks precisely the beginning of Cromwell's emergence as unassailable leader, recording Marvell's perceptions of him at the moment when the first chairman of the new civilian authority, the Council of State, had also just become the military commander-in-chief. Up to this moment, Cromwell had been second-in-command to Thomas, Lord Fairfax, but Fairfax declined to lead the invasion of Scotland, choosing instead to go into retirement, and so his inevitable successor was Cromwell, freshly home from the campaign in Ireland. Equally precisely, 'The First Anniversary' marks the pivotal moment when, late in 1654, Cromwell's first attempt at establishing an elected body to balance the power of his adventitious *de facto* monarchy under the Protectorate is unmistakably faltering. The third poem's occasion speaks for itself: it has been written not only on the subject of the death of Oliver Cromwell; but hard upon the death, and before Cromwell's son Richard has yet had the opportunity to prove himself. The elegy is a public poem, but private to the extent that it has been written in the first wave of personal grief; it is not a reflective piece looking back on Cromwell's death across an objectifying distance of intervening time, and yet it shows that Marvell has already begun to see his own earlier poems on Cromwell as part of an irrevocable past. Taken together, then, these three poems document the beginning, middle and end of Cromwell's ascendancy in the form of an accidental triptych. Although the textual transmission of these three poems is not a straightforward issue, there is no evidence that they have reached us in substantially revised or expurgated form.[2]

In the three poems Marvell addresses himself to giving an account of the personality, the political attitudes, and the progress of Oliver Cromwell, and yet the poems tell us at least as much about Andrew Marvell as they do about Cromwell. What emerges is the portrait of Marvell himself as an essentially peaceable man living through a convulsive civil war and its unquiet aftermath; and only someone who has lived through a civil war may be able to appreciate fully the tensions set up by such an experience. For us, renegotiating the Cromwell poems from across the centuries, it is especially important to be conscious not only of our own limitations in experience but also of the distortions wrought by our own vantage point of a safe distance: nothing changes so much as a political crisis in retrospect.

All three Cromwell poems are occasional pieces. As such, however, they are paradoxical, adhering to a social milieu that is somewhat at odds with the political milieu. A lot of occasional poetry was written during the years 1640 to 1660, but most of it came from the conservative side of politics. Owing poetic allegiance to Ben Jonson – whose later career was closely associated with the royal court and court values – and political allegiance to the Royalist party, the writers of occasional poetry used this mode to include a personal address in the poem's title or its dedication in order to proclaim shared attitudes and beliefs. During the years when Royalists were most embattled, the occasional poem afforded solace to the one or the few to whom it was addressed and amounted to a declaration of loyalty by its author. Among the more successful poets in this mode are Lovelace, Herrick, Fane, Benlowes, and, of course, Andrew Marvell. Among the many kinds of irony in Marvell's poetry, one that is very strong but has been little noticed is that which places him socially and culturally with his political antagonists. His occasional poems on Cromwell and his interstitial poems addressed to Lord Fairfax during the Appleton House period (1650–52) show Marvell's somewhat tricky accommodation between his politics and his poetry.

In the case of all three poems, occasion is enhanced in its poetic commemoration through the use of appropriate genre (ode, panegyric and elegy, respectively). What is remarkable is that in each case the appropriate genre does not quite fit. Nevertheless, there is no basis for the common critical opinion that Marvell uses genre subversively in the Cromwell poems. To suggest that Marvell has not really come to praise Cromwell but to bury him is wilful misreading or, at best, an over-reading of what is a much more subtle dynamic in the poems.

When Marvell came to write the first of his Cromwell poems he had already lived in and travelled through Europe at a time when the continent was dangerously unstable, racked with tensions that had been expressed from Sweden to Spain in intermittent warfare throughout the thirty years of his own lifetime. This foreign warfare had been rounded off at home with a civil war of unprecedented ferocity which had but lately culminated in a form of government hitherto unknown in England, unthought-of and almost unthinkable until it became a sudden fact: both the war and its conclusion had taken England by surprise. By the year 1650 Cromwell must have represented the main hope for stability to many who did not necessarily agree with him on all political points. To Andrew Marvell, the decisive figure of Cromwell appears to have been especially attractive. In the opening section of the 'Horatian Ode', Marvell seems to be identifying himself so closely with Cromwell that it is very hard to tell which of the two is the subject of the first eight lines. What Marvell's three Cromwell poems do is record the process by which Marvell came first to admire Cromwell, with some hesitation and almost grudgingly; then to revere Cromwell as elder statesman; and finally to lament his passing as the end of hope for a new order in England.

'Much to the Man is due'

W.B. Yeats's remark that 'We make out of the quarrel with others, rhetoric, but the quarrel with ourselves poetry' has with some justice been applied also to Marvell.[3] In choosing the Horatian genre, Marvell knew what he was doing. The very mention of Horace in his title proclaims Marvell's concern simultaneously with classical humanism and with current politics at a time when extreme attitudes in politics in sub-literary propaganda writing in prose and verse seemed to threaten humanism and all it stood for.

The much-discussed vein of irony in Marvell's 'Horatian Ode' was already there in the genre he took as his model and in the poet Marvell named as its masterly practitioner, as was the complexity of mood. A modern translator has said of Horace:

> In the Odes Greek sophistication and melancholy alternate with Italian vigour and rhetoric, and behind both there lurks a personal irony, the intensity of which it is hard to gauge. Sometimes it gleams dubiously in a word. One has the impression of a strong but elusive personality, one whose solidity is enhanced rather than diminished by surface inconsistencies . . .[4]

Much the same may be said of Marvell, but it is in political situation that the two poets are, perhaps, most similar. Both had been on the wrong side in a civil war and it seems probable that, like Horace of the Odes, Marvell had already begun to find favour with a magnanimous former enemy, for within a few months of composing the 'Horatian Ode' Marvell would enjoy the privileged position of tutor to Maria Fairfax. To what extent Marvell's irony is self-directed is a hard matter to determine and one may only begin to understand the direction of irony in the 'Horatian Ode' by finding for the poem an overall sense of direction.

The poem's outward purpose is to mark Cromwell's return from Ireland as an occasion of dignity and relief, if not rejoicing. To extract a reading that is thoroughly subversive and hostile to Cromwell one has to ignore some plain speaking or to assert that it is not what it is,[5] though one is nevertheless aware of contrarieties within the poem. Internal contexts become important for discerning Marvell's stance. For example, readers have noted that someone nominated as the scourge of God is not necessarily a good man but such readers have too easily ignored the contextualizing couplet that follows:

> 'Tis Madness to resist or blame
> The force of angry Heavens flame:
> And, if we would speak true,
> Much to the Man is due . . .
>
> (lines 25–28)

Within a further two lines of this passage, Cromwell is described as having lived quietly until called to public office and shortly afterwards as having come to power because it is a law of nature that the weak 'must make room/Where greater Spirits come' (lines 43–44). However much we may doubt that the Irish could ever have confessed.

> How good he is, how just,
> And fit for highest Trust:
>
> (lines 79–80)

after the merciless drubbing they received at Cromwell's hands, the fact remains that Marvell attributes such sentiments to them. As if to allay any possible doubt about Cromwell's benignity as military leader of the new republic, Marvell represents his homecoming from Ireland as a process of decorous and ceremonial obedience:

> He to the *Commons Feet* presents
> A *Kingdome*, for his first years rents:
> And, what he may, forbears
> His Fame, to make it theirs:
> And has his Sword and Spoyls ungirt,
> To lay them at the *Publick's* skirt.
>
> (lines 85–90)

Marvell constructs Cromwell as incarnating the old Roman virtues of the republic, in his *virtu* combining modesty with *gravitas*. Marvell's future hopes for Cromwell are tentatively expressed in over-confident assertion, but it is worth noting that the limits to presumption are not visited upon Cromwell but upon England:

> What may not then our *Isle* presume
> While Victory his Crest does plume!
> What may not others fear
> If thus he crowns each Year!

> (lines 97–100)

It takes a lot of contortion to read all of these instances of praise as being ironically directed. The title to the poem strongly implies too that Cromwell's return is an occasion to celebrate. The moving and, no doubt, sincere lines on Charles I's deportment at the scene of his execution are made more rather than less remarkable for being in contrast to or as a cross-current underlying the theme of celebration. But, for the moment captured in the poem, all that lies in the past. The Cromwell of the 'Horatian Ode' is the man of action who pauses briefly in England between his return from Ireland and his promised campaign against the Scots. In that way Cromwell is Marvell's true protagonist: by contrast, the role of Charles I is a passive one, of suffering, and of dignity, but he is yesterday's man. Marvell is by no means devoid of human feeling, but in the 'Horatian Ode' he is writing a political poem that subordinates personal views to public issues.

The form of the 'Horatian Ode', is a complex and fascinating matter in its own right. In this discussion, we may discern in Marvell, as in Horace, echoes of the Pindaric dialectic, but only echoes. The Pindaric ode had already been partially recovered by Spenser in his thalamic poems, by Ben Johnson in his 'Ode on the Death of Sir H. Morison', and by Milton in his magnificent 'Ode on the Morning of Christ's Nativity'. Within a few years Abraham Cowley would publish a whole volume of *Pindaric Odes*[6] but the Pindaric dialectic is preserved in Marvell's poem more through its *personae* than through its outward form. Marvell's section on Charles I should probably be seen as constituting an antistrophe or, to give it Jonson's English term, 'counter-turn', it allows the contrary view, but without disrupting the unity of the poem.

The third, synthesizing *persona* is, of course, the poet himself. Marvell's ode, whether Pindaric or Horatian or hybridized, is characterized by the proclamatory voice of the poet: as I have already suggested, it is a poem that in its very title self-consciously declares itself to be a poem and to be the work of a sentient, deliberatively-inclined poet. As an ode it is quite the opposite of that other form of political poem so common during the Civil War period, the ballad or pseudo-ballad, for the ballad is anonymous and the pseudo-ballad shelters behind a self-effacing affectation of anonymity.[7] From the start, Marvell's 'Horatian Ode' has that 'strong but elusive personality' we have previously noticed and its personality is largely the poet's. 'The forward youth' with whom the ode begins, and who reluctantly 'must now forsake his muses dear', must surely be identified with the poet himself. Or partly: the eight introductory lines voice a conventional reluctance *topos*, though in an unusual way. For whereas Milton uses this *topos* to admit himself to the poem in 'Lycidas' and Ben Jonson uses it similarly in his elegy on Shakespeare, Marvell evades the first person singular and neither here nor anywhere else in the poem does he employ it. As we read on we become aware of Marvell's implicit comparison of himself with Cromwell. In Cromwell's departure from the obscurity of private life for politics and war, Marvell seems to find a model for his own removal from private poetry to the public poem he is now in the act of writing.

I think that here is a vital piece of evidence in our discovery of the political identity of Andrew Marvell. In times of crisis it is not unusual for citizens to look to a person rather than to policies for salvation and deliverance. Much of the political poetry and the polemical writing of the time indicates that the Civil War was no exception: while there were coherent political positions being argued by numerous groups within the three main sectors of the King's party, the Parliamentarians and the Army, loyalties were often personal. Marvell's friend, Richard Lovelace, for example, seems to have been imbued with the political theories of Sir Robert Filmer and was probably an intimate of the Great Tew circle, but in the stormy seas of the Civil War he simply put his faith in the King. There is little indication in Marvell's poetry before the 'Horatian Ode' to suggest that he had reached any sense of commitment to ideas or to ideas above personalities. That came much later, in the relatively quiet waters of his membership of Parliament after the Restoration of the monarchy. In 1650, Marvell was looking to someone rather than to a set of ideas to rescue England from its current perils. Certainly, many of Cromwell's political (as distinct from military) actions up to that point had been dictated by exigency rather than by careful long-range planning or ideology. In the 'Horatian Ode', Marvell is not identifying himself with Cromwell the political thinker but with Cromwell the leader and man of action, the man most likely to pull England through its current crisis.

And yet the 'Horatian Ode' is not in any way a poem of slavish or sycophantic adulation. It is full of subtle complexities that prevent a simple or even straightforward response. The question is how to place these complexities in context in order to render them intelligible. As R.I.V. Hodge has put it in one of the most penetrating recent studies of Marvell: 'The poem does not need a new interpretation so much as a new context, or a renewed sense of it as a political poem growing out of Marvell's deep involvement with the issues of the age.'[8] To place the poem in political context is not to reduce it to something less than itself or to dismiss the many and diversely-directed ironies that contribute to its complexities.

This poem addresses itself to both the theoretical and the practical issues of the age. First and foremost, it treats Cromwell as an astonishing and extraordinary political phenomenon, as someone who had come from the unlikely origin of

> . . . his private Gardens, where
> He liv'd reserved and austere
>
> (lines 29–30)

to prominence among his own factious party as he

> Did thorough his own Side
> His fiery way divide.
>
> (lines 15–16)

There is no debate in the poem as to whether the republic *should* exist, only the affirmation that, given its existence, there is no one better equipped to rule than Cromwell:

> Nor yet grown stiffer with Command,
> But still in the *Republick's* hand:

> How fit he is to sway
> That can so well obey.

(lines 81–84)

So much for the pragmatic necessity to have a man like Cromwell in charge of England. It remains to be seen whether the 'Horatian Ode' hints at any theoretical basis for supporting Cromwell.

For the political ideas behind the 'Horatian Ode', we have only the 'Horatian Ode' itself to work from. Marvell has left no prose writings from that period and the other politically-connected poems from about that time – the elegies on Villiers and Hastings, together with the commendatory verses to Lovelace, coming a year or more before the 'Horatian Ode' and 'Tom May's Death' coming some months after it – are too problematical in their own several ways to tell us much that is reliable.[9] However, the 'Horatian Ode' offers some indications towards one system of ideas in particular, that of Thomas Hobbes.

Connections between Marvell and Hobbes have been seen before, but to my knowledge only a few parallels with Hobbes's thought have been noticed in the 'Horatian Ode'.[10] Much more effort has gone into establishing the political ideas of the poem by tracing parallels in the early imperial Rome of Horace's time and deducing from them Marvell's opinions as being either straightforwardly or ironically referenced to classical sources.[11] I would not suggest that the 'Horatian Ode' is a Hobbesian set-piece but I am sure that the voice of Hobbes is at least as strong as many of the others that have been heard in this poem and that it needs to be identified as a corrective.

The last eight lines of the 'Horatian Ode' constitute a conclusion or epilogue in which Marvell addresses Cromwell directly. Following a restatement of Cromwell's *virtu* as an indefatigable warrior and an expression of confidence in his righteousness, Marvell ends by reminding Cromwell, rather unnecessarily one would have thought, of the way he must work in the world:

> But thou, the Wars and Fortunes son,
> March indefatigably on:
>   And for the last effect
>   Still keep thy Sword erect:
> Besides the force it has to fright
> The spirits of the shady Night,

The same *Arts* that did *gain*
A *Pow'r* must it *maintain*.

(lines 113–120)

The sentiment contained in the final couplet is something of a commonplace and has been variously attributed to Sallust, Machiavelli and Anthony Ascham.[12] Commonplace or not, it is a significant summary of Marvell's attitude to the situation facing Cromwell in mid-1650 and a precise source may be both more remote and more immediate than those already suggested. The remote source is Thucydides; the immediate one, Thomas Hobbes, his translator.

The 'Horatian Ode' is imbued with Hobbes's way of looking at the world. But, to appreciate the nuances of the epilogue to the 'Horatian Ode', we should consider Hobbes in relation to Thucydides. Hobbes translated Thucydides' *History of the Peloponnesian War* long before he made any major excursion of his own into writing about politics. Hobbes's Thucydides first appeared in 1629 and was an immediate success, being reprinted in 1634 and 1648[13]; it was widely known in Marvell's circle of social and literary acquaintance.

One passage is particularly instructive. In a speech attributed to Pericles, urging the Athenians to treat no further with the Spartans, Pericles makes his auditors aware of hard political reality:

> You must not think the question is now of your liberty and servitude only. Besides the loss of your rule over others, you must stand the danger you have contracted by offence given in the administration of it. Nor can you now give it over: for already your government is in the nature of a tyranny, which is both unjust for you to take up and unsafe to lay down.[14]

Exactly what Hobbes meant by 'tyranny' at this time is not certain, the Greek term could be more neutral than English usage; but there does not seem to be any ground for supposing that he had changed his opinion when he wrote the *De Cive* (1642), some twelve years later. So, lest it be assumed that Marvell was recalling these lines from Hobbes's Thucydides with opprobrious implications for Cromwell in the final couplet to the 'Horatian Ode', we should bear in mind that in the English version of the *De Cive*, which Hobbes himself later possibly translated the headnote to Chapter VII contains the declaration 'That a tyranny is not a diverse state from a legitimate monarchy.'[15] The only difference between monarchy and tyranny in Hobbes's view is the way in which a particular sovereign is popularly perceived.[16] It may well be that in the 'Horatian Ode' Marvell chose to find praise for Cromwell even from the most unlikely quarter of the subjugated Irish (lines 73–84) precisely to deflect accusations that Cromwell had become a tyrant.[17]

A defence against any accusation of tyranny, however, would seem to be Marvell's second line of defence for Cromwell. Beneath the decorous and ceremonial obedience that we have already noticed in Marvell's construction of Cromwell (lines 85 to 90), there is also the assertion that Cromwell has not laid claim to sovereignty at all because, since the departure of Charles I, sovereignty has been vested in the House of Commons acting in concert with the Council of State. Hobbes has no difficulty in accepting sovereignty of either a single person or an assembly of persons: what he objects to most vociferously is the concept of a mixed government, or power-sharing between an individual and an assembly – a point to which I shall return when discussing 'The First Anniversary'. In the 'Horatian Ode' Marvell is studious in avoiding celebrating Cromwell's ascendancy in terms that would at this time be an embarrassment: later on, in 'The First Anniversary', he will be prepared to make wider claims for Cromwell's constitutional role, but only by leaving Hobbesian theory behind him.

There is an unresolved nervous uncertainty in the epilogue to the 'Horatian Ode'. For all Marvell's earlier confidence that Cromwell is 'still in the Republic's hand' (line 82), at the finish his advice to Cromwell is in terms of the reality of power: that reality is Cromwell himself.

In Hobbesian terms, power is all. Fundamentally, it is what determines where sovereignty is. Also, it is what determines all categories of ethical and aesthetic perception; and one of the most brilliant passages in *Leviathan* sees all public virtue in terms of power.[18] In this scheme of things, justice is one responsibility of power. So, furthermore, the righteous 'sword erect' (line 116) of Cromwell may well be an allusion to Hobbes's concept, previously enunciated in the *De Cive*, of 'the Sword of Justice' which is necessary 'for the security of particular men, and, by

consequence for the common peace'; and which sword is 'transferred to some Man or Counsell ... necessarily understood by
Right to have the supreme power.'[19] Certainly images of the
governmental sword were common, but Marvell's allusion may
also include more precisely what Hobbes terms 'the Sword of
War' that 'belongs to the same Man or Counsell to whom the
Sword of Justice belongs', for 'both Swords doe belong to the
chiefe command.'[20] Given the circumstances under which the
'Horatian Ode' was written, as acknowledged in its peroration on
the imminent invasion of Scotland, both applications of 'sword'
may be equally present.[21]

In the 'Horatian Ode', Marvell seems equally aware of what
Hobbes thought people who were subject to a sovereign were
entitled to expect in return:

1. That they be defended against forraign enemies.
2. That Peace be preserved at home.
3. That they be enrich't as much as may consist with publique
   security.
4. That they enjoy a harmlesse liberty.[22]

The last word of the poem – 'maintain' – has more to it than the
simple holding-on to power. The removal of outside threats by
war on the one hand, and the establishment of internal peace,
security and liberty on the other, are obligations which the sovereign power reciprocally owes to obedient subjects. Maintaining
power, then, involves a continuous process of leadership: the 'arts'
of Marvell's penultimate line are those which have won loyal
regard from within as well as awe from outside. Peace at home
and war abroad: this binary role of the sovereign in Hobbes's
view underlies the 'Horatian Ode'. Cromwell, who is so meek
and reasonable among his English, promises to be:

> A *Caesar* he ere long to *Gaul*,
> To *Italy* an *Hannibal*.

> (lines 101–102)

Finally, the most Hobbesian characteristic in Marvell's representation of Cromwell is evident in the dynamic personality given to
England's new leader in the poem. Cromwell is described as 'restless' (line 9) and as seeking his destiny under an 'active star' (line
12); his progress is rehearsed throughout the poem in verbs of

power and action, of which there are an extraordinary quantity; and towards the end he is apotheosized as 'falcon high' (line 91) or noble predator. As such, Cromwell who has been seen as exhibiting Machiavellian virtues is also the paradigm of Hobbes's theory of human life.

Hobbes draws his model for human behaviour by extrapolation from – or, as we would see it, by analogy with – new notions in physics and astronomy. The old Aristotelian view of the universe was that objects were naturally at rest and sought a state of rest: however, in the new view, Galileo 'postulated that motion was the natural state – things moved unless something stopped them. Hobbes would apply this to the motions of men, would get a system which would explain their motions relative to one another, and would then deduce what kind of government they must have to enable them to maintain and maximize their motion.'[23] For Hobbes, it is but a short step from physics to politics:

> These small beginnings of motion, within the body of Man, before they appear in walking, speaking, striking, and other visible actions, are commonly called Endeavour. This Endeavour, when it is toward something which causes it, is called Appetite or Desire . . .[24]

For the motion of desire manifests itself principally in the desire for power:

> The Passions that most of all cause the differences of Wit, are principally, the more or lesse Desire of Power, of Riches, of Knowledge, and of Honour. All which may be reduced to the first, that is Desire of Power.[25]

Like Hobbes, Marvell does not maintain that what is natural is necessarily good and he presents Cromwell's career as an instance of a rise to power, rather than as an ethical issue. The 'Horatian Ode' is what Hobbes himself termed an 'Oration of Prayse' in which 'the designe is not truth, but to Honour.'[26] To suggest, as some critics have done, that Marvell's emphasis on Cromwell's essential quality of activity becomes a subtle means of dispraise is to misunderstand the intellectual milieu out of which the 'Horatian Ode' emerges. If Marvell indicates that Cromwell's rise to power has been a good thing for England, it is in no stronger or weaker a sense than that Cromwell has put an end to a civil war he did not start, for which too Hobbes would have praised him. For it is to the situation of civil war that Hobbes's most famous statement about the state of nature ominously alludes; it is in civil war that

> ... there is no industry; because the fruit thereof is uncertain: and consequently no Culture of the Earth; no Navigation, nor use of the commodities that may be imported by Sea; no commodious Building; no Instruments of moving, and removing such things as require much force; no Knowledge of the face of the Earth; no account of Time; no Arts; no Letters; no Society; and which is worst of all, continuall feare, and danger of violent death; And the life of man, solitary, poore, nasty, brutish, and short.[27]

Cromwell has delivered England from the continuance of this experience, or so Marvell's poem implies. Lest it be objected that *Leviathan* appeared after the 'Horatian Ode', it should be remembered that Hobbes had said much the same, though in less finely-honed rhetorical prose, years earlier in the *De Cive*. While relief is undoubtedly mixed with apprehension in the 'Horatian Ode', it is in the dual context of this experience and Hobbes's political meditations upon government that Marvell is able to say with straightforward sincerity in an utterance that is guarded but without reserve: 'Much to the Man is due.'

'If these the Times, then this must be the Man.'

Most of us come to 'The First Anniversary' from other poems that have already set in our minds notions of what is best in Marvell or what is most 'Marvellian'. 'The First Anniversary' is generally thought of as belonging with his later body of political poems, which are often deemed to be less worthy of notice than the earlier lyrics.[28] And yet, many of Marvell's finest lyrics undoubtedly come from the short period of some four years between 'An Horatian Ode' and 'The First Anniversary'. Preference for the lyrics dates from the 'rediscovery' of the so-called metaphysical poets by Sir H.J.C. Grierson, T.S. Eliot and their circle; and this preference is at least partly to be accounted for by prevailing taste of that time (c. 1920). The separation between the lyrics and the political poems has persisted, largely unchallenged, to this day. Margoliouth's otherwise splendid edition of 1927 takes the liberty of reinforcing the preference by shuffling the order of poems as they had appeared in the 1681 edition to put the lyrics first.[29]

One of the reasons why 'The First Anniversary' has not been much admired or liked may have something to do with the metric form in which it is cast. For most of his lyrics Marvell had favoured a form that was distinctively terse, even elliptical – the iambic tetrameter couplet. This is probably the most distinctive prosodic characteristic of the whole period in lyric poetry: before Marvell, it had been put to elegant service by Thomas Carew, Richard Lovelace, Edmund Waller and Robert Herrick, to name but a few. Marvell took on this demanding form and made it his own.

Marvell, however, extended his use of the iambic tetrameter couplet form, or 'Cavalier couplet', beyond the lyric and into his best-liked political poetry: he used it in four-couplet stanzaic units in 'Upon Appleton House', in 'Upon the Hill and Grove at Bilborough' and in his quasi-lyrical masterpiece, 'The Garden'. In these three poems addressed to the recently-retired Fairfax, Marvell may well have used this form in deference to his patron's tastes and interests: one of the projects which Fairfax took up while Marvell was with him was a commentary on the *Pimander*. Marvell's poems of this sojourn certainly bear the intellectual signs of Fairfax's influence and it may be inferred that Marvell chose the tetrameter couplet for the Fairfax poems as being especially suitable for conveying hermetically-tinged ideas.[30] 'The Horatian Ode', an avowedly political poem, is cast in tetrameter couplets that alternate with even more compact trimeters. It is a unique experiment in form appropriate to its political subject: Marvell is also echoing, as closely as he may in English, the Latin form of Horace's odes, themselves adapted from Greek Alcaics.

One way or another, then, the shorter-lined poem has been associated with Marvell at his best. His earlier pentameter poems – his commendatory verses for Richard Lovelace's *Lucasta*, his 'Elegy upon the Death of My Lord Francis Villiers', his elegy 'Upon the Death of the Lord Hastings', and 'Flecknoe, an English Priest at Rome' – receive mention chiefly for their historical interest. As the main stream of poetry in the second half of the seventeenth century moved progressively towards a more public and political-satirical stance, so there was a move away from the tetrameter to the pentameter line (both in blank verse and in heroic couplet form). Marvell's career straddled this perceptible change, which was to find its most polished expression in the work of Milton, Dryden and Pope. The modern reader of 'The First Anniversary' and 'The Death of Oliver Cromwell' is likely to be influenced by long-standing critical categories, to find these poems neither metaphysical or Augustan, and therefore to reject them as inferior works.

'The First Anniversary', though very different from 'An Horatian Ode' in a number of ways, not least metrically, shows continuity in some respects. It continues Marvell's association with the ode, but has little of the Horatian about it, being a more elaborate and extended exercise in the Pindaric mode.[31] We have already noticed Pindaric elements in the substratum of the Horatian form of Marvell's earlier poem on Cromwell. Though both the Horatian and the Pindaric odes are in some measure poems of public declamation, the Pindaric is more pervasively so, not permitting the dreamy introspection that is sometimes found in Horace. Being a more fully public poem in stance than its Horatian predecessor, 'The First Anniversary' is more Pindaric.

Circumstances surrounding the composition of Marvell's first two Cromwell poems suggest that in each case he was deliberately choosing a form that would suit his intentions. Although Marvell's 'Horatian Ode' affects a public voice, it is predominantly a poem of personal readjustment, very like some of Horace's own odes. And although the conclusion moves outwards into a direct exhortatory address to Cromwell himself, there is no internal or external evidence to suggest that Marvell had much of a public at this time: we do not know how widely 'An Horatian Ode' circulated in manuscript or, indeed, whether Cromwell himself read it before going off to hunt 'the Caledonian deer'; at this stage Cromwell may not even have heard of Marvell. With 'The First Anniversary' the situation was entirely different. Marvell, an established member of Cromwell's intimate circle, was on the way to becoming his unofficial laureate.[32] In January 1655 'The First Anniversary' was advertised in *Mercurius Politicus*, the propaganda mouthpiece of Cromwell's regime and, furthermore, it seems that Cromwell 'used some phrases from the poem in the speech with which he dismissed Parliament at the end of that month.'[33] Marvell's decision to shift his emphasis towards the Pindaric form of ode is significant in general terms.

'The First Anniversary' seems to be directly related to Pindar's *Pythia I* which had been commissioned by the tyrant Hieron of Sicily in 470 B.C. to celebrate the foundation of the new city of Aetna.[34] By now Cromwell, like Hieron, had become an enlightened dictator and each of the poems involves 'an investigation of the problem (the dictator) faces in wielding absolute power.'[35] Both had come suddenly to power, and were non-hereditary leaders, but the essential difference between them, however, was that Hieron *enjoyed* power in every sense, whereas Cromwell found himself called to an office he had never sought; and he was at pains to divest himself of as much power as he could without returning his unstable country to civil war. At the time of the writing of 'The First Anniversary', Cromwell was witnessing the beginning of the end of his latest attempt to share power with an elected assembly. The fact that Cromwell could not find any effective accommodation between himself and a succession of parliaments and assemblies, continuing to be a dictator almost by default, would have made the implied comparison between himself and the Hieron of Pindar's ode a rueful piece of irony indeed had he been aware of it. We must assume, of course, that Marvell was aware of it, for – contrary to received opinion – there is much of his customary irony in 'The First Anniversary', though it operates within a much narrower compass than usual. While there is no room to doubt whether Marvell was really praising Cromwell, there is ample space for reflection within the poem on whether Cromwell, given his rightful role, was making the best use of it. At all events, both Pindar and Marvell have found poetry a suitable medium for debating 'the subject of the ideal state.'[36] Marvell was by no means unique among poets of his time in using the Pindaric for political purposes.

Rather than rehearse the full extent of Pindaric elements in 'The First Anniversary', which Revard has ably done, I would prefer to move on to an aspect of the poem which has not received adequate attention: the imagery of water. 'The First Anniversary' begins and ends with imagery of water.[37] This imagery seems at first glance to be placed as a decorative frame to the body of the poem, but it is central to the poem, both thematically and structurally. In the exordium, 'Flowing Time', when it flows smoothly, sustains those who would otherwise sink or keeps them close to the surface. This is not a situation to be commended: the words 'vain' and 'maze' in the first line resonate with associations of time mis-spent in a delusive world. Both words had come together in disapprobation only a year or two before in the line 'How vainly men themselves amaze' with which Marvell's 'The Garden' begins. In both poems the biblical and medieval sense of *vanitas* as worldly folly is closely annexed to the Renaissance idea of a maze as metaphorical representation of man's dangerous path through the world.[38] Cromwell's 'vigour' (line 7) alone runs counter to the 'smooth streams' (line 2) of easy sloth. While mankind itself is 'declining always' (line 3), Cromwell's activity takes him into another dimension of being, beyond the watery element of sublunary mortality and into the skies where, circling 'Sun-like' (line 8) in the quintessential world of eternity, he masters time:

> 'Tis he the force of scatter'd Time contracts,
> And in one Year the work of Ages acts.
>
> (lines 13–14)

How different is Cromwell's circling from the 'weak Circles of increasing Years' (line 4) sent out from the spot where lesser men have disappeared and gone into oblivion.

The imagery of water continues through the central sections of the poem in which Cromwell is likened to three Old Testament figures whose several and distinct attributes he incorporates. What all three have in common is that each has been called by God to a specific mission as deliverer of the chosen people. They are Elijah (by strong implication rather than by direct invocation), Gideon and Noah. Marvell has taken these three for their complementary diversity: Elijah as prophet and spiritual leader; Gideon as judge and leader in time of war; and Noah as patriarchal leader in peace-time.

Cromwell's divinely-appointed mission, however, places him beyond such identifiable roles and the terminology used to describe them:

> For to be *Cromwell* was a greater thing,
> Than ought below, or yet above a King.
>
> (lines 225–26)

The thing-king rhyme points to a dichotomy that cannot adequately be encompassed in words. At this point in the poem Marvell is ingeniously converting the disaster of Cromwell's nearly-fatal coaching accident into a triumphant revelation: the incident serves to remind England that Cromwell is 'the headstrong Peoples Charioteer' (line 234) in a 'fertile Storm' (line 236) in the time of a recalcitrant king, a new Ahab, worshipping false gods.[39] Like Elijah, he has attempted to warn the king of the impending fertile storm

> Which to the thirsty Land did plenty bring,
> But, though forewarn'd, o'r-took and wet the King.
>
> (lines 237–38)

It seems likely that Marvell is here seeking to exculpate Cromwell from guilt for the fall of Charles I, and with some justice, for Cromwell spent much time trying to treat with the King after the end of the first Civil War. Whether Cromwell had later changed his attitude towards the King, and what his motives were, are matters which lie outside the poem. For the poem, it remains that Elijah's rain and Cromwell's bring relief to the parched earth along with the omen of drowning for those whose impiety has caused spiritual drought.

The role of Cromwell as the new Elijah would have had an additional significance for the percipient reader of 'The First Anniversary' when published in 1655. At that time the return of Christ to rule over the elect in his new Jerusalem of England was almost daily expected by many.[40] Whether Marvell was party to the excited mood of apocalyptic expectation we are not certain, but there can be little doubt that in casting Cromwell thus Marvell was playing up to it, for the return of Elijah was the sign of the second coming for which the millenarian English were waiting. The Old Testament ends with God speaking through his prophet, Malachi:

> Behold, I will send you Elijah the prophet before the coming of the great and dreadful day of the Lord; and he shall turn the heart of the fathers to the children, and the heart of the children to their fathers, lest I come and smite the earth with a curse.[41]

Marvell may be seen as making a renewed appeal for the national unity that he identifies, earlier in the poem, as a precondition for the great event (see lines 131–44).

More politically pointed still is Marvell's association of Cromwell with Gideon. Gideon, as a judge from the earlier and

better era before the reign of kings, had long been associated with
anti-monarchical sentiments and had been used by Milton in this
way some three years earlier, in the *Pro Populo Anglicano Defensio*
(1651).[42] The 'two Kings' (line 250) defeated by the new Gideon
would seem to be Charles I and Charles II, the former in the
civil wars and the latter at Worcester after his abortive attempt to
invade via Scotland. More problematical, though, is the reference
to '*Succoths* Elders' (line 253) and the 'Tow'r' (line 252) of Penuel:
the dissolution of the Long Parliament has been seen as a parallel.[43]
I think it more likely that the reference is a general warning to
those who resist the power of God's agent. As such, it echoes a
warning previously given in 'An Horatian Ode':

> 'Tis Madness to resist or blame
> The force of angry Heavens flame.
>
> (lines 25–26)

Water imagery does not have any biblical basis in relation to
Gideon, but Marvell applies to his rule the commonplace Renaissance trope, partially derived from Plato and from Stoicism, of the
ship at sea as representing both self-control and good government.
'So have I seen at Sea . . .' (line 265) says Marvell of his Cromwell-
Gideon, characterizing Cromwell as the 'lusty Mate' (line 273)
who takes the helm from the 'artless Steersman' (line 275) during
a mighty storm in order to save the ship and its crew.

From the example of his Cromwell-Gideon as saviour of the
ship of state, Marvell draws a political inference that is valid for
all circumstances:

> 'Tis not a Freedome, that where All command;
> Nor Tyranny, where One does them withstand;
> But who of both the bounders knows to lay
> Him as their Father must the State obey.
>
> (lines 279–82)

The need for power to be centralized in one who takes responsibility for the state, which, in return, acknowledges his ascendancy,
together with the renewed emphasis on Cromwell's vigour (lines
7–48) take us back to Marvell's Hobbesian figure of Cromwell as
leader in 'An Horatian Ode'.

The last of the three Old Testament figures, Noah, is invoked
briefly in a curiously limiting fashion, with emphasis on Noah's
unconscious self-exposure in his drunkenness. This unfortunate

incident is not compared but contrasted with Cromwell's deportment in Marvell's poem (lines 283–92), but one cannot resist the
innuendo that Noah's failing is offered as an admonition to
Cromwell not to rely too much on his own uprightness.

Marvell proclaims the survival of Cromwell's family of eight
through the Civil War period as being 'like *Noah's* Eight' (line
283), but the image is grotesquely distorted. Cromwell has sur-
vived 'the Wars Flood' (line 284), which is, by implication, a sea
of blood. While Marvell asserts Cromwell's superiority to Noah
in his unfailing sobriety, there is not, it seems, the same innocence
or cleanness in the survival of the cataclysm. We are momentarily
back with the troubled vision of 'Upon Appleton House', where
the victorious armies of Fairfax and Cromwell are imaged as
mowers who are not innocent pastoralists but figures of death
with their scythes as they 'massacre the grass' that is, the people,
leaving behind them a plain not stooked with hay but 'quilted
o'er with bodies slain.'[44]

When Cromwell's stature is confirmed by a spokesman for the
hostile but admiring foreign princes in the oddly-voiced peroration
to 'The First Anniversary', it is largely Cromwell's authority as
master of a sea power that receives notice (lines 349–72). In view
of Cromwell's measure of success in re-establishing England as a
sea power there is nothing out of the way in Marvell's decision
to emphasize the area of Cromwell's success in his panegyric,
especially when other ventures were proving less successful. And
yet, significant or not, here is another instance of disturbing imagery in relation to water: Cromwell's navies are not so much ships
as a deadly 'new Hatched Nest' of ominously 'floting Islands'
(line 359); in their manufacture not a beneficent portion of nature
but rather 'An hideous shole of wood-Leviathans' (line 361), great
wooden whales which threaten destruction. Again, we are
reminded of the disturbing imagery of civil war in the Fairfax
poems, as where the grove and hill of peaceful Bilborough are
contrasted with the 'groves of pikes' and 'mountains raised of
dying men' that had formerly provided vistas for Fairfax during
the Civil War.

It is only at the very end of 'The First Anniversary' that Marvell
resolves the uncertainties and ambiguities posed by the water
imagery. Cromwell, says Marvell, goes far beyond his capacity
for praise:

And as the *Angel* of our Commonweal,
Troubling the Waters, yearly mak'st them Heal.

(lines 401–402)

We have heard previously in the poem of 'Angelique *Cromwell*' (line 126) as the militant force in the battle against the great monster of evil which retreats to her predictably '*Roman* den' (line 129) in the face of his onslaught. At the end, however, it is a peaceably angelic Cromwell who troubles the political waters like the angel at the pool of Bethesda, stirring it only in order to activate its healing properties.[45] Water, which may warn an Ahab or vindicate a Gideon or drown the ungodly outside the chosen family of a Noah, symbolizes the mysterious operation of the divine in its contrary manifestations and Cromwell as its appointed agent.

'The First Anniversary' is a panegyric that literally praises Cromwell to the skies, but the fulness of Marvell's almost metonymic association of Cromwell with angelic powers extends beyond praise to persuasion: it is a deliberative poem as well. This combination is hardly surprising when one recalls the circumstances surrounding its composition. Marvell is doing what he can to support Cromwell's Protectorate. As mediators between God and man, angels are agents of enforcement for the divine will, often expressed through laws given to men. In the Acts of the Apostles, the betrayers and murderers of Christ are those 'Who have received the law by the disposition of angels, and have not kept it.'[46] Again, in St. Paul's Epistle to the Galatians, the law 'was ordained by angels';[47] and in his Epistle to the Hebrews: 'If the word spoken by angels was steadfast, and every transgression and disobedience received a just recompense of reward: how shall we escape if we neglect so great salvation?'.[48] Such texts would not have been far from recall to Marvell's readers when they heard their lawgiver described as an angel. There is in these texts the same admixture of threat and promise as there is in the water imagery that flows through the poem from beginning to end. What will save a Noah, will destroy an Ahab.

Cromwell's role as lawgiver in 'The First Anniversary' brings together the Old Testament figures and the mythological Amphion. There is nothing new, of course, in the conjunction of biblical types with gentile types to form an antitype who is their composite Christian fulfilment: the medieval encyclopaedic tradition annexed to humanistic syncretism is familiar enough in sixteenth- and seventeenth-century poetry.[49] Since the poem celebrates the anniversary of a system of government, the centrality of lawgiving as a theme is hardly surprising: so the types are primarily types whose significance is political. Amphion is a particularly appropriate figure to take from classical mythology for, like Theseus, he represents the advance of civilization but, unlike Theseus, he is creator of his *polis* rather than its inheritor. Marvell spends considerable space in justifying the parallel between Cromwell and Amphion, suggesting that Cromwell has effectively brought into being something new and wonderful that was not there before.

As angelic intermediary between God and man, Cromwell is distinguished from lesser mortals in a passage that compares the inevitable failures of merely earthly governors unfavourably with a divinely-inspired political order:

> While indefatigable *Cromwell* hies,
> And cuts his way still nearer to the Skyes,
> Learning a Musique in the Region clear,
> To tune this lower to that Higher Sphere.

(lines 45–46)

This bridging passage at the end of the *exordium* skilfully prepares for the *narratio* introducing Amphion, in a vein reminiscent of Marvell at his most lyrical:

> So when *Amphion* did the Lute command,
> Which the God gave him, with his gentle hand,
> The rougher Stones, unto his Measures hew'd,
> Dans'd up in order from the Quarreys rude;
> This took a Lower, that an Higher place,
> As he the Treble alter'd, or the Base:
> No Note he struck, but a new Story lay'd,
> And the great Work ascended while he play'd.

(lines 49–56)

Marvell's characteristically witty word-play in 'Measures' and 'order', terms also used for parliamentary process, has been noticed.[50] We should also consider that these and other allusions to the circumstances of contemporary government in what purports to be an account of the founding of an ancient Greek city state – like the 'gentle'-man with a god-given mandate to rule the 'rougher' stones of proletariat and peasantry – add up to an inference that true government was ever like this. For the moment, at least, we are close to the world of Sir Robert Filmer and other royalist advocates of hierarchical patriarchy.

Indeed, Marvell affirms:

> Such was that wondrous Order and Consent,
> When *Cromwell* tun'd the ruling Instrument.
>
> (lines 67–68)

By his conceit that the Instrument of Government establishing the Protectorate is also like a musical instrument, Marvell makes a direct link between the original Amphion and 'our *Amphion*' (line 73). Marvell uses the extended analogy to make subtle distinctions between the Theban achievement and the English one, pointing out how much more difficult Cromwell's task has been. The fault, Marvell suggests, is not with the instrument or he who devised it or the model it seeks to re-create, but with the inferior materials upon which the new Amphion's magical powers have to work:

> The Commonwealth then first together came,
> And each one enter'd in the willing Frame;
> All other Matter yields, and may be ruled:
> But who the Minds of stubborn Men can build?
> No quarry bears a Stone so hardly wrought,
> Nor with such labour from its Center brought;
> None to be sunk in the Foundation bends,
> Each in the House the highest Place contends,
> And each the Hand that lays him will direct,
> And some fall back upon the Architect;
> Yet all compos'd by his attractive Song,
> Into the Animated City throng.
>
> (lines 75–86)

These English stones, unlike those of Thebes, have wills of their own, and are quarrelsome and vexatious. Only Cromwell's personal charisma offers any hope that he will not eventually be crushed. Marvell's hope against hope is that enough downward force will neutralize opponents by turning them into petrified human caryatids. Hardly probable! One senses desperation in Marvell's over-extended ingenuity:

> The Common-wealth does through their centers all
> Draw the circumf'rence of the publique Wall;
> The crossest Spirits here do take their part,
> Fast'ning the Contignation which they thwart;
> And they, whose Nature leads them to divide,
> Uphold, this one, and that the other Side;
> But the most Equal still sustein the Height,
> And they as Pillars keep the Work upright,
> While on the Basis of a Senate free,
> Knit by the Roofs Protecting weight, agree.

(lines 87–98)

The first parliament elected under the Protectorate was doomed when Marvell wrote these lines and, almost certainly, Marvell knew it. The building is impossibly precarious. There is an empty hollowness at the centre too. It is not the hollowness of the sycophantic flatterer, or of a cynical or sceptical time-server, that reverberates through these lines and their imagery, but rather the anguish of someone who has come to believe in Cromwell and who wants the system to work, knowing it cannot.

Marvell's faith in Cromwell as 'the common power to keep the people in awe', as Hobbes frequently describes the effective sovereign in *Leviathan*, is perhaps what he means to convey by 'the Roofs Protecting weight'. We do not know, however, whether Marvell had followed Hobbes's thought from the *De Cive* through to *Leviathan* and we cannot be sure what Cromwell thought of it either.[51] Cromwell's concept of power-sharing in the Instrument of Government was in direct opposition to Hobbes's view that there could be no such thing as a mixed government.

For Hobbes, it was the folly of attempting to divide power in a mixed government that had helped lead to the civil war:

> And this division is it, whereof it is said *a kingdome divided in itself cannot stand*: for unlesse this division precede, division into opposite Armies can never happen. If there had not first been an opinion received of the greatest part of England, that these Powers were divided between the King, and the Lords, and the House of Commons, the people had never been divided, and fallen into this Civill Warre.[52]

Whatever the reason, there is less of Hobbes in 'The First Anniversary' than in 'An Horatian Ode'. It may have been that the issue of naked power – the Hobbesian motif so strong in the 'Horatian Ode' – was not in itself a problem for Marvell now that Cromwell was in firm control. It has been cogently argued that the essentially Ramist construction of Marvell's Amphion is an indication of affinity with the equally Ramist Hobbes.[53] But there can only be a Hobbesian interpretation of the poem if it is also contended that Marvell is subtly using, through the Amphion passages, a Hobbesian paradigm to point out Cromwell's error to the great man himself. That is possible, but unlikely.

'The First Anniversary' is written at the intersection of religion with politics. In it we notice the apocalyptic strain evident in much of Marvell's poetry. Millenarian fervour in England, which had surfaced at various times and with varying degrees of intensity since the inception of Protestantism, was undoubtedly at a new pitch when Marvell was writing his 'First Anniversary' tribute to Cromwell. Indeed, Cromwell had permitted the Jews to return to England after centuries of exclusion, not only as an act of religious tolerance but also in order to create the circumstances for their promised conversion. But to unravel the connections between popular millenarianism and government policy and to distinguish between the variant forms of millenarian thought is a large subject beyond the scope of this essay. Our concern must be with what Marvell makes of it all in his poem.

One would expect a poem of this kind to acknowledge the ideas circulating in the government and we do, in fact, find such ideas, among them that which looks on Cromwell as the only man to usher in the reign of Christ on earth. Much of the familiar rhetoric of standard seventeenth-century millenarian discourse is represented in 'The First Anniversary'. Marvell turns his thoughts to 'The great Designes kept for the latter Dayes' (line 110) and allows himself conventional references to Antichrist as 'the Whore' (line 113), 'the Beast' (line 124), and 'the Monster' (line 128). The question is what these references signify.

Having built a shaky structure for Cromwell, held together only by 'the Roofs Protecting weight' Marvell proceeds to concentrate most of the negatives in his prophetic vision into the passage from which I have just been quoting. It leads into Marvell's positive vision for Cromwell:

> Hence oft I think if in some happy Hour
> High Grace should meet in one with highest pow'r,
> And then a seasonable People still

> Should bend to his, as he to Heavens will,
> What we might hope, what wonderful Effect
> From such a wish'd Conjuncture might reflect.
> Sure, the mysterious Work, where none withstand,
> Would forthwith finish under such a Hand:
> Fore-shortned Time its useless Course would stay,
> And soon precipitate the latest Day.
>
> (lines 131–40)

The remarkable thing about these lines is that, considering the occasion and the public nature of the poem, Marvell's hope for Cromwell is so doubtfully expressed. All depends upon the conditional 'if'; and the verbs that follow are cast in the subjunctive mood of uncertain possibility.[54] Far from penning an enthusiastically apocalyptic paean, Marvell goes on to dissociate himself from the chiliasts; while giving full credit to Cromwell for having done the best any man could do, he permits himself no more than a further, conditional appraisal of Cromwell himself which falls far short of what would be required of a straightforward propaganda piece:

> But a thick Cloud about that Morning lyes,
> And intercepts the Beams of Mortal eyes,
> That 'tis the most which we determine can,
> If these the times, then this must be the Man.
>
> (lines 144–147)

Cromwell's personal worth is in no way lessened by this perception, but Marvell refuses to commit himself or Providence. The Marvell who wrote 'The Picture of Little T.C. in a Prospect of Flowers' and the Mower poems is too well aware of the dangers that attend upon presumption.

'I saw him dead.'

If 'An Horatian Ode' has met with considerable approbation and 'The First Anniversary' has been the subject of serious analysis, then 'A Poem on the Death of O[liver] C[romwell]' has been cursorily praised and consigned to oblivion.[55] It is not so much that 'The Death of Cromwell' (as I shall refer to the poem hereafter) has been unfairly judged as that it has been unjustly ignored.

Marvell's political hopes had been sustained by his faith in Cromwell and when he died part of Marvell died too. He would never again write political poetry with any degree of affirmation; from now on he would write satirically only, from the cool distance of Restoration parliamentary politics.

Although 'The Death of Cromwell' is within the tradition of the English funeral elegy, it is a highly individual work and more deeply felt than many of its antecedents. As an elegy that does not take death as an opportunity or excuse to write about something else, 'The Death of Cromwell' is not primarily a political poem. There are important points of political contact in it, however, to the extent that the farewell to Cromwell virtually admits that the political order represented by Cromwell is over: the concluding address lacks all conviction. It may be debated whether this conclusion represents subtle art or tired artlessness but, either way, there is no persuasive power in the statement that Richard 'where his great parent led,/Beats on the rugged track' (lines 305–306) or that 'A Cromwell in an houre a prince will grow' (line 312). In these last twenty lines Marvell tries out a number of images as metaphors for Richard Cromwell's succession to power. They are garnered to affirm the hope that 'calm peace succeeds a war' (line 321), and they culminate in the couplet:

> Tempt not his clemency to try his pow'r,
> He threats no deluge, yet foretells a showre.
>
> (lines 323–24)

Whatever else this conclusion means, it implicitly acknowledges that the age of heroic action and grand cataclysm are over.

In 'The Death of Cromwell' Marvell takes us back to the great days of past action. We recall that it was Cromwell's activity that had fascinated Marvell in his earlier poems, and so it is appropriate for Cromwell to be remembered now in terms of *res gestae*. Marvell recalls the deeds of Joshua, for whom 'the commanded sun' (line 192) stood still; of Moses, who led God's elect out of Egypt (line 294); and of David, renowned alike 'for the sword and harpe' (line 294). We should not be surprised to hear or half-hear muted echoes of earlier poems. In as much as Marvell is mourning for Cromwell he is mourning for mortality itself and for his own past experience. Marvell is surely remembering here that he had characterized Cromwell in terms of Old Testament types, in 'The First Anniversary'. Further evocation of the scriptural past in 'The Death of Cromwell' is both complementary and confirmatory. In Cromwell's lifetime, Marvell had not ever, except perhaps in the excitement of one moment, joined his voice to those that urged Cromwell to become king.[56] In retrospect he has taken the progression from Moses to Joshua to David (lines 293–94) as a hint at Cromwell's kingly qualities, but as in 'The First Anniversary' he has evoked these figures typologically rather than literally. With reference to England's own past, Marvell proclaims that Cromwell in terms of *'British Saints and Worthy's'* (line 176):

> ... in a valour less'ning *Arthur's* deeds,
> For Holyness the *Confessor* exceeds.
>
> (lines 177–78)

Granted, both Arthur and Edward the Confessor were kings, but Marvell is more interested in their attributes than their royal titles. They separately represent perfection in the active and the contemplative lives, which have since come together in the single person of Cromwell. The closest Marvell comes to calling Cromwell king is in his maritime role as *'Monarch'* (line 169) of the seas.

Active and contemplative are not exact terms to describe a Christian spirituality that has moved as far away from medieval Catholicism as the puritan spirit of a Cromwell or a Marvell, but they will have to suffice. In these terms, Marvell's Cromwell poems show a shifting balance in his perception of Cromwell's role as a political leader with a religious mission. The 'Horatian Ode' celebrates Cromwell almost exclusively as a man of action. Marvell grants Cromwell a capacity for quietness and contemplation but the poem is much more concerned with how Cromwell has followed 'his active Star' (line 12) in recent times. In 'The First Anniversary', the balance has shifted perceptibly. There is still zestful activity as Cromwell 'alone with greater Vigour runs' (line 7), and yet the man who so energetically devised a new system of government has done so through an energy born of inward spirituality (lines 45–48).

In 'The Death of Cromwell' this active life now seems a long way in the past, and although Cromwell's valour is remembered intermittently throughout, it is his daughter Eliza who is at the poem's centre. There is the same motif of a world in mourning as the result of the death of a young woman that one finds in Donne's two anniversary poems on the death of Elizabeth Drury, but here the mourning world is concentrated in the person of the Grieving Cromwell; and whereas Donne's Elizabeth Drury is virtually an abstraction, Marvell's Elizabeth Cromwell is someone known, if only through Marvell's testimony to the intensity of her father's passionate love for her. Consequently, there is none of Donne's extravagant posturing. In 'The Death of Cromwell' Marvell is more sparing than usual in his recourse to biblical echo and classical allusion. It is as though Marvell has sloughed off conventional trappings in his search for a sincerely personal expression of grief. There are also echoes from Milton's great elegy, 'Lycidas', but they are muted, and there is no place in Cromwell's grief-stricken household for pastoral appurtenances.[57] Indeed, Cromwell's *Love* and *Grief* for Eliza have executed 'the fatal Writ' (line 21) for his own death. She represents what in Jungian terms might be accounted his *anima*, the sensitive and feminine side to his being. Of all humans, only she

> . . . with Smiles serene and Words discreet
> His hidden Soul at ev'ry turn could meet.
>
> (lines 41–42)

Once she is dead, he no more has the will to live:

> Nature it seem'd with him would Nature vye;
> He with *Eliza*, It with him would dye.
> He without noise still travell'd to his End,
> As silent Suns to meet the Night descend.
>
> (lines 133–36)

All that is left of the old Cromwell is the energy with which he seeks his death:

> And now his life, suspended by her breath,
> Ran out impetuously to hasting Death.
>
> (lines 71–72)

Undoubtedly Cromwell was deeply affected by his favourite daughter's illness and agonizing death.[58] Nevertheless, his own health had been declining for years and ever since his invasion of

Ireland he had been plagued with recurrent bouts of malaria. That
Andrew Marvell has chosen to relate the two deaths so closely in
his poem is a deliberate act and, in part, a political act. Behind
the structuring of 'The Death of Cromwell' is a shaping will to
represent Cromwell in a specific way. Marvell was writing at a
time when Cromwell's power base had been perilously eroded.
Between the Republicans on one side and those who favoured the
return of the Monarchy on the other, Cromwell's support
remained strong only among his committed personal adherents.
Marvell was one of these. The best Marvell could do, on
Cromwell's death, was to represent him to succeeding generations
as a man of spirituality and sensitivity rather than as an unrepent-
ant regicide or an aspirant to autocratic power.

'The Death of Cromwell' is in every way the most reflective of
the three major poems Marvell wrote on Cromwell. The poem is
a retrospective view of a relatively short but momentous epoch
and we should not conclude without indicating how extensive this
process of retrospection is. Marvell begins by asserting Providence
in Cromwell's death, as he had previously asserted it in his political life in both 'An Horatian Ode' and 'The First Anniversary'.
The idea that Cromwell loved peace but had been called to war
by an 'angry Heaven' (line 16) is a direct recollection of 'An
Horatian Ode', where the same phrase occurs (line 26).[59] The
anger of God is less directly but as forcefully bodied forth in 'The
First Anniversary' when Gideon punishes the elders of Succoth
and razes the tower of Penuel (lines 249–56).

In 'An Horatian Ode' and 'The Death of Cromwell' those who
enjoy watching the fall of a great one are described in similar
terms as ignoble groundlings in search of unwholesome diversion.
In 'An Horatian Ode' there are those who gather round at the
execution of Charles I as though at a play:

> That thence the *Royal Actor* born
> The *Tragick Scaffold* might adorn:
> While round the armed Bands
> Did clap their bloody hands.
>
> (lines 53–56)

In 'The Death of Cromwell' the end is eagerly awaited by the
sorts of ghouls who

... blame the last *Act*, like *Spectators* vain,
Unless the *Prince* whom they applaud be slain.

(lines 9–10)

Beyond this, however, there seems to be no comparison being made, for the two deaths are very different.[60]

The stature of Cromwell and his accretion of offices and powers are attended in Marvell's poems with the imagery of natural immensity and growth. In 'The Death of Cromwell', Marvell describes the late Protector in terms of 'huge Trees, whose growth with his did rise' (line 119). Later in the poem, Cromwell is 'Not much unlike the sacred oak' (line 261) that has been blasted by 'angry Jove' who does not spare his own plant when striking 'at mortalls sins' (lines 265–66). It has been suggested that there is an indirect use here of Lucan, one of Marvell's sources for 'An Horatian Ode': Pompey, Caesar's defeated antagonist, had been described as a decayed oak, so now Cromwell's 'shape decay'd' (line 257) marks the completion of another political life cycle.[61]

In 'The First Anniversary', Marvell had found Cromwell 'Sun-like' (line 8) and had said of Cromwell's fall in the coaching accident in Hyde Park: 'It seem'd the Sun was faln out of the Sphere' (line 206). In 'The Death of Cromwell' he remembers this imagery poignantly in line 136: 'As silent Suns to meet the Night descend.'[62] With the light of Cromwell's sun has gone too the heavenly music heard in the great work of England's Amphion.

There are more cross-references and backward glances which connect the three Cromwell poems. What, finally, connects them most completely is the process within the poet's consciousness. Marvell begins with admiration in 'An Horatian Ode', continues with loyalty in 'The First Anniversary', and concludes with desolation in 'The Death of Cromwell'. Marvell's most moving statement of his feelings is contained in the simple cry: 'I saw him dead' (line 247).

Many years later Marvell would write differently about the Cromwell years. In a very different political climate, and with motives that are not entirely clear to the modern reader, he would record another view of the past:

Whether it were a War of Religion, or of Liberty it is not worth the labour to enquire. Which-soever was at the top, the other was at the bottom; but upon considering all, I think the Cause was too good to have been fought for. Men ought to have trusted God; they ought and might have trusted the King with the whole matter. . . . For men may spare their pains where Nature is at work, and the world will not go the faster for our driving.[63]

Whatever this passage may be interpreted to mean, and with whatever subtlety it may be glossed, its tone is unmistakable as one of wistful regret that the events which are the subject of his three long poems on Cromwell had ever happened. Two decades on, when he wrote this passage in *The Rehearsal Transpros'd*, Marvell was a much older and, evidently, a wearier man. Nevertheless, the flexibility of mind that had allowed him to pass from being a quiescent royalist to a committed supporter of the charismatic Cromwell had not gone; indeed, it had now taken him beyond his former opinions. The three Cromwell poems were by now a part of history. England had moved on, and so had Marvell.

Notes

1. The commonly-held notion that the world had been strangely inverted is discussed by Christopher Hill in *The World Turned Upside Down: Radical Ideas during the English Revolution*, 1972; Harmondsworth: Penguin, 1975 *passim*. See also Leah S. Marcus, *The Politics of Mirth: Jonson, Herrick, Milton, Marvell and the Defense of Old Holiday Pastimes*, Chicago: University of Chicago Press 1986; her chapter entitled 'Pastimes without a Court: Richard Lovelace and Andrew Marvell', pp. 213–63, is most instructive on the theme of topsy-turviness in England at this time.

2. The preservation and transmission of these poems is discussed in the 'General Note on the Text' and in the headnotes to individual poems in Pierre Legouis and E.E. Duncan-Jones' third, revised edition of *The Poems and Letters of Andrew Marvell*, ed. H.M. Margoliouth, Oxford: Clarendon Press, 1971. All further references are to this edition.

3. *Mythologies*, New York and London: Macmillan, 1959, p. 331. Lawrence L. Hyman uses this passage to distinguish between Marvell's 'Horatian Ode' and his later political poems in *Andrew Marvell*, New York: Twain, 1964. However, the distinction is under strain in Hyman's own discussion of 'The First Anniversary', when he acknowledges that 'beneath the conventional praises of Cromwell

there is clear evidence of the same conflict within Marvell's own attitude that was expressed in "An Horatian Ode" ' (Hyman 95).

4. James Michie, ed. and trans., *The Odes of Horace*, Harmondsworth: Penguin, 1967, p. 13.

5. Marvell's attitude towards Cromwell in the Ode has long been in contention. Cleanth Brooks, in 'Marvell's "Horatian Ode" ', *English Institute Essays, 1946*, New York: Columbia University Press, 1947, pp. 127–58 found it 'as heavily freighted with admiration as it is with a great condemnation'. Douglas Bush, in 'Marvell's "Horatian Ode" ', *Sewanee Review* 60 (1952), pp. 363–76 queried the 'darker connotations' found by Brooks. Brooks rejoined in 'A note on the Limits of "History" and the Limits of "Criticism" ', *Sewanee Review* 61 (1953), pp. 129–35, suggesting that 'Mr Bush and I are much more in agreement about the speaker's admiration for Cromwell than his reading of my essay has led him to believe.' A classic study of Marvell's Ode in relation to current political events is John M. Wallace's *Destiny His Choice: The Loyalism of Andrew Marvell*, Cambridge: Cambridge University Press, 1968, pp. 69–105. Rosalie L. Colie considers the poem in relation to its generic antecedents in *'My Ecchoing Song': Andrew Marvell's Poetry of Criticism*, Princeton: Princeton University Press, 1970, pp. 62–71 and reviews the debate on Marvell's stance since Brooks and Bush. Annabel M. Patterson, in *Marvell and the Civic Crown*, Princeton: Princeton University Press, 1978, pp. 60–68, finds a rhetorically-constructed 'tension between different kinds of responses'. Warren Chernaik, in *The Poet's Time: Politics and Religion in the Work of Andrew Marvell*, Cambridge: Cambridge University Press, 1983, pp. 15–22, finds the poem's greatness 'lies in its ability to rise beyond . . . the natural human need to choose sides', but concludes that in the Ode 'power and right cannot be entirely resolved'. Robert Wilcher, in *Andrew Marvell*, Cambridge: Cambridge University Press, 1985, pp. 113–24 finds 'very mixed feelings' in the Ode, but that in the closing lines 'Marvell allows the tone of admiration to dominate'. Margarita Stocker, in *Apocalypric Marvell: The Second Coming in Seventeenth Century Poetry*, Brighton: Harvester Press, 1986, pp. 67–104, finds in Marvell a 'personal antipathy to Cromwell' that is subsumed into the irony of God.

6. For a few hints of Pindar's influence, see Colie, pp. 66–68. In a recent essay Stella P. Revard has paid attention to the Renaissance resurgence of interest in the Pindaric Ode, with special reference to Marvell's 'First Anniversary': see 'Building the Foundations of a Good Commonwealth: Marvell, Pindar, and the Power of Music' in Claude J. Summers and Ted-Larry Pebworth eds., *'The Muses*

Common-Weale': Poetry and Politics in the Seventeenth Century, Columbia: University of Missouri Press, 1988, pp. 177–90.

7. As an example of the self-effacing pseudo-ballad that does not strike a posture on behalf of its poet, and on the very same subject of Oliver Cromwell's success, see Richard Lovelace's 'A Mock-Song'. Although Lovelace's poem is not in ballad metre it projects the subversive anonymity of verses in political broadsheets of the time.

8. R.I.V. Hodge, *Foreshortened Time: Andrew Marvell and Seventeenth Century Revolutions*, Cambridge: D.S. Brewer, 1978, p. 117.

9. Apart from the question of doubtful authenticity in some cases ('Villiers' and 'Hastings'), and possible later revision in another ('Tom May'), these other poems have heavily contextualized meanings that necessitate extreme caution in their use.

10. Hodge, pp. 123–24, 130.

11. Many of the writings noted above (note 5) refer to Marvell's classical sources. For intensive treatment of classical sources and allusions, see R.H. Syfret, 'Marvell's "Horatian Ode" ', *Review of English Studies* n.s. 12 (1961), pp. 160–72; and John S. Coolidge, 'Marvell and Horace', *Modern Philology* 63 (1965), pp. 111–20. Syfret sees Marvell as hostile to Cromwell; Coolidge as guardedly approving.

12. Margoliouth (3rd ed.), pp. 302–303; Chernaik, p. 45; and Stocker, p. 327, n. 85.

13. Arnold A. Rogow, *Thomas Hobbes: Radical in the service of Reaction*, New York: Norton, 1986, p. 79.

14. William Molesworth, ed., *The English Works of Thomas Hobbes*, vol. 8 (*The History of the Grecian War Written by Thucydides* trans. by Thomas Hobbes; London, 1843), p. 217.

15. Molesworth, p. 106.

16. Molesworth, p. 108.

17. The English had a surprising amount of support in Ireland, or at least genuinely thought they had. See Wallace, pp. 85–88.

18. Thomas Hobbes, *Leviathan*, ed. C.B. MacPherson, Harmondsworth: Penguin, 1968, pp. 150–160.

19. Thomas Hobbes, *De Cive*, ed. Howard Warrender, Oxford: Clarendon Press, 1983, pp. 93, 94.

20. Hobbes, *De Cive*, p. 94.

21. For other possible significances see E.E. Duncan-Jones, 'The Erect Sword in Marvell's "Horatian Ode" ', *Etudes Anglaises* 15 (1962), pp. 172–74.

22. Hobbes, *De Cive*, p. 158.

23. MacPherson, introduction to *Leviathan*, p. 19.

24. Hobbes, *Leviathan*, p. 119.

25. Hobbes, *Leviathan*, p. 139.

26. Hobbes, *Leviathan*, p. 136.

27. Hobbes, *Leviathan*, p. 186.
28. See Note 3, above, on Hyman's classification.
29. Annabel Patterson has argued in her article 'Against Polarization: Literature and Politics in Marvell's Cromwell Poems', *English Literary Renaissance* 5 (1975), pp. 251–73, that, as with the *Sylvae* of Statius and the later *sylva* of Jonson's *Forrest* and *Underwoods*, the apparent randomness of Marvell's 1681 edition may have been to a purpose. For further development of this argument, see also Patterson, *Civic Crown* 50–59; and this volume, pp. 188–212.
30. For discussion on Marvell's Hermeticism, see Maren-Sofie Roestvig, *The Happy Man: Studies in the Metamorphosis of a Classical Ideal* Vol. 1 (1956); Oslo: Norwegian University Press, revised 1962.
31. The Pindaric elements in 'The First Anniversary' are closely examined by Revard (see note 6, above).
32. See the chapter 'Cromwell's Laureate', in Hilton Kelliher, *Andrew Marvell: Poet and Politician*, London: The British Library, 1978, pp. 55–65.
33. Kelliher, p. 60.
34. Revard, p. 177. She also suggests parallels, which there is not space to elaborate upon here, comparing the structure of Pindar's Ode with Marvell's.
35. Revard, p. 180.
36. Revard, p. 177.
37. The water imagery is noticed but not fully discussed by James F. Carens in 'Andrew Marvell's Cromwell Poems', *The Bucknell Review* 7 (1957), pp. 41–70, at 66.
38. For a thorough and informative treatment of the maze motif in Renaissance literature, see David Ormerod, '*A Midsummer Night's Dream*: The Monster in the Labyrinth', *Shakespeare Studies*, 11 (1978), pp. 39–52.
39. On the subject of Elijah, see Patterson, *Civic Crown*, pp. 79, 84; also note in Margoliouth, p. 325.
40. See Stocker *passim*; also Graham Parry, *Seventeenth-Century Poetry: The Social Context*, London: Hutchinson, 1985, pp. 221–46. There is excellent background material for the seventeenth-century scholar in Richard Bauckham's *Tudor Apocalypse*, Cambridge: Cambridge University Press, 1978.
41. Malachi 4: 4–5.
42. Patterson, *Civic Crown*, p. 85. The relevant biblical passages on the transition from judges to kings are Judges 21:25 and 1 Samuel 12.
43. Patterson, *Civic Crown*, p. 86.
44. 'Upon Appleton House', lines 394 and 422.
45. John 5:2–4.
46. Acts 7:53.

47. Galatians 3:19.
48. Hebrews 2:2–3.
49. Jean Seznec, *The Survival of the Pagan Gods: The Mythological Tradition and Its Place in Renaissance Humanism and Art*, trans. Barbara F. Sessions, Princeton: Princeton University Press, 1953, is instructive throughout. For a significant instance of the tradition in practice, see Milton's 'Nativity Ode'.
50. Hodge, p. 109.
51. It has been suggested that Hobbes caused the engraving of sovereignty on the title page of the first edition of *Leviathan* to look like Cromwell, Rogow, pp. 159–60.
52. Hobbes, *Leviathan*, pp. 236–37.
53. Hodge, pp. 7–16, pp. 106–13.
54. Patterson, *Civic Crown*, p. 69.
55. Only Patterson, *Civic Crown*, p. 90–94, and Donald M. Friedman in *Marvell's Pastoral Art*, London: Routledge and Kegan Paul, 1970, pp. 285–90 give it any sustained attention.
56. In 'Blake's Victory', pp. 39–40. For an outstanding scholarly essay on possible constructs of kingship in relation to Cromwell's position, see J.A. Mazzeo's 'Cromwell as Davidic King', in *Reason and the Imagination*, New York: University of Columbia Press, 1962, pp. 229–55. However, in my opinion Mazzeo over-reads the vital passage in 'The First Anniversary', pp. 131–44, seeing it as affirmative rather than conditional. See also Chernaik, pp. 43–62.
57. For instance, compare line 167 with 'Lycidas', lines 132–34 (noticed by Margoliouth, p. 334).
58. Maurice Ashley, *Oliver Cromwell and his World*, London: Thames and Hudson, 1972, p. 110.
59. Margoliouth, p. 332; and Friedman, p. 286.
60. Friedman, p. 286.
61. Patterson, *Civic Crown*, p. 93.
62. Friedman, p. 287.
63. From *The Rehearsal Transpros'd*, in *Complete Works*, ed. A.B. Grosart, vol. 3, 'The Fuller Worthies Library': Lancaster, 1873, pp. 212–13.

2 Marvell's 'Upon Appleton House, to my Lord Fairfax' and the Regaining of Paradise

A.D. Cousins

In the English country house poems which precede Marvell's 'Upon Appleton House', one often sees arcadian visions mingle with visions of perfect moral commonwealths.[1] The country house poems before Marvell's, that is to say, frequently offer images of pastoral ease and plenty, of life in harmony with the cycle of the seasons, of the Golden Age come again, centred upon the image of the great house itself.[2] The image of the country house tends also in those poems to be central to depictions of microcosmic, and politically specific, ideal societies. *To Penshurst*, 'To Saxham', *To my friend G.N. from Wrest*, and *A Panegerick to Sir Lewis Pemberton*, for example, represent life in and immediately environing the country houses which they respectively celebrate as essentially feudal, decorous, and benign. The moral, no less than the political, order of life is shown in each poem to derive from the houses' owners: the constant and untroubled social concord which seemingly pervades relations between the owners of the houses and their various dependents is indicated to arise primarily from the owners' courtesy (usually accompanied by *caritas*) in the regulation of community – their true 'civility'.[3] It could reasonably be argued that country house poems prior to 'Upon

Appleton House' tend to express royalist views of little worlds in which the active virtue of royalist families – in conjunction with fruitful natural surroundings (the portrait of Saxham differs slightly here) – fashions, in effect, ideally coherent commonwealths.[4]

In what follows I want to suggest that 'Upon Appleton House' is at once an appropriation and, theologically as well as politically, a comprehensive rewriting of the country house poem. Marvell directs the poem, as its title announces, not to a supporter of the late King but to the Independent general who was one of his more notably successful opponents.[5] With that transference of the country house poem appears to occur its transformation. As has been proposed above, the royalist predecessors of Marvell's poem incline towards depicting pleasant places and towards envisioning small, ideal societies; so does 'Upon Appleton House'. The royalist poems, moreover, usually make the great house emblematic of its owner's moral attributes; again, so too does Marvell's work.[6] Yet the differences would seem to be these. Through its description of the great house (lines 1–80) and then in its account of Fairfax's ancestry and of the man himself (lines 281–368), Marvell's country house poem represents Fairfax not as primarily courteous and charitable, nor as an epitome of the virtues (so Herrick images Pemberton in *A Panegerick*, lines 133–136), but as virtually embodying the Calvinist idea of moderation – in fact, as an embodiment of Protestant heroic virtue.[7] Having thus characterized Fairfax, the persona goes on to develop the poem as an apology for the general's retirement from public life. Marvell's persona, drawing on or paralleling a main strand of Calvin's theology, represents Fairfax not merely as someone whose active virtue makes the little world of his estate, with its pleasant and fertile landscape, a perfect moral commonwealth but as someone whose regenerate private life will enable him – through the most immediately consequential product of his regenerate state, his daughter Mary – to contribute significantly to the renewal of a devastated England that has only recently emerged from civil war: to help bring the 'dear and happy Isle' (line 321), a second but violently lost 'Paradise' (line 323; cf. lines 324–344), closer to being paradise regained.[8]

At the start of 'Upon Appleton House' Marvell's persona confronts the reader with a description of the great house itself (lines 1–80), yet with one that reveals little of the house's appearance. Instead, the persona reveals and elaborates on what he identifies as at once its shaping principle and that which is predominant in the life of its owner, Lord Fairfax. The description begins:

I

Within this sober Frame expect
Work of no Forrain *Architect*;
That unto Caves the Quarries drew,
And Forrests did to Pastures hew;
Who of his great Design in pain
Did for a Model vault his Brain,
Whose Columnes should so high be rais'd
To arch the Brows that on them gaz'd.

II

Why should of all things Man unrul'd
Such unproportion'd dwellings build?
The Beasts are by their Denns exprest:
And Birds contrive an equal Nest;
The low roof'd Tortoises do dwell
In cases fit of Tortoise-shell:
No Creature loves an empty space;
Their bodies measure out their Place.

III

But He, superfluously spread,
Demands more room alive then dead.
And in his hollow Palace goes
Where Winds as he themselves may lose.
What need of all this Marble Crust
T'impark the wanton Mote of Dust,
That thinks by Breadth the World t'unite
Though the first Builders fail'd in Height?

IV

But all things are composed here
Like Nature, orderly and near:
In which we the Dimensions find

Of that more sober Age and Mind,
When larger sized Men did stoop
To enter at a narrow loop;
As practising, in doors so strait,
To strain themselves through *Heavens Gate*.

The opening line of the poem, with its famous reference to Appleton House as 'this sober Frame', indicates the unpretentious appearance of the house but, more important, also initiates a discourse on moderation as the house's principle of design. That discourse is developed as a dialectic between architectural moderation and its opposite. In the remaining lines of the first stanza, Marvell's persona goes on to stress that Appleton House does not bear the mark of any 'Forrain *Architect*': if to any degree it were to do so, he suggests, then it would somewhere manifest extravagance. His assertion of the house's native Englishness is of course – as the amplification, in lines 3–8, on the extravagant designs of foreign architects implies – an insistence on sobriety, moderation, as rather the house's shaping principle than merely its appearance. What emerges from this early phase of the dialectic thus established is a twofold analysis of excess as a principle of architectural design. One aspect of the analysis is social, the idea being put forward that the lavish schemes of foreign architects deplete nature for the private good of the individual or of the few (lines 3–4; cf. lines 17–24). The other, and more significant, is psychological. The persona indicates that, as a principle of architectural design, excess expresses a disordered, distorting *phantasia* and, at the same time, the destructive impulse to overreach (lines 5–8). Both aspects are elaborated upon as the dialectic unfolds.

Marvell's persona does continue to focus on the social implications of an architecture shaped by extravagance, as can be seen from much of what he says in the third stanza (lines 17–22, especially 'superfluously', 'hollow', 'lose', 'impark', 'Mote of Dust'). However, he considers at greater length the connection between excess as a shaping principle and the impulse to overreach. Asking, 'Why should of all things Man unrul'd / Such unproportion'd dwellings build?' (lines 9–10), he then proceeds in most of what follows (until line 32) to define that aspect of architectural extravagance against the moderation expressed both in the dwellings of the creatures (lines 11–16) and in the house of the Fairfaxes (lines 25–32). His allusion to the creatures' instinct for making modest 'Denns' (line 11) or 'Nest[s]' (line 12) clearly links moderation as a principle of design with natural law, so defining its opposite as unnatural. And as he proposes that idea the persona seems to affirm it with another no less forceful. The only creature specifically mentioned at this moment of the text is the tortoise ('The low roof'd Tortoises do dwell / In cases fit of Tortoise-shell . . .,' lines 13–14). As critics have often pointed out, the tortoise was emblematic of self-containment.[9] But if the image of the tortoise here can reasonably be seen to imply an association between moderation as a natural principle of design and a cautious self-containment – something of obvious relevance to the persona's subsequent picture of Fairfax – it has, too, another and equally apt emblematic connotation. In treating of '*Honos et Virtvs*' Valeriano remarks about a representation of Virtus, armed, standing with one foot on a tortoise: '*Deinde quia pedes & crura imbecillitatem, quā ex hoc terreo corpore suscipimus, quae nos cupiditatum ictibus obnoxios reddit Prudētia, cuius symbolum est testudo, quam sub pede habet, diligenter muniamus. . . .*'[10] The implication of the persona's use of the creatures as evidence, then, would appear to be that 'Man unrul'd', in building extravagant dwellings, reaches beyond natural law, beyond – in particular – nature's rule of self-containment, and beyond *prudentia* (moderation therefore being linked, logically enough, with prudence as well as with the law of nature).

The climax to the persona's study of the connection between excess as a principle of design and the impulse to overreach occurs in the immediately following description of the individual amidst a 'hollow Palace' (lines 17–24). The description stresses the double vanity of architectural extravagance: the pride that it expresses, and its nothingness ('hollow', 'lose', 'Marble Crust'). The specific function of the vanity of vanities motif evoked from the very beginning of the set-piece becomes clear in the pair of conceits that end it. The first pictures man as a 'wanton Mote of Dust' (line 22) and thereby foregrounds the notion that man is an insignificant creature filled with unrestrained, wilful desire. The second identifies excess, as a shaping principle expressive of the impulse to overreach, with the construction of the Tower of Babel (lines 23–24). In other words, the two conceits iterate the vanity of vanities motif but in doing so posit the source of the connection between architectural extravagance and overreaching. They suggest, climactically, that excess as a principle of design expresses an impulse to overreach which is, in fact, the archetypal human yearning for infinite self-extension, for divinity: the *cupiditas* of the Fall.

The persona's conclusion to the dialectic between architectural excess and its opposite – and thus the conclusion to his discourse on moderation as the shaping principle of Appleton House – turns the poem's focus directly again on the house itself (lines 25–32). Fairfax's residence is, the persona declares, 'Like Nature, orderly and near . . .' (line 26). The persona indicated mere 'Marble Crust' to manifest at once unnaturalness and imprudence; he implies that Appleton House manifests both prudence and harmony with nature (cf. lines 13–14). Yet if at first and briefly he proposes that the house resembles nature in structure, he goes on to amplify the idea that its moderate design reflects primitive Christian virtue. '[A]ll things' (line 25) may be so brought together in Appleton House that it is '*Like* Nature . . .' (my emphasis), but in them

> we the Dimensions find
> Of that more sober Age and Mind,
> When larger sized Men did stoop
> To enter at a narrow loop;
> As practising, in doors so strait,
> To strain themselves through *Heavens Gate*.
>
> (lines 27–32)

The persona asserts that in the house's design can be seen the moderation which informed the times and temper of the Early Church, his reference to 'that more sober Age and Mind' distinctly recalling his initial reference to the 'sober Frame' of the house itself. Moreover, in remarking on the sobriety of the Early Church he emphasizes the humility of its members, which he connects with their desire for a house not made with hands. In contradicting excess as a principle of architectural design, the persona thus seems finally to suggest, the moderation of Appleton House sets the self-denying, God-seeking spirit of primitive Christianity against fallen mankind's hubris.[11]

The opening four stanzas of the poem have been discussed in some detail because in them the principle of design that supposedly shapes Appleton House is closely considered. The remaining stanzas given over to formal description of Fairfax's residence affirm rather than add to what has gone before; however, they also proceed to identify the principle shaping of the house as that which shapes Fairfax's life (and his wife's).[12] The presence of *'Vere and Fairfax'* (line 36) at Appleton House, according to the persona, makes it 'sacred' (line 35) and the site of future *'Pilgrimage[s]'* (line 34). Whilst the suggestion of their sanctity is probably linked with an idea that they incarnate Republican ideals (cf. lines 345–360 and, for example, Livy, *Ab urbe* . . ., 3, 26–30), the persona links it here more directly with the Christian moderation which he has just before revealed as Appleton House's shaping principle. The persona implies that the house's Christian moderation of design, expressing *'Humility'* (line 41) and therefore a *'holy Mathematicks'* (line 47), at once 'delights' Fairfax (line 56) and articulates his own humility (lines 57–60), his own moderation (lines 61–64 – especially the reference to 'Pride'). That the Christian moderation of the house can be seen too in Fairfax (the persona alludes to Anne Vere, in the poem's first section, only at lines 36–37) is indicated perhaps most succinctly by the persona's observation: 'A Stately *Frontispice of Poor* / Adorns without the open Door' (lines 65–66). The stateliness of the house's entrance derives, the reader learns, not from Fairfax's addition to it of imposing decoration but instead from his adornment of it with *caritas*. His aristocratic *grazia* ('Height with a certain Grace does bend', line 59) is thus shown to be born of true grace (cf. lines 69–70, with their possible play on the phrase *'Mark of Grace'*), his *virtù* (lines 49–53) to be born of true virtue (cf. line 56, lines 65–66). In 'Upon Appleton House' as in 'To Penshurst', then, description of the country house serves to represent its owner; however, the emblematic blazon in Marvell's poem differs significantly from that in Jonson's – and from such blazons in other previous country house poems. To examine how it differs is to recognize the political strategy directing the poem as a whole.

Perhaps the best way to begin is by glancing at the start of 'To Penshurst': 'Thou art not, Penshurst, built to envious show / Of touch or marble, nor canst boast a row / Of polished pillars, or a roof of gold. . . .'[13] The lines echo Horace's *'Non ebur neque aureum / mea renidet in domo lacunar, / non trabes Hymettiae / premunt columnas . . .'* (lines 1–4), and in doing so suggest that Stoic moderation – in conjunction with 'religion', alluded to near the end of Jonson's poem – is elemental to life in the great house.[14]

The main difference between the Marvell persona's account of Appleton House and the Jonson persona's of Penshurst is, of course, the emphasis in the former on Christian moderation as a shaping principle of both architecture and life. That emphasis, furthermore, also distinguishes the description of Appleton House from depictions of country houses in poems by Marvell's other predecessors (the distinction being heightened by the Marvell persona's pervasive emphasis on the truly Christian life as a transcendent good). How the emphasis on Christian moderation in Marvell's poem functions becomes clear, it seems to me, when one relates the idea of Christian moderation presented by Marvell's persona to Calvin's idea of it.

According to Calvin, with the Fall the human personality lost its God-centred order, becoming subject to an egocentric disorder marked by inordinate desire and excess: '[I]n consequence of the corruption of nature, all our faculties are so vitiated and corrupted, that a perpetual disorder and excess are apparent in all our actions, and ... the appetites ... are inordinate, and inordinate because nothing pure and upright can proceed from a corrupt and polluted nature'.[15] Again: '[N]o moderation can be seen in the depravity of our nature, in which all affections with turbulent impetuosity exceed their due bounds. ...'[16] It is understandable, therefore, that Calvin emphasizes moderation as elemental to the regenerate life:

> We say ... that the worship of God is the beginning and foundation of righteousness; and that wherever it is wanting, any degree of equity, or continence, or temperance, existing among men themselves, is empty and frivolous in the sight of God. We call it the source and soul of righteousness, inasmuch as men learn to live together temperately, and without injury, when they revere God as the judge of right and wrong.[17]

There one can see that Calvin clearly suggests moderation (in fact, all virtue) to derive from God alone – a thought that he proposes even more distinctly elsewhere.[18] In keeping with both that thought and his emphasis on moderation's importance in the regenerate life is his imaging of Christ as the perfect example of and instructor in moderation. For instance, Calvin writes: '[A]s he [Christ] was upright, all his affections were under such restraint as prevented everything like excess'.[19] He also writes: 'Our feelings are sinful because they rush on unrestrainedly and immoderately; but in Christ they were composed and regulated in obedience to God and were completely free from sin. . . . He had [no passion] that was not right and founded on reason and sound judgment.' In the same passage Calvin calls Christ our 'example', adding: '[W]here should we seek for the rule of supreme perfection but in Him?'[20] Calvin seems to identify moderation as a basic need of, a prime virtue in, the human personality.

Whilst Calvin stresses the significance of moderation for the individual, however, he does not imply that it solely benefits the individual; furthermore, he does not consider moderation to be independent of everything other than the grace of God, from which it springs. Inasmuch as moderation, in Calvin's view, is elemental to the regenerate life, and because he asserts that from personal emerges social renovation ('Renovation is afterwards manifested by the fruits produced by it – viz. justice, judgment, and mercy') then moderation has to be seen as elemental to the good of society.[21] Calvin draws attention to humility and prudence as reinforcing moderation. Although he points to God as the ultimate source of that virtue, he describes 'humility' as 'the mother' of moderate behaviour.[22] Of prudence and moderation he observes: 'We should always prudently reckon what the Lord bids us, what He requires from each of us, in case the exuberance of our zeal boils over without reason or restraint'.[23] There the words 'reason' and 'restraint' connect his advice with his description of Christ as moderation's exemplar. Calvin indicates that moderation extends beneficently from the individual into the community, that it is born of one of the primary Christian virtues and is – or should be – accompanied by wisdom.

The similarities between the idea of Christian moderation presented by Marvell's persona and Calvin's idea of it can be summed up as follows. To begin with, in 'Upon Appleton House' and in the *Institutes* moderation is indeed described as a Christian, a God-derived, virtue – though in the former it is implied to be ultimately and essentially Christian (see lines 27–32) whereas, in the latter, ultimately and solely so. When, in Marvell's poem, the persona describes moderation as a Christian virtue, he emphatically associates it with the truly Christian life (see especially lines 31–32); when, in *Institutes* 2,8,11, Calvin represents moderation as a Christian virtue he suggests it to be elemental to the regenerate life.[24] (Of course, Calvin appropriates moderation for Christianity and identifies it as elemental to spiritual renovation in many passages and many works. It is worth mentioning here that both Marvell's persona and Calvin link excess with the Fall.) Marvell's persona distinctly connects moderation with humility, and Calvin does also; moreover, the persona apparently connects moderation with prudence, which Calvin certainly does. Finally, as regards similarities, in both Marvell's poem and in Calvin's writings personal moderation is shown to benefit society (see 'Upon Appleton House', lines 65–66).

Although those likenesses indicate that the Marvell persona's description of Appleton House and thus of Fairfax may be predominantly based on Calvin's view of Christian moderation, Marvell's direct indebtedness to Calvin cannot be demonstrated. What can reasonably be suggested, however, would seem to be this: the Marvell persona's emblematic blazon of Appleton House reveals – deliberately or otherwise – Fairfax as conforming to, as in effect incarnating, Calvin's thought on moderation. In other words, Fairfax is characterized not merely as moderate and devout, nor in broad terms as regenerate; rather, he is characterized in terms which are at once specific and (at the least) concordant with those of a central, Protestant authority as being regenerate. That presentation of Fairfax is, I think, crucial to the main political strategy of 'Upon Appleton House' and how it would appear to work comes into focus when one considers the account of Fairfax's ancestry and of the man himself (lines 281–368) that follows soon after the description of the house.

The initial line in that section of the poem ('From that blest Bed the *Heroe* came', the trope 'blest Bed' referring to the marriage between Sir William Fairfax and Isabel Thwaites) glances back to the imaging in the previous section (lines 81–280) of William, Lord Fairfax's ancestor, as a type of Protestant – in spirit, if not in actuality – heroism (see especially lines 201–248). Whether, then, the rest of the thirty-sixth stanza alludes to William Fairfax's son, or to the first Lord Fairfax, or to the Great Lord, Marvell's persona clearly introduces the portrait of Fairfax which pervades this part of 'Upon Appleton House' with an allusion to his (supposedly) illustrious Protestant lineage. That portrait amplifies both the image of William Fairfax as exemplifying Protestant heroism and the particularized image of Fairfax himself as regenerate. Marvell's patron is first pictured with his family amidst his gardens, whose flowers in 'five imaginary Forts' (line 350) – suggestive, according to the persona, of moral guardedness (lines 285–288) – imply that higher nature immediately environs Fairfax's home. The flowers are whimsically personified as the former general's pacific soldiery (lines 289–320), but the quaint personification of them emphasizes harmless innocence and creative order; moreover, Fairfax's daughter, in the idealized guise of 'Virgin Nymph' (line 300), is identified with them (lines 301–303, in which she is also said to transcend them). Thus caritas (lines 65–66) and higher nature combine to adorn Fairfax's house, indicating it to be the centre of a small, perfect, moral commonwealth.

More striking than that association of Fairfax with higher nature, however, is the conclusion to his portrait, which touches upon his retirement from public life. His retirement is attributed to the dictates of 'Conscience, that Heaven-nursed Plant' (line 355). The persona then remarks:

> A prickling leaf it [Conscience] bears, and such
> As that which shrinks at ev'ry touch;
> But Flowrs eternal, and divine,
> That in the Crowns of Saints do shine.
>
> (lines 357–360)

The image of 'the Crowns' is a reference to the New Testament 'crown of life' / 'crown of glory' and emphasizes that Fairfax's retreat to Appleton House was a sign of his commitment to heavenly rather than to mundane values (cf. line 354): Fairfax is proleptically identified with the 'Saints'. Especially, if not solely, through that identification, the poem's earlier image of Fairfax as regenerate is brought to a climax; at the same time, furthermore, Fairfax is in effect shown to be the fulfilment of William Fairfax's Protestant heroism (as stanza 31, and arguably stanza 36, seem to foreshadow). When reflecting on the Civil War – which he does amidst his portraying of Fairfax – Marvell's persona observes that 'had it pleased [Fairfax] and God,' the former general '[m]ight once have made our Gardens [that is, presumably, England just after the second Civil War] spring / Fresh as his own and flourishing' (lines 346–348). The persona appears there to be playing on the idea of renovatio, his assertion apparently being that the regenerate Fairfax (compare lines 347–348 with sts 5–9, and sts 37–40), while yet involved with public affairs, could possibly have effected social regeneration, renewing a country fallen (cf. st. 41) into discord. Of course, in what follows the reader is immediately told of Fairfax's retreat from public life because of '*Conscience*'. Even so, the portrait of the Great Lord is that of William Fairfax writ large: the latter is imaged as devout, the former (emphatically) as regenerate; the latter's virtuous action is described as having *directly* benefited an individual, the former's (by implication) as having benefited, and (overtly) as promising further benefit to, his country (see st. 44); finally, if William Fairfax's moment of glory, according to the poem, was his virtuous overcoming of false religion, his descendant's penultimate moment of glory, foretelling apotheosis, is shown to have been the overcoming of '*Ambition*' (line 354) by choosing retreat from the public sphere, which he might well (the persona says) have dominated (see lines 349–352).[25]

In combination, the first and third sections of 'Upon Appleton House' indicate Fairfax to be a virtually complete embodiment of (Calvinist) Protestant heroic virtue – that is, to possess a triumphant, a virtually perfect, regeneracy (revealed as according, at the least, with Calvin's thought on *renovatio*, particularly with regard to moderation) which informs and perfects his military heroism. Their doing so, it will now be argued, seems to form the poem's main political strategy. To begin with, through representing Fairfax in such a way Marvell's persona can imply that the former general has not, in a sense, retired at all. Fairfax's abandonment of *negotium* for *otium* could hardly be denied, and the persona does not seek to deny it; however, through his idealized, religious image of Fairfax he does suggest that the Great Lord may have forsaken *negotium* but retains – in Calvin's phrase – *negotium cum deo* (sts 4–9, 44–45).[26] Fairfax, in other words, is acknowledged as having turned away from dealings with the world, yet is suggested to have maintained dealings with God: in an obvious sense, he can be said to have retired; in another and more important, he cannot. Furthermore, just as the image of Fairfax as a type of Protestant heroic virtue enables the Marvell persona to put forward a discriminating account of Fairfax's retirement, so it lets him imply that even amidst political retirement Fairfax can still benefit society.

The Protestant heroic virtue revealed as expressing Fairfax's continuous *negotium cum deo* is indicated in the first and third parts of the poem to shape, as has been proposed above, a small and perfect moral commonwealth centred upon Fairfax's house. Throughout the poem, the principles of that microcosm of the ideal society are implicitly set against others that inform different versions of the ideal society, different visions of true community – each counterpart to the idyllic Protestant realm of the Fairfaxes being dismissed in the contrast (as indeed each would have to be, given the terms of the emblematic blazon of Appleton House and of Fairfax's portrait). Marvell's persona clearly suggests that in the little society focused upon the Great Lord's residence can be seen the principles which should direct society as a whole.

But the persona represents the former general as more actively and creatively virtuous, for all his being politically retired, than that: his retirement is not pictured as having only a localized beneficence which is usefully symbolic. In the poem's final section (approximately lines 617–776), Mary Fairfax appears as a numinous figure – at once sapiential and a correlative type of the Virgin Mary – whose eventual marriage will effect, the persona asserts, 'some universal good' (line 741). It seems the persona prophesies that Fairfax's daughter will one day confer on society at large (in fact, is destined to do so – see line 744) some undefined blessing. The persona's idealized presentation of Mary Fairfax and his hyperbolic prophesy about her are, of course, legitimized by his claim that she has been

> In a *Domestick Heaven* nurst,
> Under the *Discipline* severe
> Of *Fairfax*, and the starry *Vere*;
> Where not one object can come nigh
> But pure, and spotless as the Eye;
> And *Goodness* doth it self intail
> On *Females*, if there want a *Male*.
>
> (lines 722–728)

That is to say, the persona has laid the foundations for his assertion of Mary Fairfax as able to bring about 'some universal good' in the description of her home and in the portrait of her father. They enable him to image her as at once an offspring and an exemplar of the regenerate life, who will one day embody *renovatio* in the world beyond that of Nun Appleton. How Mary

Fairfax, as an exemplar of *renovatio*, will bring about through her marriage a 'universal good', what exactly that 'good' will be, and how it will relate exactly to her regenerate existence need not, then, in the end be defined proleptically by Marvell's persona, since the very fact of her making *renovatio* signally present (due doubly to her parentage) in a supposedly once paradisal (lines 321–344) society emerging from its fall (lines 321–328) into civil war must, for that is the implication of the persona's demonstrative rhetoric, draw it closer to a renewing of its former state. Mary Fairfax is depicted in the poem's final section as truly a manifestation of her father's personal regeneration, and as destined to return (in recreated and rarefied form) his Protestant heroic virtue to English society – an image in accord with Calvin's thinking on the social consequences of personal regeneration.[27]

To begin making more specific the argument that the representation of Fairfax as a type of Protestant heroic virtue is the main political strategy of 'Upon Appleton House', I should like now to turn to the poem's second section: the nunnery episode (lines 81–280). There the persona unfolds a dynastic myth, a tale of origins and of transformations, in which caricatures of nuns are contrasted with the simple and elevated figures of William Fairfax and of Isabel Thwaites. However, in unfolding that tale the persona does not offer merely a contrast between two sets of characters; rather, he opposes the nunnery – which he pictures as a dystopia disguised as an ideal society informed by Christian belief – directly to the genuinely '*Religious House*' (line 280) into which he claims Fairfax and Thwaites transformed it, and also indirectly to the perfect, if microcosmic, moral commonwealth that he claims is centred upon the Great Lord and his family.

The nun whose monologue occupies just over half (lines 97–196) of the nunnery episode describes the nunnery as containing a society in which peace and heroic Christian virtue (lines 105–116), greatness and humility (lines 117–144), dominance by the self and self-submission (lines 145–168), the sensuous and the spiritual (lines 169–196), holiness and pleasure (*passim*) are accommodated to each other, harmonize in a little state which has imprisoned the world (with its 'wild Creatures, called Men' – line 102, cf. lines 97–104) and liberated the happy few. The paradoxicality of the nun's monologue, and thus the vision of an ideal society that it presents, is less harmonious than the nun suggests – as the reader, if not Isabel Thwaites, recognizes at once. For a start, in trying deceitfully to identify her companions and herself as spectacular *milites Christiani* the nun unconsciously parodies the *miles Christianus* concept through the '*Virgin Amazons*' image (line 106); more important, she then no less unknowingly – and her various, but not innocent, unknowingness is part of the point at issue in her monologue – elaborates that image into a parody of the parable about the wise and foolish virgins (lines 107–108). Her deliberative speech begins by parodying not merely the *miles Christianus* topos but also the words of the Word. Just as she simultaneously asserts and denies the presence of heroic Christian virtue in the nunnery, so she reveals that the calm to be thought co-existent with it is in fact physical and emotional complacency (see her remarks on 'Our *Orient* Breaths' and 'our Tears', lines 109–116).

Discordant, too, are the nun's accounts of power, sensuousness, and spirituality in the nunnery. When feigning to consider the advantages that Thwaites would gain from submitting herself to the rule of the religious life (line 116), the nun tempts Thwaites by appealing to the desire to overreach. Each of the nuns, she says, 'must be seen' (line 117) as in fact 'a *Spouse*' and 'a *Queen*' (line 118); she adds that the nuns 'can in *Heaven* hence behold / [their] brighter Robes and Crowns of Gold' (lines 119–120). The nun's words there seem conventional and unremarkable enough, but her reference to queenship is cunning. It introduces, of course, both the nun's hint that Thwaites is an antitype in beauty of the Virgin (thus transcending in that respect the Virgin herself – see lines 131–136) and her attempt to impose on Thwaites the fantasy of receiving apotheosis (lines 141–144). In addition to that vision of Thwaites as a numinous figure who is an intermediary between the human and the divine (cf. lines 160–168), the nun puts before Thwaites the prospect of mundane authority as future '*Abbess*' (lines 157–160) – again parodying the words of Christ as she does so (line 159). Humility and self-submission are connected in the monologue, then, with an irreligious desire for infinite self-extension and with the will to power. As those appeals to Thwaites show, the nun is interested in tempting her in terms of excess, and in that vein the nun subsequently sets out before her the nunnery's supposed reconciliation of sensuous delight with spirituality. The nun implies that in the nunnery spirituality perfects sensuous delight – one 'Sweet' perfects 'the other' (line 171) – as grace perfects nature. However, her monologue indicates that the sensuous pleasures enjoyed by the nuns are diversely precious and many (see especially lines 177–182): the nuns are revealed not merely as self-indulgent but as luxuriating in the senses, one aspect of that seeming to be a uxoriousness in unnatural parody of Christ the Bridegroom (lines 185–192; cf. line 108). The nun's attempt to picture a Catholic ideal society has been deftly managed by Marvell's persona (for her monologue is *sermocinatio* at two removes) to delineate something quite different.

What the nun's speech actually describes is a hedonistic and narcissistic little community organized and maintained by human artifice, not by divine grace, and so dystopian rather than at once Christian and ideal. How the nuns and their way of life differ from William Fairfax, Isabel Thwaites, and their way of living seems to be made clear enough and need not be dwelled on for long. The nun's extravagant account of her companions and herself as '*Virgin Amazons*' (line 106) – revealing them to be parodic, not spectacular, *milites Christiani* – expresses the desire to overreach, and through that desire she tries to tempt Thwaites (lines 141–144). She also tries to appeal to Thwaites through terms suggestive of excessive sensuous pleasure (lines 169–182) and of unnaturalness (lines 185–192). On the other hand, William Fairfax is represented as a true *miles Christianus* (st. 29) whose moderate temper at first delays, and then espouses when legally sanctioned (lines 229–236), action against the nuns as agents of false religion (cf. lines 201–224, lines 249–272). Thwaites' chastity in marriage (lines 277–279) is contrasted with the nuns' sexual unnaturalness – and with their pretended chastity (lines 97–108, line 118, lines 219–220). Finally, here, Thwaites is indicated to be more truly an adherent to the restraint of the religious life than were the nuns (lines 278–280; cf. line 263). Other differences between the caricatures of the Cistercian nuns and the portraits of William Fairfax and of his wife could be suggested, but those seem to be the most prominent.

In pointing to the differences between the lives of the nuns and the lives of Lord Fairfax's ancestors, however, Marvell's persona at the same time implicitly contrasts the nunnery as a dystopia with the ideal community centred on the Great Lord and his family. That contrast can be partly seen as one reads the nunnery episode, because what the nun's monologue reveals about her little world – its parodic Christian heroism, its overreaching, its excess and so on – differentiates it immediately from the description, in the poem's foregoing section, of Lord Fairfax's residence, of Fairfax himself, and of his social relations. The contrast is completed in the poem's third section, with its portrayal of Fairfax, as William Fairfax writ large, amidst his gardens. Marvell's persona, then, unfolds in the nunnery episode a myth of dynastic origins for Lord Fairfax in which is imaged the displacement of a pseudo-Christian, dystopian community by the household of Fairfax's truly Christian ancestors; he frames that myth with portraits of Fairfax and, to lesser degrees, of his family which represent them as having been merely prefigured by those ancestors (st. 31; cf. sts 35 and 38) – to be, as is most forcibly and directly visible in the heroic figure of Fairfax himself, amplifications of those truly Christian ancestors and central presences in a small society which triumphantly inverts the dystopian qualities of the long since vanished nunnery. Thus it can be suggested that by depicting Fairfax as a type of Protestant heroic virtue and primarily using that image of him to frame the nunnery episode, Marvell's persona both establishes the idea of Fairfax as a man of high destiny – a destiny that the close of the poem implies will be fulfilled through his daughter – and indicates that the principles of ideal community lie not in Catholicism (pictured as belonging to the past) but are rather to be found in the singular, Protestant world of Nun Appleton.

The privileging of the little society focused on Fairfax's residence can also be seen in the poem's fourth section, the meadow sequence (lines 369–480). There Marvell's persona playfully celebrates the natural as well as the human environs of Appleton House and studies its historical environment. So elaborately and self-consciously playful is the persona's celebrating of the physical and human surrounds of Fairfax's residence that his description of them could, in rhetorical terms, better be called *topothesia* – rather than *topographia* – and *pragmatographia*, and it is through the shifting perspectives, the sudden juxtapositions and dissolutions, of the description that he examines history. Particularly significant is that, towards the end of the meadow sequence, he briefly sets the principles of the Levellers against those that he has earlier revealed as informing at once the architecture of Appleton House and the life of its owner.

The meadow sequence begins (st. 47) and ends (sts 58–60) with the world-upside-down topos; that is to say, its opening and closing emphasize dislocation, inversion of the familiar order of things. Within the sequence, as has been often pointed out, Marvell's persona describes the altering views before him in terms of theatrical illusion (lines 385–386, line 441). The altering views that he describes, moreover – and that are bounded by changes of physical perspective – are considered from changes of figurative perspective: biblical; military; mock-heroic; fabulous, and so on. The play of mind here recalls (or perhaps anticipates) what is said in 'The Garden' about the mind's recreative/creative power (lines 43–48); it recalls, too, what is said about the imagination by Sidney and, earlier, by Gianfrancesco Pico della Mirandola. One result of this flamboyantly imaginative play of mind is that it presents the persona as having a unique perception of Appleton House's physical (as well as social) site and site in history: it affirms his role – established at the poem's outset – as the house's interpreter. Thus it helps to foreshadow and to justify the persona's serio-comic portraying of himself, in the poem's next section (lines 481–approximately 616), as a visionary, as the poet-priest of Fairfax's estate (see especially stanzas 71–74). Another result, however, is that the persona's examining of recent history has a shrewd mixture of reticence and assertiveness.

Of the different views set before the reader by Marvell's persona, that containing the mowers occupies most space in the meadow sequence (lines 385–440) and is, I would argue, the most important. The mowers are initially described as 'tawny' (line 388) figures 'Who seem like *Israalites* to be, / Walking on foot through a green Sea' (lines 389–390). That image of the mowers is, of course, continued and developed when 'bloody *Thestylis*' (line 401) cries, referring to the persona, '[H]e call'd us *Israelites*; / But now, to make his saying true, / Rails rain for Quails, for Manna Dew' (lines 406–408). The persona depicts the actual work of the mowers in military terms: there is the 'Massacre' of 'the Grass' (line 394), involving the death of the '*Rail*' (line 395); allusion to

'A Camp of Battail newly fought' (line 420); comparisons involving 'Bodies slain' (line 422), 'Pillaging' (line 424), 'careless Victors' (line 425), '*Roman Camps*' (line 439) and 'Soldiers Obsequies' (line 440). Especially because of that pervasive, military imagery, the representation of the mowers has sometimes been read as an allegory of the Civil War. It is not difficult to connect the portrayal of the mowers as Israelites with the account in stanza forty-one of England as God's own country – and both with the widespread notion in Renaissance England that the English were, in effect, God's chosen people (cf. the first four stanzas of Phineas Fletcher's *The Locusts, or Apollyonists*). It is more difficult, though, to see the military perspective on the mowers' work as effecting either a schematic allegory of the Civil War or even an allegory at all. That is not to deny the insistence of the military imagery, nor to ignore the fact that Marvell's persona is very conscious throughout the poem of the Civil War's closeness to the world of Nun Appleton, both chronologically and because Fairfax had acted so prominent a part in the conflict. Perhaps, then, another and not entirely discontinuous way of reading the long account of the mowers would be to see the military perspective on them at work as offering, if not an allegory of the Civil War, yet a twofold postscript to it. First, the military perspective seems to suggest that the mowers' labour parodies warfare: their work is violently energetic, organized, and brings death; but the mowers' work as a whole destroys in order to create, and the death that it brings is, moreover, animal not human, pathetic as well as slyly ironic (as pictured through the persona's play with stoic commonplaces) rather than tragic (see lines 409–417). The mowers' work, in other words, seems distantly to mirror the greater and tragic violences of recent history, and to indicate that (relatively) harmless violences of more familiar kinds have supplanted them. On the other hand, however, the apparently parodic, military perspective seems also to suggest that the mowers' labour – harmless or not – is unavoidably overshadowed by recent history. Having thus indicated (whether deliberately or otherwise) two results of the Civil War, Marvell's persona then dissolves the view just presented and proceeds to consider, briefly, a post-Civil War way of life alien to that centred on Appleton House.

After the account of the mowers, with its reflections of warfare, and before the 'Villagers' and their cattle come into view (lines 451–464), the persona describes what he sees as 'A new and empty Face of things; / A levell'd space, ... smooth and plain ...' (lines 442–443). Thereupon he calls that 'space' a 'naked equal Flat, / Which *Levellers* take Pattern at ...' (lines 449–450). The *adnominatio* 'levell'd' / '*Levellers*' indicates that the persona's mention of the Levellers is not to be seen as haphazard; furthermore, as a specific, topical reference it stands out in the meadow sequence as distinctly as do the references to '*Lilly*' (line 444) and to '*Davenant*' (line 456). The reason for that pointed and brusquely dismissive political allusion is no doubt partly because Fairfax had personally confronted, at different times, various of the Levellers.[28] But it is arguable that the mention of them has another and more specific cause, one directly related to the persona's identification of Fairfax and of his residence with moderation – with Protestant heroic virtue.

It was proposed above that the view of the mowers at work can be seen as offering a postscript to the Civil War. The subsequent reference to the Levellers would seem to offer an abrupt focus on/dismissal of one recent and influential (and also many-sided) model for a post-Civil War society (the study of the nunnery implies, clearly enough, that Catholicism cannot provide a model for contemporary English society). The persona ironically suggests, in lines 449–450, that the Levellers base their notions of society on the idea of bare, reductive sameness ('naked equal Flat'). What he thereby does, I think, is to indicate that Appleton House embodies those principles which should now inform the once 'dear and happy Isle' (line 321). In minimal terms, one can say that just as Marvell's persona earlier depicts the nunnery as containing a little society expressive of luxuriant sensuousness and of sensuous self-indulgence, so here he characterizes the Levellers' vision of society as being expressive of drab austerity, of deprivation; one has to add, though, that just as earlier he implicitly opposed the fruitful, Protestant moderation of the Fairfaxes and of Appleton House to the irreligious excesses of the Catholic nunnery, so here the Levellers' Protestant excess is also contrasted implicitly by him with the moderation essential to the Fairfaxes' estate. Yet the simultaneous repudiation of the Levellers and celebration of Fairfax (as well as of Appleton House) is in fact more thorough than that.

In the emblematic blazon of the house and the portrait of Fairfax amid his gardens, Marvell's patron is represented as a type of (Calvinist) Protestant heroic virtue. When, not long before the writing of Marvell's poem, Fairfax confronted the 'True Levellers' he encountered Gerrard Winstanley, one of their leaders. Winstanley's pamphlets of the time cast him in the role of prophet – the prophet of political equality – and in that of true Christian hero, leading the vanguard of a new, Christian society (see especially 'To the City of London, Freedome and Peace Desired' and *The New Law of Righteousnes* . . .; Leveller writings other than Winstanley's frequently put forward an heroic image of those in that heterogeneous 'movement').[29] There is, of course, room in 'Upon Appleton House' for only one Christian hero, Fairfax, and consequently the pretensions to Christian heroism of Winstanley in particular and of the Leveller project in general have no place in the poem; the dismissive allusion to the Levellers indicates them to be dull, ridiculous, unheroic.[30] Something similar seems to happen in the mower poems, most notably in 'Damon the Mower'. There, Damon tries to describe his experience of unrequited love not in a plain manner appropriate to his class but in an elevated one – ranging, as it happens, from the middle style to the high – and in doing so he tries to represent himself as heroic (see, for example, stanzas 4 and 5). When seeking to put himself forward as heroic, he asserts, in the medial stanza of the poem, his centrality to and dominance of the natural world in which he works (see especially his reference to the sun in lines 45–46). Yet the narrator's satiric framing of Damon's monologue (sts 1 and 10), Damon's naivete and unwitting satirizing of himself (as shown, for instance, in lines 57–60), and his awkward – presumably unwitting – fashioning of a counterpart to the language of literary pastoral, ridicule his overreaching. Damon's very name, insofar as it belongs to the sophisticated realm of literary pastoral (as does that of his mistress), emphasizes the disparity between what he is and what he imagines himself to be.

Neither the nunnery nor the Levellers, then, can be seen to provide the principles for a post-Civil War society. (What might be called High Anglicanism has been discredited, in stanza 46, for its worldliness: the '*Prelate* great' in '*Cawood Castle*' is identified in terms of 'Ambition' – associated with *negotium* rather than with *negotium cum deo*.) Through the Marvell persona's portrayals of Fairfax and of Fairfax's residence, and through his strategic use of those portrayals, the poem implies that pre-eminently if not only in Appleton House can be discerned the principles of a truly Christian social order.

It has been argued above that in the final and climactic section of 'Upon Appleton House' (approximately lines 617–776) Mary Fairfax is presented as at once an offspring and an exemplar of the regenerate life, who will one day embody *renovatio* in the world beyond that of her father's estate. What I want to focus on now is the nature of that presentation and how it suggests she will bring English society closer to renewal – closer, that is, to being once more the supposed '*Paradise* of four Seas . . .' (line 323).

That Marvell's persona does indeed image Mary Fairfax as born of and embodying regeneration is made clear in stanza 91:

> This 'tis to have been from the first
> In a *Domestick Heaven* nurst,
> Under the *Discipline* severe
> Of *Fairfax*, and the starry *Vere*;
> Where not one object can come nigh
> But pure, and spotless as the Eye;
> And *Goodness* doth it self intail
> On *Females*, if there want a *Male*.

The image of the Fairfaxes' '*Domestick Heaven*' and the reference to their '*Discipline* severe,' evoking the poem's emblematic blazon of Appleton House and portrait of the Great Lord, indicate distinctly that Mary Fairfax has been born to and nurtured by regenerate parents. The persona goes on to emphasize that Mary has grown up in a virtually immaculate family environment ('Where not one object can come nigh / But pure, and spotless as the Eye . . .'), and subsequently announces that '*Goodness* . . . it self' has become her spiritual inheritance, thus distinctly and logically implying that she embodies the regeneration evident in her parents. What stanza 91 suggests about Mary Fairfax, however, is also if not always as directly suggested earlier in this part of the poem, for the stanza concludes a portrait of Fairfax's daughter which variously represents her as an exemplar of *renovatio*: the stanza at once triumphantly ends and affirms a representation of Mary Fairfax as manifesting regeneration in a number of different ways.

The portrait of Fairfax's daughter begins in stanza 82, and from the start she is described as a numinous figure. The persona, calling her '[t]he *young Maria*' (line 651), tells of her 'judicious Eyes' (line 653) and asserts that '*She* ... already is the *Law* / Of all her *Sex*, her *Ages Aw*' (lines 655–656). The words 'judicious' and '*Law*', which in part define the phrase '*Ages Aw*', imply rational discrimination, rational order, self-control, and thereby associate Mary with the Christian moderation, and so the Protestant heroic virtue, of her father. But the words have another aspect. They foreshadow the association of Mary with wisdom. In stanza 89 the persona says:

> *She* [Mary] counts her Beauty to converse
> In all the Languages as *hers*;
> Nor yet in those *her self* imploycs
> But for the *Wisdome*, not the *Noyse*;
> Nor yet that *Wisdome* would affect,
> But as 'tis *Heavens Dialect*.
>
> (lines 707–712)

There the persona emphatically connects Mary with Christian wisdom. She is, he suggests, interested in the languages, the babel ('*Noyse*', line 710), of the (fallen) world not for their own sakes, nor just for the sake of the wisdom which their acquisition can bring (lines 710–711), but because in gaining wisdom from them she gains something of the divine – something of the language of heaven itself (line 712). That connection of Mary with Christian wisdom, moreover, amplifies the association of her in stanza 82 with her father's Christian moderation (see lines 709–711) and hence with his regenerate state, her association with the latter of course being affirmed more directly by the persona's reference to her desire for the heavenly (lines 711–712 having, it seems to me, a general as well as a specific application to her). From one angle, so to speak, Mary Fairfax appears numinous because portrayed as supranaturally judicious, as sapiential – each of which is implied to express her spiritual regeneracy. But the depiction of her as numinous because regenerate is more ambitious than that.[31]

In portraying Fairfax's daughter, the persona describes nature itself as responsive to her. 'See how loose Nature, in respect / To her, it self doth recollect' (lines 657–658), he says, adding, 'The *Sun* himself, of *Her* aware, / Seems to descend with greater Care;

/ And lest *She* see him go to Bed; / In blushing Clouds conceales his Head' (lines 661–664). He proceeds, in a famous simile, to claim that her effect on nature is in fact like the halcyon's: just as '[t]he modest *Halcyon*' (line 669) makes silent and still '*Admiring Nature*' (line 672 – for the creature's like effect on humanity, see lines 679–680), so does Mary (lines 665–682).[32] To amplify that claim he concludes his comparison of Mary to the halcyon with a contrast between her and a comet (lines 683ff.), at the close of that contrast observing: '[B]y her *Flames*, in *Heaven* try'd, / *Nature* is wholly *vitrifi'd*' (lines 687–688). The dominant idea in those final lines seems to be that through Mary's spiritual incandescence, which is divine (unlike the merely physical incandescence of exhalations from 'the putrid Earth' – see lines 685–686), the landscape around her becomes at once clarified and deprived utterly of motion. The contrast amplifies the preceding comparison's assertion, then, by heightening its images of stillness through the allusion to nature's total vitrification, and by suggesting that Mary Fairfax can impose stasis on the world around her because of her divinely refined/proved spirituality. That emphasis on her spiritual power iterates forcibly the idea of her regeneracy, making as it does so her spiritual power appear at least similar in stature to the heroic spirituality of her father – but a restatement of his spirituality in more rarefied form. Thus as an embodiment of *renovatio* Mary Fairfax is revealed to be not only judicious, or even sapiential: she is indicated both to resemble and to transcend the halcyon, and to transcend analogy to a comet, in her effect on her surroundings.

That diverse imaging of Mary Fairfax as regenerate helps to illuminate, I think, the persona's declaration, after his celebration of her in terms of halcyon and comet:

> 'Tis *She* that to these Gardens gave
> That wondrous Beauty which they have;
> *She* streightness on the Woods bestows;
> To *Her* the Meadow sweetness owes;
> Nothing could make the River be
> So Chrystal-pure but only *She*;
> *She* yet more Pure, Sweet, Streight, and Fair,
> Then Gardens, Woods, Meads, Rivers are.

(lines 689–696)

The persona's announcement that the natural world of her father's estate derives its beauty and order from her would seem to be legitimized, within the frame of his portrait of her, insofar as he has revealed her to be an embodiment of the truly *vita beata*, of *rectitudo* – as able to confer the grace of a regenerate existence on her environment and thereby to perfect it. According to the persona, it is through her, and not directly through her parents, that the landscape of the Fairfax estate becomes '*Paradice's only Map*' (line 768; see lines 749–767).

Just before the persona uses that phrase – in fact, when he is introducing the antitheses which it will conclude (lines 745–752 introducing the antitheses of lines 753–766) – he speaks of Mary Fairfax in words that indicate concisely what his portrait of her has in effect been designed to manifest: '[A]ll *Virgins* She precedes' (line 751). Near the start of the poem's final section he refers to her as 'The *young Maria*' (line 651), and it appears from his subsequent portrayal of her as an exemplar of *renovatio* that the young Mary, preceding all virgins in her spiritual purity (see especially lines 737–738), is a correlative type of the Virgin Mary (rather than an antitype of the Virgin as – so the persona's fable runs – a nun once implied Isabel Thwaites in part to be).[33] Earlier in the poem, Mary's father is suggested to be his ancestor William Fairfax writ large; here, Mary herself is suggested to be at once 'the . . . Virgin *Thwates*' (line 90) writ large and another, greater Isabel Thwaites awaiting another William Fairfax ('Till Fate her [Mary] worthily translates, / And find a *Fairfax* for our *Thwaites*,' lines 747–748).[34]

Recognizing that the persona fashions an implicitly typological portrait of Mary Fairfax would seem to clarify his notion that her marriage, and so her entry into the world beyond that of her parents' estate, will evoke 'some universal good' (line 741). Given that, as has just been argued, Mary is represented as a correlative type of the Virgin, then the logic of a Marian depiction of her points to her marriage as possibly bringing into post-revolutionary English society a child who will enact a religio-political messianic role (line 741 being, as has been previously observed, benignly but, of necessity, vaguely prophetic). In that case, the '*Destiny*' to be chosen (see line 744) by Mary's parents will be socially renovative in a quite specific sense. Whether or not, however, Marvell's persona is actually gesturing towards such a prophecy about Mary Fairfax, his depiction of her as exemplifying regeneracy suggests that her entry into the world of post-Civil War England must draw it closer to a renewal of its (supposedly) prewar peaceful and flourishing state, and thus broadly supports the idea of her as able one day to evoke 'some universal good'. The persona's association of Mary, through her regeneracy, with judiciousness and with wisdom certainly contributes to the notion that she will benefit society. More important, though, is his emphatic indication that because of her regeneracy she can convey peace to her surroundings, and that in doing so she manifests a spiritual power akin to, but more rarefied than, her father's. The account of the mowers at work (in the poem's fourth section) reveals contemporary English life as emerging from yet as still overshadowed by or, so to speak, echoing the discords of recent history. After the account of the mowers immediately follows a curt dismissal of the Levellers, implying that their political ideals cannot provide a model for post-Civil War society. Here, on the other hand, the spirituality intimated by the persona to be incarnated in Mary Fairfax is indicated to offer, if hardly a distinct social programme, a pacifying and harmonizing influence on her environs, heightened by her capacity to perfect the natural by the graciousness of her presence. Furthermore, it is indicated that when one day she conveys those attributes into society, she will be translating an amplified restatement of her father's Protestant heroic virtue from the inner world of his retirement back into the outer world where his heroic virtue was, according to the persona, pre-eminent. Through the portrait of Mary Fairfax, then, the persona can confirm the notion raised earlier in the poem that the Great Lord's retirement has been, in a sense, no retirement at all. The first and third sections of 'Upon Appleton House' imply that Fairfax's retirement has meant his leaving negotium but maintaining negotium cum deo; the portrait of Mary signals that he has been nurturing in his retirement a daughter whose departure from his estate will (to whatever degree he has been aware of it) bring again his power for good – perhaps even increased – into the world.[35] Thus in the portrayal of Fairfax as a type of (Calvinist) Protestant heroic virtue lies the foundation for the climactic argument in the Marvell persona's political defence of Fairfax's withdrawal into private life.[36]

In 'Upon the Hill and Grove at Bill-borow . . .,' the Marvell persona celebrates hill and grove respectively in terms of perfect proportion (lines 1–8), humility (lines 9–16), courtesy (lines 21–24), beneficent grandeur (lines 25–32), and flourishing uprightness (lines 55–56) allied with prudence (line 60). Fairfax himself is celebrated as a numinous figure (lines 35–40), as an embodiment of heroic love (lines 43–48) and an exemplar of heroic virtue (lines 65–72), and for his humility (lines 75–80). Those categories are also (if not identically) used in the demonstrative rhetoric of 'Upon Appleton House' but there they seem to be centred on the idea of Christian moderation, and so to become part of the Marvell persona's honouring of not merely arms and the man but rather of arms and the Christian man. As I have been attempting to argue throughout this essay, however, in apparently making the idea of Christian moderation central to the representation of Fairfax, Marvell's persona seems to depict him as being more than *miles Christianus*: as a virtually complete embodiment of (Calvinist) Protestant heroic virtue. And I have tried to suggest that, through fashioning such an icon of Fairfax, Marvell's persona can at once celebrate the Great Lord and defend his retreat from public life, the icon therefore appearing to have a deliberative as well as a demonstrative function, and the fashioning of it therefore to be a political strategy – the poem's dominant one – as well as an act of praise. Marvell's achievement in 'Upon Appleton House' would thus seem finally to be both the honouring, the defence, of his patron and (to those ends) the appropriation, the political/-theological transformation, of the country house poem.

Notes

1.   Reference to Marvell's verse is from the first volume of H.M. Margoliouth, ed., *The Poems and Letters of Andrew Marvell*, 3rd edn rev. Pierre Legouis with E.E. Duncan-Jones, 2 vols, Oxford: Oxford University Press, 1971. I use the phrase 'perfect moral commonwealths' approximately in the sense given to its singular form by J.C. Davis, *Utopia and the Ideal Society: A Study of English Utopian Writing 1516–1700*, 1981; reprinted Cambridge: Cambridge University Press, 1983, pp. 26–31. I use the term 'arcadian' in a more general sense than that given it in his book, pp. 22–26. On varieties of 'Utopian' thought in the English Renaissance, I have also con-

sulted the studies by Frank E. and Fritzie P. Manuel, and by M. Eliav-Feldon.

2. See, for example: 'To Penshurst', lines 19–44; 'To Saxham', lines 1–3; 'To my friend G.N. from Wrest', lines 1–20, lines 69–106. Reference to Jonson is from Donaldson's edition, to Carew from Dunlap's.

3. Cf. 'To Penshurst', lines 45–75, 'To Saxham', lines 11–14 and 35–58, 'To my friend G.N. . . .', lines 20–57, 'A Panegerick to Sir Lewis Pemberton', *passim*. Reference to Jonson and Carew as given above; to Herrick, from Patrick's edition. On the idea of 'civility' in those contexts, see my 'The Cavalier World and John Cleveland', *Studies in Philology*, 78 (1981), pp. 61–86, at pp. 76–8. (The article's account of Marvell's verse differs in some respects from that put forward here.)

4. Those perfect, microcosmic commonwealths are usually pictured as being beyond the range of current political disturbances, and so are in part defined (deliberately or otherwise) against them.

5. Fairfax was also, of course, one of his more politically conservative opponents.

6. On the debate about which Appleton House was the one described in Marvell's poem, see Lee Erickson, 'Marvell's "Upon Appleton House" and the Fairfax Family', *English Literary Renaissance*, 9 (1979), pp. 158–168. I find Erickson's arguments persuasive; the phrase 'the great house' may be only loosely applicable to the house described by Marvell's persona.

7. Fairfax is represented as primarily embodying Christian virtues, whereas Pemberton is pictured as embodying a range of classical virtues in conjunction with those which are specifically Christian.

8. For other views of the poem, see especially: Ruth Wallerstein, *Studies in Seventeenth-Century Poetic*, 1950; reprinted. Madison and Milwaukee: University of Wisconsin Press, 1965, pp. 295–318; Don Cameron Allen, *Image and Meaning: Metaphoric Traditions in Renaissance Poetry*, Baltimore: Johns Hopkins University Press, 1965, pp. 115–153; Kitty W. Scoular, *Natural Magic: Studies in the Presentation of Nature in English Poetry from Spenser to Marvell*, Oxford: Oxford University Press, 1965, pp. 120–190; Harold E. Toliver, *Marvell's Ironic Vision*, New Haven and London: Yale University Press, 1965, pp. 113–129; Harry Berger, Jr, *'Upon Appleton House*: An Interpretation', *Southern Review*, 1 (1965), pp. 7–32; M.J.K. O'Loughlin, 'This Sober Frame: A Reading of "Upon Appleton House" ', in George de F. Lord, ed., *Andrew Marvell: A Collection of Critical Essays*, Englewood Cliffs, N.J.: Prentice Hall, 1968, pp. 120–142; John M. Wallace, *Destiny His Choice: The Loyalism of Andrew Marvell*, 1968; reprinted. Cambridge: Cambridge Univer-

sity Press, 1980, pp. 232–257; J.B. Leishman, *The Art of Marvell's Poetry*, 2nd edn, London: Hutchinson, 1968, pp. 221–291; Pierre Legouis, *Andrew Marvell Poet Puritan Patriot*, 2nd edn, Oxford: Oxford University Press, 1968, pp. 27–90; Maren-Sofie Röstvig, ' "Upon Appleton House" ', in Michael Wilding, ed., *Marvell: Modern Judgements*, London: Macmillan, 1969, pp. 215–232; David Evett, ' "Paradice's Only Map": The *Topos* of the *Locus Amoenus* and the Structure of Marvell's "Upon Appleton House" ', *PMLA*, 85 (1970), pp. 504–513; Rosalie L. Colie, *'My Ecchoing Song': Andrew Marvell's Poetry of Criticism*, Princeton: Princeton University Press, 1970, pp. 181–294; Donald M. Friedman, *Marvell's Pastoral Art*, Berkeley and Los Angeles: University of California Press, 1970, pp. 213–246; Barbara Kiefer Lewalski, *Donne's Anniversaries and the Poetry of Praise: The Creation of a Symbolic Mode*, Princeton: Princeton University Press, 1973, pp. 355–370; Jim Swan, ' "Betwixt Two Labyrinths": Andrew Marvell's Rational Amphibian', *Texas Studies in Literature and Language*, 17 (1975), pp. 551–572; Isabel G. MacCaffrey, 'The Scope of Imagination in *Upon Appleton House*', in Kenneth Friedenreich, ed., *Tercentenary Essays in Honor of Andrew Marvell*, Hamden, Conn.: Shoestring Press, 1977, pp. 224–244; Maren-Sofie Röstvig, *'In ordine di ruota*: 'Circular Structure in "The Unfortunate Lover" and "Upon Appleton House" ', in K. Friedenreich, ed., *Tercentenary Essays . . .*, pp. 245–267; William A. McClung, *The Country House in English Renaissance Poetry*, Berkeley, Los Angeles, London: University of California Press, 1977, pp. 157–174; John Dixon Hunt, *Andrew Marvell: His Life and Writings*, London: Elek, 1978, pp. 80–112; Annabel M. Patterson, *Marvell and the Civic Crown*, Princeton: Princeton University Press, 1978, pp. 95–110; Frank J. Warnke, 'The Meadow-Sequence in "Upon Appleton House": Questions of Tone and Meaning', in C.A. Patrides, ed., *Approaches to Marvell: The York Tercentenary Lectures*, London, Henley, Boston: Routledge and Kegan Paul, 1978, pp. 234–250; R.I.V. Hodge, *Foreshortened Time: Andrew Marvell and Seventeenth Century Revolutions*, Cambridge: Brewer, Rowman and Littlefield, 1978, pp. 132–158; Michael O'Loughlin, *The Garlands of Repose: The Literary Celebration of Civic and Retired Leisure*, Chicago and London: University of Chicago Press, 1978, pp. 157–224; Warren L. Chernaik, *The Poet's Time: Politics and Religion in the Work of Andrew Marvell*, Cambridge: Cambridge University Press, 1983, pp. 23–25, 28–42; Robert Cummings, 'The Forest Sequence in Marvell's "Upon Appleton House": The Imaginative Contexts of a Poetic Episode', *Huntington Library Quarterly*, 47 (1984), pp. 179–210; Harold Skulsky, ' "Upon Appleton House": Marvell's Comedy of Discourse', *ELH*, 52

(1985), pp. 591–620; Margarita Stocker, *Apocalyptic Marvell: The Second Coming in Seventeenth Century Poetry*, Sussex: Harvester, 1986, pp. 46–66; Michael Wilding, *Dragons Teeth: Literature in the English Revolution*, Oxford: Oxford University Press, 1987, pp. 138–172; Patsy Griffin, "'Twas no *Religious House* till now': Marvell's "Upon Appleton House"', *Studies in English Literature 1500–1900*, 28 (1988), pp. 61–76.

9. Kitty Scoular was the first, I think, to connect Marvell's tortoise with an emblem of self-containment; the tortoise has, of course, a range of other emblematic associations but many of those are connected with behaviour supposedly desirable for women.

10. G.P. Valeriano Bolzani, *Hieroglyphica* (1602) ed. Stephen Orgel, New York and London: Garland, 1976, p. 629. This emblem may illuminate [Sir] Politic Wouldbe's appearance as 'most politic tortoise' near the end of *Volpone*: a parodic emblem of *prudentia* – the politician's special attribute.

11. The 'sober . . . Mind' of the Early Church is thus implicitly opposed to the overreaching *phantasia* expressed in foreign architecture. If Marvell's persona is not referring to the primitive Christian virtue of the Early Church, then he would seem to be referring to that of earlier, less sophisticated, English society. My point is the same in either case.

12. If Lee Erickson is right (see n. 6), then the structure of the house is also revealing of Fairfax's ancestors.

13. Reference is to Ian Donaldson's edition of the poems, Oxford: Oxford University Press, 1975.

14. *Odes* II, 18; reference is to the Loeb edition.

15. John Calvin, *Institutes of the Christian Religion*, trans. Henry Beveridge, 2 vols, 1845; reprinted. Grand Rapids: Erdmans, 1983, vol. 1, p. 518. Further reference to Calvin's *Institutes* is from this edition. I am indebted to the studies of Calvin by Wallace, Wendel, Kendall, Höpfl, and Bouwsma.

16. *Institutes*, vol. 1, p. 445; cf. vol. 2, p. 26 and p. 33.

17. *Institutes*, vol. 1, p. 324.

18. John Calvin, *The Epistles of Paul the Apostle to the Galatians, Ephesians, Philippians and Colossians*, trans. T.H.L. Parker, Edinburgh: Oliver and Boyd, 1965, p. 105.

19. *Institutes*, vol. 1, p. 445.

20. John Calvin, *The Gospel according to St John, 11–21 and The First Epistle of John*, trans. T.H.L. Parker, Edinburgh: Oliver and Boyd, 1961, pp. 12–13.

21. *Institutes*, vol. 1, p. 515. Cf. vol. 1, p. 324.

22. John Calvin, *The Epistles of Paul the Apostle . . .*, trans. Parker, p. 245.

23. John Calvin, *A Harmony of the Gospels Matthew, Mark and Luke*, vol. 3, trans. A.W. Morrison, Edinburgh: Oliver and Boyd, 1972, p. 158.

24. For Calvin, there could be no 'worship of God' without Christ's mediation.

25. The implication seems to be that William Fairfax indirectly benefits his country by founding the Fairfax dynasty. It is also implied that Fairfax had, of course, the same heroic power now possessed before the war's end, that he was regenerate before his retirement, and that he had, after all, fought on the right side – and therefore that he could have perhaps singularly benefited his country had he not retired.

26. For acquaintance with Calvin's idea of *negotium cum deo* I am indebted to the notes in the McNeill and Battles translation of the *Institutes*, at pp. 212, 598, 610, 691, 891.

27. Barbara Kiefer Lewalski, in *Donne's Anniversaries and the Poetry of Praise* (see n. 8), also describes Fairfax's daughter in terms of personal regeneration, though her interpretation of the image of Mary Fairfax differs in many ways from that argued below. Some of the views on Mary Fairfax – and on the poem in general – put forward in this discussion also have counterparts in Patsy Griffin's "Twas no *Religious House* . . .' (see n. 8).

28. See John Wilson, *Fairfax*, New York: Watts, 1985, pp. 123–130 and 154–162. I have also drawn on the biography by Clements R. Markham.

29. See Gerrard Winstanley, *The Works*, ed. George H. Sabine, 1941; reprinted. New York: Greenwood Press, 1965, especially at pp. 315–316, 150. See also: Christopher Hill, *The World Turned Upside Down: Radical Ideas During the English Revolution*, 1972; reprint Penguin, Harmondsworth, 1975, pp. 107–150; T. Wilson Hayes, *Winstanley the Digger: A Literary Analysis of Radical Ideas in the English Revolution*, Cambridge, Mass. and London: Harvard University Press, 1979.

30. The nuns, too, are presented as unheroic: as parodic Christian heroines.

31. D.C. Allen, in his *Image and Meaning* . . . (see n. 8), does not merely connect Mary with Christian wisdom but identifies her with Wisdom itself.

32. Mary is imaged as certainly affecting nature; her effect on humankind is also implied, however, by the halcyon image.

33. In using the phrase 'correlative type' – coined, as far as I know, by Barbara Kiefer Lewalski – I want to emphasize that Mary Fairfax is implied to have necessary limitations, rather than actual flaws, in being presented as a counterpart to the Virgin.

34. Even if it were not agreed that she is being represented typologically, because '[A]ll *Virgins* She preceds' she can still nonetheless be seen as the figure of Isabel Thwaites writ large.
35. Whilst it is obvious that Fairfax has physically retreated from public life, it is apparent that, paradoxically, he has done so only to send a more refined version of his heroic virtue into society.
36. Cf. 'The Garden', lines 57–64, especially lines 63–64, where the persona tries to legitimize his notion of retreat by an appeal to Scripture – which undercuts his idea instead of supporting it.

3   Virgins and Whores: the Politics of Sexual Misconduct in the 1660s

Steven N. Zwicker

Just past the middle of 'The Last Instructions',[1] Marvell slackens the restless pace of his satire; he turns from abuse and excoriation to pastoral and panegyric. Set deep within the argument of this epic satire are two pastoral episodes that counterpoint the poem's dominant idiom; but these vignettes do more than play country virtue to court corruption. Their position within the structure of the poem argues the vulnerability of pastoral, but, more urgently, they fix a model of physical innocence in a poem whose most fundamental corruption is sexual violence. The pastoral moment in which Marvell sets the portraits of Michael de Ruyter and Archibald Douglas suggests how powerful and pervasive is the matter of sexual corruption with which the poem opens, how crucial the attempted rape at the poem's close, and how intimate are the relations throughout this poem, and in the culture more broadly, between sexual appetite and political corruption. The Stuart court would prove vulnerable to the force of this association not only in the mid–1660s, the first moment of serious literary assault on the court, but throughout the 1670s, in Exclusion, and indeed through the final assault on James and Mary of Modena in the satires on the supposititious Old Pretender.

The body politic is a familiar literary trope; it is also a fundamental of political thought and political theory, nowhere more forcefully argued than in the 1651 frontispiece to Hobbes's *Leviathan*.[2] It may not be a novel observation that the body politic took on an explicitly sexual life after 1660, but the power of this topic, the danger and vulnerability of its terms, the force of its polemical meaning have not been fully charted in our reading of the satiric attacks levelled steadily and brilliantly against the persons of the Stuart court or in the explication of Restoration court culture. It is, of course, difficult to read Lord Rochester's verse of the 1670s without acknowledging the brutal and relentless equation between sexual excess and corruption at court. But Rochester is not the daring exception. 'The Last Instructions' gives us an occasion to chart the metaphor in the most important satiric text of the first decade of the Restoration and to map the political argument of innocence and appetite into the larger rhetorical field of the 1660s.

First, perhaps, an acknowledgement that the sensibility of our poet might make us hesitant to generalize beyond the borders of his work. But even in the delicacy, the decay and indulgence, of the lyric Marvell we can sense the larger public argument. The dating of Marvell's lyrics is vexed, but we can arrange a background for the whores and virgins of 'The Last Instructions' out of the pastoral materials that marked the poet's sojourn at Lord Fairfax's estate. That background should enable us to see not only the continuity of Marvell's sensibility from lyric to satire but its larger cultural meaning. The pastoralist of 'The Garden' and 'The Nymph Complaining', and most especially the satirist and idler of 'Upon Appleton House' was possessed of a peculiar and exquisite refinement; but the lyrics and lyric history suggest more than idiosyncrasy. They acknowledge the force of sexuality in imaginative exploit, in the argument of heroic venture, in the calculation of human potential, and in the luxuries of retreat. There is in the lyrics and in 'Upon Appleton House' something close to an equation of sexual, ethical, and civic misconduct. The indulgence of 'The Garden' is an invitation to moral disintegration; the corruption of sexual appetite in the nunnery of 'Upon Appleton House' is a perversion not simply of sacred retreat but of national destiny. The ethical force of monogamous heterosexual coupling is unmistakable throughout the historical drama of 'Upon Appleton

House'. Destiny recognizes only one appropriate sexual model; all others are corrupt or immature. Both Maria and the angler are virgins awaiting the force of destiny; Maria is on its verge, the marital and sexual fate of the angler is unknown. But there can be little doubt about the public values the angler projects: the great vehicle of history is monogamous, reproductive union.

While the body politic is a continuous theme in renaissance political discourse, we must acknowledge as background to the satires of the 1660s not only that continuity, Marvell's own absorption in this subject, but its more immediate cultural and political resonance. The cult of Platonic love in the court of Charles I suggests the subtle and rarified ways in which the language of love relations might articulate political culture.[3] Sexual exploit displaced Platonic love as a civic language in the 1660s, but at both Caroline courts there was a keen appreciation, at the centre and at the margins, of the ways in which the taste and exploits of the monarch defined and publicized the quality of the body politic.

Of course, the address to sexual power in the Restoration did not begin with satire; it had begun as early as the panegyrics welcoming the restoration of monarchy and pleasure.[4] Not that the invocation of pleasure signalled sexual profligacy. The public themes of those first months argued the Restoration as a return of the person of the King and the office of kingship, and these were coupled with broader renewal: a restoration of arms and arts; a reinvigoration of science and letters; a revival of wit and eloquence; an elevation of style and manners; and for our purposes, most especially, a restoration of abundance and pleasure.[5] At the centre of these hopes and idealizations stood the King whose words announcing return, and spoken frequently thereafter, promised forgiveness and liberality.[6] And these were ideals not difficult to embrace. Not many in 1660 would have gainsaid forgiveness and liberality, a mythic English past of carolling and delight,[7] or the more immediate pleasures of the alehouse. Charles's return to London on May 29 was a bacchanalian triumph, 'This day, his Majesty, Charles II came to London . . . with a triumph of above 20,000 horse and foot, brandishing their swords, and shouting with inexpressible joy; the ways strewn with flowers, the bells ringing, the streets hung with tapestry, fountains running with wine . . . the windows and balconies, all set with ladies;

trumpets, music, and myriads of people flocking . . . such a restoration was never mentioned in any history, ancient or modern,
since the return of the Jews from their Babylonish captivity; nor
so joyful a day and so bright ever seen in this nation.'[8] But the
pleasures and arts of this Court would prove rather more complex,
strategic, and finally more subversive than could have been
reckoned in the early months of the Restoration. What seem to
our eyes gestures of bucolic innocence, indeed the entire culture
of pleasure, formed an important polemical position in the 1660s.
Delight and abundance played a crucial role in repudiating a once
much trumpeted piety and saintliness. That the 1650s were a good
deal more complex hardly needs assertion; but what does need
stressing is that the themes of this restoration not only projected
ideals for the future and idealized images of the present, they also
allowed in quite conscious and perhaps not quite so conscious
ways a powerful engagement with Puritan moral regulation and
reformation; in that project, abundance, liberality, and pleasure
played a significant role.[9]

It may have been chance that the person of Charles II allowed
so much of this double-edged work to be done, that his history
of exile and restoration offered the parallel with David in godly
election as in sexual history, and that the King's personal inclinations so fully accommodated the themes of liberality and abundance that were claimed for the restoration as a whole. But the
generosity of spirit that the King announced at Breda would, in
significant ways, come to characterize his reign. Nor can the
King's wit and playful sense of irony be doubted; it is not difficult
to believe that the restored Court provided a model for repartee
in the comedy of manners, that the satires of Rochester, scurrilous
and brilliant, found a forgiving audience in the king, or that he
would have grasped immediately the ironies and pleasures of the
opening lines of *Absalom and Achitophel*. And while abundance,
generosity, and pleasure took their cue from the person of the
King, they had also a broader life in the literature promoting,
celebrating, and defending his kingship. On the abundance of the
King turned the patronage system in its entirety: both the literal
and figurative systems of rewards and generosity of personal attention, protection, place, and pension. It was not only in the defensive and partisan gestures of *Absalom and Achitophel* that the
paternalism of the King was urged as an aspect of patronage,

stability and national abundance; those combined hopes were expressed in the first poems written to greet his return and frequently thereafter.[10] And though the public assumed that sexual abundance would be harnessed by marriage and progeny, the twinning of personal and national fertility, of sexual abundance and commercial triumph, is repeatedly found in the Restoration pronouncements.[11]

Indeed, the King's procreative promise formed the very centre of a politics of abundance. Charles's return is celebrated in the language of passion and penance, pleasure and fertility, bounty and leisure, marriage and fecundity. The explicitness of this language derived not simply from what was known or rumoured of the King's private pleasures, but from conventional assumptions about the role of those pleasures in the state.[12] As the panegyrics and nuptial verse make clear, the royal capacity for abundance promised civic stability and continuity, qualities much prized after two decades of political turbulence. We have come to associate the Court of Charles II with bawdry and heartless licence, but there is nothing in the slightest licentious in the high-minded verse that celebrates this sexual restoration. At its centre were lineage and political continuity; from the promise of the royal line issued a series of topics that bound sexual fertility to those very qualities which the King had pronounced on his return home: liberality, generosity, and forgiveness.

We cannot grasp the political issues or the complex polemical atmosphere in which the domestic politics of the early 1660s unfolded without allowing pleasure and abundance their full political meaning. Nor can we properly read the literature of the mid–1660s without contemplating how these themes might have turned in the minds of a public disappointed by the barrenness of the royal marriage and the unbridled licence of the court. But when the King returned, pleasure and fertility meant a repudiation of the immediate past and the continuity of the future. The King himself observed to his second Parliament, 'I have been often put in mind by my friends, that it was now high time to marry, and I have thought so myself ever since I came into England. But there appeared difficulties enough in the choice, though many overtures have been made to me; and if I should never marry till I could make such a choice, against which there could be no foresight of any inconveniences that may ensue, you would like to see me an old batchelor, which I think you do not desire to do. I can now tell you ... that I am resolved to marry if God please ... which I look upon as very wonderful, and even as some instance of the approbation of God himself.'[13] The mood of buoyant optimism and godly approbation which had greeted the Restoration and the nuptials of the King did not last very long into the 1660s.

The disappointment of returning cavaliers has been amply documented,[14] but it was not only those trying to get back their own who were not completely gratified by the Restoration settlement. Dissenters were harried and threatened and had not of course disappeared, though some had turned to quietism under the new régime. The so-called Clarendon Code was harshly restrictive, and though the King attempted Indulgence in 1662, his Cavalier Parliament was not in a mood to grant such an indulgence to dissenters.[15] And while the King and many in Parliament had spoken against division and recrimination, sharp words were not long in coming.[16] The first real crises of the restoration arrived, however, with a force beyond anyone's reckoning.[17] The middle years of this decade brought military, fiscal, natural, and political disaster: the Dutch invasion of the Thames and destruction of a good part of the English fleet; the Great Plague and Fire that decimated London's population, levelled huge tracts of the city, and left rumours of conspiracy in its wake; and the hounding from office of the Lord Chancellor in a parliamentary mood that reminded some of the destruction of Strafford.[18] The combination of fire, plague, and military defeat gave some observers the impression that the four horsemen of the apocalypse had descended on to London in rapid order; cries of divine judgment were not long in coming, nor was the apocalyptic significance of the year lost on millenarian sensibilities.[19] To suggest that by 1667 the court was harried and beleaguered is to argue the mildest version of this crisis. Although political resentments had not yet hardened into a system of opposition politics as they would in Exclusion,[20] they nevertheless opened a floodgate of polemical activity: sermons, broadsides, pamphlets, petitions, lampoons, and satires as well as an heroic literature of the Anglo-Dutch war, including Edmund Waller's 'Instructions to a Painter' (1665) and Dryden's 'Annus Mirabilis' (1667).

Waller's celebration of the English victory at Lowestoft was the opening and hopeful gesture in an heroic and highly decorative idiom,[21] and it was quickly answered not only by the events of the Anglo-Dutch war but also by satires that engaged the premise, the topics, tropes, and style of Waller's verse.[22] In the satiric reversals of Waller's piece, the conduct of the war, the character of the Admiralty, the quality of the Court, and finally the negligence and indulgence of the King himself were put under harsh satiric scrutiny. The breadth and density of the satiric attack were such that the polemical literature itself can be said to have become part of the crisis. The Court was put on the defensive not only against defeat and disaster but also against the scurrilous charges levelled at its conduct and character, and at the suggestion that such conduct was itself responsible for the divine judgment now so clearly visited on the nation. The poems of praise and blame addressed the prosecution of the war, its heroes and heroics, and the conduct of the Ministry and Admiralty; they also undertook to manage the image of the Court and King, and rather more specifically and daringly, the King's sexual conduct.

By the mid–1660s that bacchic moment in which the King and nation first embraced had long ago disappeared; the failure of the King's legitimate sexual abundance was only too obvious, and the morals of the royal family were searched for explanations of that failure. Licence and fornication had, by the mid–1660s, an urgent moral and political significance. Who could have missed the application implied by publishing in 1667 a sermon on Hebrews 13.4 entitled 'Fornication Condemned',[23] or the significance of the sermons preached before the King at Whitehall in 1667 on sensuality, lust, and passion.[24] In the midst of disaster, these were subjects as dangerously charged as ministerial incompetence and greed, naval mismanagement and cowardice, fire and plague. The royal extravagance came under parliamentary scrutiny and displeasure in 1667;[25] but the licentiousness of the Court was addressed in other forms, no less significant for the political culture, including squibs, pamphlets, broadsides and lampoons, and of course the series of advice poems that culminated in 'The Last Instructions'.

Waller's 'Instructions to a Painter'[26] may not have been the very first effort in politicizing pleasure for the mid–1660s, but it was a visible and vulnerable move; in its optimistic elevation of tone it gave an opening to satirists sceptical of its attempt to claim for this court the authority of high culture. For example, the short, complimentary episode depicting the Duchess of York's visit to Harwich in May of 1665 is scornfully replayed in 'The Second Advice' and 'The Last Instructions', and refurbished in Dryden's dedicatory verse to 'Annus Mirabilis'. Waller inserts the scene between two naval battles and suggests that the resupply not only refreshed the naval stores but renewed valor itself:

> But who can always on the billows lie?
> The wat'ry wilderness yields no supply:
> Spreading our sails, to Harwich we resort,
> And meet the beauties of the British court.
> Th' illustrious Duchess and her glorious train
> (Like Thetis with her nymphs) adorn the main.
> The gazing sea-gods, since the Paphian queen
> Sprung from among them, no such sight had seen.
> Charm'd with the graces of a troop so fair,
> Those deathless powers for us themselves declare,
> Resolv'd the aid of Neptune's court to bring
> And help the nation where such beauties spring,
> The soldier here his wasted store supplies
> And takes new valor from the ladies' eyes.
>
> (lines 77–90)

For the moment, Waller would have us contemplate the Duchess of York as Aphrodite and Thetis, goddess of the sea, divinity of love and fertility, supplier of arms to Achilles. Innocent enough; but in 'The Second Advice' (1666),[27] both the subject and Waller's literary manners come under scornful attack. Here is no Aphrodite and her train of nymphs, but sexual caricature:

> But, Painter, now prepare, t' enrich thy piece,
> Pencil of ermines, oil of ambergris:
> See where the Duchess, with triumphant tail
> Of num'rous coaches, Harwich does assail!
> So the land crabs, at Nature's kindly call,
> Down to engender at the sea do crawl.
> See then the Admiral, with navy whole,
> To Harwich through the ocean caracole.
> So swallows, buri'd in the sea, at spring
> Return to land with summer on their wing.
> One thrifty ferry-boat of mother-pearl
> Suffic'd of old the Cytherean girl;
> Yet navies are but properties, when here
> (A small sea-masque and built to court you, dear)

Three goddesses in one: Pallas for art,
Venus for sport, and Juno in your heart.
O Duchess! if thy nuptial pomp were mean,
'Tis paid with int'rest in this naval scene.
Never did Roman Mark within the Nile
So feast the fair Egyptian Crocodile,
Nor the Venetian Duke, with such a state,
The Adriatic marry at that rate.

(lines 53–74)

The Duchess's 'glorious train' has become a triumphant tail, Waller's elevated tone is ridiculed, his mythology exploded, his extravagance regretted. And 'The Last Instructions' provides a harsher and nastier explicitness. Through the satires, in 'The Second Advice', 'The Third Advice', and in 'The Last Instructions', the elevated, heroic, and complimentary materials of Waller's *Advice* and, more largely, of the literature of court compliment are inverted vividly and exactly. Rather than nymphs, gods, and goddesses, Marvell gives us anatomy and appetite, grossness and sexual license. The satirist exposes vice, extravagance and folly, but in 'The Last Instructions' the particular aim, the nearly obsessive fix on enormity and appetite, is to connect sexual greed and political corruption. Marvell addresses himself to poetics, but the fundamental issue is politics. The satirist is keen to lower the tone, to debunk epic gestures and claims, to debase and embarrass; but what he angles after throughout the satire is the matter of governance. And it was clear by the mid–1660s that a deep vulnerability in the Court's armoury was the King's morals: his appetites, his personal indulgences and sexual follies.

It may seem puzzling that these attacks should have been repeatedly directed against the Duchess of York, and by implication at the Duke of York, rather than against the King himself. But the accounts of the King's sexual appetite that would come in 1670s should not obscure the fact that direct attacks on the person of the King were quite new in the polemic of the mid–1660s. Just as it had been customary to attack a King's policies through his supposititious 'evil ministers', so was it now easier to attack Charles's morals through his relatives and mistresses. And the Duchess of York was particularly vulnerable to such attack, both as the subject of scandalous rumours circulated at the time of her sudden marriage to the Duke, and as the daughter of the reviled and by the middle of 1667 discredited person of her father, Lord Chancellor Hyde, Earl of Clarendon.[28] One of the charges against Clarendon was his aim to load the King with a barren wife so that he might ascend, through his grandchildren, to the throne.[29] It was an accusation frequently repeated and coupled with other charges against his appetite, grandeur, and arrogance. The 'Third Advice' poses the simplicity and honesty of the Duke and Duchess of Albemarle against Clarendon.[30] But in 'The Last Instructions' the address to luxury and vice could hardly be more sharply focused on the Court or more centrally concerned with the relations between sexual indulgence and political folly. What had been indirection and innuendo becomes in 'The Last Instructions' direct assault. Here the poet is concerned with a 'race of Drunkards, Pimps, and Fools'; and steadily, both in blame and praise, the aim of this poem is to argue sexual and political issues as one. So the poem begins, and so the poem ends in that daring portrait of Charles II in his bedchamber. Between lies a world of appetite, vice, and folly.

The attribution of corrupt politics and sexual profligacy to a single court appetite begins with a portrait of Henry Jermyn, Earl of St. Albans, at the French court:

> Paint then St. Albans full of soup and gold,
> The new Courts pattern, Stallion of the old.
> Him neither Wit nor Courage did exalt,
> But Fortune chose him for her pleasure salt.
> Paint him with Drayman's Shoulders, butchers Mein,
> Member'd like Mules, with Elephantine chine.
>
> (lines 29–34)

Although succeeding portraits are more daring and violent, the sketch of Jermyn has a lovely economy, a neatness and efficiency that are the signature of Marvell's satire. The conjoining of soup and gold explicates the imbedded pun on bullion, linking not excrement and treasure but appetite and greed; and that argument is coupled to the crucial third term in the suggestion of Jermyn's sexual service to Henrietta Maria, 'The new Courts pattern, Stallion of the old'. At the Restoration, Jermyn was created Earl of St. Albans and posted ambassador to the French court; the Queen Mother was fifty-one in 1660 and dead at the beginning of 1666.[31] The suggestion that Jermyn, debauched in appetite, besotted with food and drink, was stallion to Henrietta Maria is both lurid and comic. Pepys records the rumour that St. Albans was married to the Queen Mother,[32] but Marvell's image does not conjure nuptial propriety. Jermyn is cast as 'pleasure salt'; the language conjoins sexual and physical appetite; ingestion and copulation are one. 'Pleasure salt' recalls the initial figure of Jermyn, bloated with soup and gold, and its implications are extended in images of lechery and force: 'Paint him with Drayman's Shoulders, butchers Mein'. Moreover the physical image is but a prelude to the figure of Jermyn as 'instrument' of political treachery. The twinning of lust and deceit is argued toward the close of the portrait: 'He needs no Seal, but to St. James's lease, / Whose Breeches were the Instrument of Peace'.[33] John Wallace has observed of this portrait that Marvell's political seriousness in 'The Last Instructions' is shown by his unusual concern with foreign policy, and his prescient grasp of France's role in English diplomatic history;[34] the portrait of Jermyn also fixes this critique in explicitly sexual terms and anticipates, in its insistent coupling of sexual defilement and political corruption, the closing portrait of Charles II.

More immediately, the portrait of Jermyn prepares the terms for the figure of Anne Hyde drawn in the succeeding lines:

> Paint then again Her Highness to the life,
> Philosopher beyond Newcastle's Wife.
> She, nak'd, can Archimedes self put down,
> For an Experiment upon the Crown.
> She perfected that Engine, oft assay'd,
> How after Childbirth to renew a Maid.
> And found how Royal Heirs might be matur'd,
> In fewer months than Mothers once indur'd.
>
> Not unprovok'd she trys forbidden Arts,
> But in her soft Breast Loves hid Cancer smarts.
> While she revolves, at once, Sidney's disgrace,
> And her self scorn'd for emulous Denham's Face;
> And nightly hears the hated Guards away
> Galloping with the Duke to other Prey.
>   (lines 49–56, 73–78)

Again the poet harshly and luridly mingles political, sexual, and physical appetites, a disorder suggesting not only a chaos of passions but a violence and degradation of taste. The portrait is crowded with particulars, with plots, treachery, ambition, hunger, and enormity; it argues a confusion of terms, it suggests that debauchery cohabits with treason. While the portrait of Jermyn glances slanderously at the Queen Mother, the address to Henrietta Maria's daughter-in-law is frontal and direct: Jermyn may be the Queen Mother's stallion, but the Duchess of York is a whore. The accusations were familiar enough by the time Marvell drew up his indictment: her sexual career preceding marriage to the Duke of York (rumoured to include the Earl of St. Alban's nephew and namesake Henry Jermyn), her political ambition to mount the royal throne, her supposed murder of Lady Denham, one of the Duke of York's mistresses, the enormity of her appetite and body, and her sexual servicing by Henry Sidney, Groom to the Bedchamber of the Duke and Duchess and her Master of the Horse.[35] The insults echo the attacks on Lord Chancellor Hyde and taint the royal family, but in their force and violence go quite beyond smearing association. Appetite and debauchery are satiric commonplaces, but the particular insults are quite this poet's own:

> Paint her with Oyster lip and breath of fame,
> Wide mouth that 'sparagus may well proclaim:
> With Chancellor's belly and so large a rump,
> There, not behind, the coach her pages jump.
>
> (lines 61–64)

The image is a further debasement of Waller's portrait of the Duchess, cruder than the figure in 'The Third Advice'. The particulars are not only degrading, gross in every sense, they also position the rule of appetites at the centre of a realm in which governance is out of control. Slandering the Duchess of York may have been good sport in the satires of the 1660s, but in the structure of this satire, the escalating attacks bring the denunciations of raging appetite ever nearer to the body of the King. Whoring and misgovernance are the central charges laid against the King at the poem's close, and they are carefully prepared at the beginning of the satire.

Pierre Legouis has assured us that 'the more revolting charges [against Anne Hyde] may be safely rejected';[36] he means of course that they were false. But they may not be rejected if we are correctly to read their most important claim. For 'The Last Instructions' attacks not simply the more revolting physical excesses of individuals, but the political deformity of the body politic, and the one is insistently metaphor of the other. Marvell's 'revolting' charges against Jermyn, Hyde, and Castlemaine are intended with the utmost seriousness; they aim to disgust in their violence and particularity, and they intend our sense of disgust to be brought finally to bear against the inmost centre of the body politic. John Wallace praises the high-mindedness of 'The Last Instructions', its avoidance of debasement, its careful exemption of the King from personal abuse.[37] But it is the low-mindedness of this poem that carries its most urgent argument. For 'The Last Instructions' insists on, and makes central to its political argument, the deformity, the appetites, the personal vulgarity of the Stuart Court. It may be difficult to reconcile the salacious and vulgar materials of 'The Last Instructions' with the delicacy of Marvell's lyric muse, but to stress only the high-mindedness of his satire is to gloss over the vigour and particularity of his opposition poetics and politics, their connection to and incorporation of cruder forms of popular print culture, and finally to slight the matter of sexual misconduct so important to the depiction of the court and Charles II's place of pride in its articulation.

The final portrait in the opening trilogy comes yet closer to the centre of the body politic; it is a portrait of the King's then most notorious whore, The Duchess of Cleveland:

> Paint Castlemaine in Colours that will hold,
> Her, not her Picture, for she now grows old.
> She through her Lacquies Drawers as he ran,
> Discern'd Love's Cause, and a new Flame began.
> Her wonted joys thenceforth and Court she shuns,
> And still within her mind the Footman runs:
> His brazen Calves, his brawny Thighs, (the Face
> She slights) his Feet shapt for a smoother race.
>
> (lines 79–86)

The portrait is exclusively sexual in content; the burden of Marvell's argument is that the servicing of Castlemaine by her lackey is a humiliation of the King's mistress and of the King himself. Love's cause in this scene is anatomy; but while Castlemaine discerns love's cause in her lackey's drawers, it is not in copulation that Marvell portrays the King's whore, but in a lurid 'rub down' of her groom:

> Great Love, how dost thou triumph, and how reign,
> That to a Groom couldst humble her disdain!
> Stript to her Skin, see how she stooping stands,
> Nor scorns to rub him down with those fair Hands;
> And washing (lest the scent her Crime disclose)
> His sweaty Hooves, tickles him 'twixt the Toes.
>
> (lines 91–96)

In a blasphemous mockery of Luke 7, this woman of sin washes and anoints not the feet of her lord but the 'hooves' of her groom. The figure cuts of course against Lady Castlemaine and the quality of the entire Court; it offers a momentary and shocking juxtaposition of high and low; the scene is aligned with and inverts the Gospel. It is a fitting culmination to the initial argument of court corruption, for the actors in the scene are unaware of the travesty, but the reader is not allowed their brazen naïveté. The opening portraits fix the terms of 'The Last Instructions', and they are nothing so simple as slander and outrage. Uncontrolled appetite, lust and debauchery confounded with greed and corruption, these are the terms important not only to the satiric portraiture but as well to the discursive passages of governance and war that they frame in conjunction with the figure of the King that closes the poem. They are also terms brilliantly rewritten in the portraits of de Ruyter and Douglas that illumine the centre of 'The Last Instructions'.

At line 523, Marvell takes up his description of the Dutch invasion of the Thames and destruction of the English fleet. What is shocking about the poet's handling of the narrative is not the violence of the scene but its elevation, the pastoral setting given to plunder and destruction. As de Ruyter sails from ocean to river the poem turns from heroic to pastoral scenery; the invasion is rendered as a panel, perhaps from an illustrated Ovid:[38]

> Ruyter the while, that had our Ocean curb'd,
> Sail'd now among our Rivers undisturb'd:
> Survey'd their Crystal Streams, and Banks so green,
> And Beauties e're this never naked seen.
> Through the vain sedge the bashful Nymphs he ey'd;
> Bosomes, and all which from themselves they hide.
> The Sun much brighter, and the Skies more clear,
> He finds the Air, and all things, sweeter here.
> The sudden change, and such a tempting sight,

Swells his old Veins with fresh Blood, fresh Delight.
Like am'rous Victors he begins to shave,
And his new Face looks in the English Wave.
His sporting Navy all about him swim,
And witness their complaisence in their trim.
Their streaming Silks play through the weather fair,
And with inveigling Colours Court the Air.
While the red Flags breath on their Top-masts high
Terror and War, but want an Enemy.
Among the Shrowds the Seamen sit and sing,
And wanton Boys on every Rope do cling.
Old Neptune springs the Tydes, and Water lent:
(The Gods themselves do help the provident.)
And, where the deep Keel on the shallow cleaves,
With Trident's Leaver, and great Shoulder heaves.
Aelous their Sails inspires with Eastern Wind,
Puffs them along, and breathes upon them kind.
With Pearly Shell the Tritons all the while
Sound the Sea-march, and guide to Sheppy Isle.

(lines 523–550)

The pastoral is finally shattered by the bombardment of Sheerness (line 560), but the long portrait of de Ruyter's invasion is rendered in a most self-conscious and heightened style. What might properly be figured as violence and plunder, rape and violation, is magically transformed into a pastoral of gallant love. And what is especially curious in its opposition to the portraits that open and close the poem is Marvell's invitation to imagine the scene as a field of modest sexual delight. The violation of English territory by the invading Dutch is softened, rendered amorous and nearly comic. De Ruyter is transformed from an aging admiral to a gallant lover; the streams are crystal, the skies clear and the air sweet. Here amorous passion is all delicacy and courtliness; rather than coarse bodily function, love in this passage is filtered through a diaphanous pastoral. Not that the matter of desire is entirely dispersed, but it is heightened, rarified, mythologized. The banks boast shy nymphs hidden in verdant green; the Dutch sailors look longingly from ships which fly streaming silks; all is rendered innocent through song and myth. The gods smile on this scene. The distance from the harsh verisimilitude and coarse imagery of the opening portraits could hardly be more pointed. Satire, now the only literary kind fitted to render the Stuart Court, is transformed when the characters change. The mixed modes of 'The Last Instructions' are made to seem determined not by the poet's will but by his subject matter. Like the commemoration of Archibald Douglas that follows, the Dutch pastoral is strikingly literary in texture and detail. The juxtaposition of pastoral and satire not only allows Marvell to play foreign virtue against native vice, it also allows the poet to remind us of the idioms and images of Stuart panegyric, of that language of abundance and pleasure so insistently invoked for our halcyon days in 1660.

The portrait of Douglas (lines 649–696) extends both the literary and political terms and makes one further point. The nymphs and lovers of the Dutch pastoral are at once shy and gallant, an inversion of love at the English Court; but the elegy for Douglas carries a more complex argument. For in this scene, the gallant is no aging admiral but an adrogynous beauty, a nymph among nymphs, a vestal virgin, yet the hero of the English fleet. The portrait of Douglas answers the figure of de Ruyter but further complicates its terms. For while de Ruyter prepares for amorous play, Douglas is a denial of sexual desire: he is innocence in a world of corruption; beauty among the deformed. It is bravery and honour that Marvell celebrates in Douglas, fortitude and constancy, virtue in all its complex senses:[39]

> Not so brave Douglas; on whose lovely chin
> The early Down but newly did begin;
> And modest Beauty yet his Sex did Veil,
> While envious virgins hope he is a male.
> His yellow Locks curl back themselves to seek,
> Nor other Courtship knew but to his Cheek.
> Oft has he in chill Eske or Seine, by night,
> Hardn'd and cool'd his Limbs, so soft, so white,
> Among the Reeds, to be espy'd by him,
> The Nymphs would rustle; he would forward swim.
> They sigh'd and said, Fond Boy, why so untame,
> That fly'st Love Fires, reserv'd for other Flame?
>
> (lines 649–660)

In part the initial terms anticipate Douglas's immolation aboard the Royal Oak; but the portrait offers other displacements and claims. Heroic and steadfast, Douglas is yet hardly of age; the valiant Scot not only shames the English youth, he also rebukes the aging pimps and whores of the English Court. But more than that, he is the very denial of sexual passion. Douglas rejects the river nymphs and embraces only the flames in which the Royal Oak is consumed:

> Like a glad Lover, the fierce Flames he meets,
> And tries his first embraces in their Sheets.
> His shape exact, which the bright flames infold,
> Like the Sun's Statue stands of burnish'd Gold.
>
> (lines 676–680)

Although Douglas was married at the time of his death, in the economy of 'The Last Instructions' his virginity denies not chaste marriage but the outrageous sexual appetites and deformities of the poem's opening scenes and yet more importantly anticipates the closing portrait of the King, itself prefaced by an anecdote of lust and infidelity. In death, Douglas is the 'glad Lover', for here passion is explicitly a civic duty, love is the embrace of honour, the defence of king and country. The sexual ambiguity of the figure allows Douglas to be hero and victim: the true embodiment of loyalty and honour, the innocent sacrificed to the flames created from the Court's lust and dishonour.

In an effort to rescue the seriousness of 'The Last Instructions', to differentiate it from the more libellous satires, several students of the poem suggest that the closing portrait of Charles II is neither harsh nor critical.[40] They assume that the envoy alters the terms of the portrait of Charles (lines 885–906), that Marvell seriously intends the device of the King's evil ministers to paper over his harsh criticism of the monarch. Such a reading would have Marvell close 'The Last Instructions' by blaming others for the havoc wreaked by the King's passions and follies. But read in terms of the other figures in Marvell's gallery, the portrait of the King dreaming in his bedchamber is the most serious and most daring satire, and quite properly the culminating argument of 'The Last Instructions'.

The portrait is immediately prefaced by a group of nasty lines on Speaker of the Commons, Henry Turner which close with an image of Turner being serviced by the wife of James Norfolk, Serjeant-at-Arms of the House of Commons:

> At Table, jolly as a Country-Host,
> And soaks his Sack with Norfolk like a Toast.
> At night, than Canticleer more brisk and hot,

> And Serjeants Wife serves him for Partelott.
> Paint last the King, and a dead shade of Night,
> Only dispers'd by a weak Tapers light.
>
> (lines 881–886)[41]

Lust and infidelity anticipate the King's vision; what the weak
tapers disclose is a scene in which the King either dreams or
envisions a bound virgin, a figure whom he would press in close
embrace:

> Raise up a sudden Shape with Virgins Face,
> Though ill agree her Posture, Hour, or Place:
> Naked as born, and her round Arms behind,
> With her own Tresses interwove and twin'd:
> Her mouth lockt up, a blind before her Eyes,
> Yet from beneath the Veil her blushes rise;
> And silent tears her secret anguish speak,
> Her heart throbs, and with very shame would break.
> The Object strange in him no Terrour mov'd:
> He wonder'd first, then pity'd, then he lov'd:
> And with kind hand does the coy Vision press,
> Whose Beauty greater seem'd by her distress;
> But soon shrunk back, chill'd with her touch so cold,
> And th' airy Picture vanisht from his hold.
> In his deep thoughts the wonder did increase,
> And he Divin'd 'twas England or the Peace.
>
> (lines 891–906)

The King's efforts to satisfy his sexual desires on the bound virgin
is an image prepared by the opening portraits and by the elegy
for Archibald Douglas. Douglas as 'the Sun's Statue of burnish'd
Gold' is the counterpart of the bound virgin illumined by candle-
light. And now the argumentative force of Douglas's virginity is
brought home, for he is both an analogue for the virgin England
and a reminder of the civic uses of passion. The slumbering monarch reaches for the captive virgin; excited by her distress, he
would satisfy his appetites on the hapless figure, and in his lust
he misreads the emblem. Luxury and sensuality at the centre of
the Court are fundamentally political in character: pleasure rather
than honour or abundance is the aim of this monarch; private
passion rather than public trust is the principle of this Court.
Though not in detail as vile as the images of the courtiers earlier
offered in the poem, the implications of the King's undifferentiat-

ing appetites are more damaging. What the scene finally urges is the recognition that England herself is matter simply to excite and relieve the King's desires. Perhaps because the indictment is read so directly against the King, Marvell casts it as dream vision, a device that allows him to soften the scene. But it also permits him to historicize the scene, to anchor it in an episode of the King's erotic history that works, with a wonderful economy, against the scene's elevation. For the allegory is a redaction of Charles's pursuit of Frances Stuart, the most protracted and least successful of the King's sexual ventures.[42] The combination of allegory and historical narrative conjoins, as does the poem throughout, politics and whoring; and rather than disperse the criticism, the covering of the narrative by allegory concentrates the indictment and sharpens the explicitness of the case.

The shape raised up of virgin's face had appeared at Court in 1662. Painted by Lely as Diana, twice by Huysmans, and by Cooper, Frances Stuart was widely admired for her beauty, and by no one more than the King.[43] Her sexual history was the focus of interest and gossip throughout the early 1660s, particularly in 1667, when first she sat in February, at the King's direction, for the figure of Britannia which appeared on the Peace of Breda Medal created by Roettier[44] – hence, her certain identity in line 906 as 'England' or the 'Peace' – and subsequently and secretly eloped from Whitehall at the end of March to marry the Duke of Richmond.[45] In so eluding the King's sexual demands and preserving her virginity, she was rumoured to have been assisted by the Lord Chancellor who, the King believed and others suggested, had arranged the secret marriage to frustrate the King's passions and correct his morals. Charles's anger and frustration help to explain the King's otherwise unaccountably vindictive attitude toward Clarendon.[46]

The brief scene records several details of Charles's pursuit of Frances Stuart: her resistance, her virtue, her fondness for games, including, suggestively, blindman's buff – a detail that renders both poignant and ridiculous the blindfolded figure in the vision – and of course her escape from the King's hold and his surprise and frustration over her disappearance into the night. The most telling juncture of detail is provided by the puns of the portrait's final line, where the language tangles together coins, whores, medals, and politics: 'England', and the 'Peace' of line 906 allowing the medal struck to celebrate naval victories in the Dutch wars to be collapsed with the meaning of piece as 'whore' and piece as 'money', a meaning already conjured with reference to Frances Stuart in line 761 where Marvell alludes to her appearance as Britannia on the farthing. The puns underscore, as does the whole scene, the compounding of lust with policy, and so serve as structural and argumentative cruxes linking the King's dream to the dismissal of Clarendon in the next scene. The fall of Clarendon is determined, so the structure of the poem argues, by the Lord Chancellor's role in the frustration of the King's appetite, and by the chief architects of the King's new policy, Bennet and Castlemaine (lines 927–942) who through the summer and early fall of 1667 had been linked in their efforts to use Frances Stuart to influence the King. In this poem, so drenched in topicality and so insistent on its author's highmindedness, the King's dream occupies a special position, conducting its argument simultaneously as allegory and gossip.

The coldness of the virgin shocks the King into an awareness of the allegory, educates him in poetics; but the King's heroic resolve proves nothing more than fixing on a device to disperse criticism. Rather than reform his own appetites and understanding, the King indulges the fiction of 'evil ministers', a fiction that was, at the close of the summer of 1667, deployed to appease the hunger of the House of Commons, and a device savagely ridiculed earlier in 'The Last Instructions' in the parliamentary chorus that would blame all the naval disasters on Commissioner Pett. The sacrifice of Clarendon fits the wise designs of Castlemaine, Bennet, and Coventry, those emblems of lechery and mistrust.[47] While Marvell hardly means to allow sympathy for Clarendon, the valour of the King's resolve is itself a disgrace.

The envoy (lines 949–990) doubtless softens the closing representation of the King; Marvell's address to the King invokes familiar literary and political sentiments and conventions – the poet's own modesty, the purity of his aims, the conservative constitutionalism of his politics[48] – but its very reliance on the trope of the King's evil ministers damages its credibility. It is difficult indeed to reconcile the formal pieties of the envoy with the scathing tone Marvell achieves at the close of the King's portrait, or to assume that the device of Hyde's disgrace would effect the restoration so affectingly glimpsed in the pastoral couplet lodged between images of scratching courtiers, 'But Ceres Corn, and Flora is the Spring, / Bacchus is Wine, the Country is the King'. Given the structure of the poem, its steady accretion of images, its length, its density and particularity, it is hard to imagine how courtly panegyric could have been successfully wrought from satire. The pastoral figures tucked into the envoy bear an inordinate weight if they are truly to counterpoise the violence and corruption catalogued in the body of the poem. I suspect that Marvell was aware not only of the failure of resolution in the envoy but also of the aesthetic and political difficulties of resolving this satire, and though the poem does indeed wander toward a conclusion with images of the good subject, of 'gen'rous Conscience and . . . Courage high', the line that finally brings the poem to a close is anxious and dissonant, 'Give us this Court, and rule without a Guard'. The reference to the King's Horse and Foot Guards in the final line of the poem conjures up the bleeding ghosts of Henry IV and Charles I (line 918); rather than resolution, the image offers a world closer to the spirits of the shady night at the conclusion of 'An Horatian Ode' than to the harmonies and abundance of the pastoral state. The restoration of Charles II in 1660 had twinned hopes of stability and abundance with the person of the King; that his private pleasures and civic care should have proved fruitless and negligent was a conclusion to which Marvell had come by the summer of 1667, and to which he gave, in 'The Last Instructions', a brilliant, implacable, and damaging form.

Notes

1. Citations are to the text in *The Poems and Letters of Andrew Marvell*, ed. H.M. Margoliouth, 3rd ed. revised by Pierre Legouis and E.E. Duncan-Jones, 2 vols., Oxford: Oxford University Press, 1971.
2. The figure can be traced to Plato and Aristotle; on the body politic in medieval political theory see Ernst H. Kantorowicz, *The King's Two Bodies*, Princeton: Princeton University Press, 1957; and on renaissance literary uses of the image see D.G. Hale, *The Body Politic: A Political Metaphor in Renaissance English Literature*, The Hague, 1971; and Leonard Barkan, *Nature's Work of Art: The*

  Human Body as Image of the World, New Haven and London: Yale University Press, 1975.

3. On the politics of Platonic love at the Court of Charles I see Kevin Sharpe, 'Cavalier Critic? The Ethics and Politics of Thomas Carew's Poetry', in *Politics of Discourse: the Literature and History of Seventeenth-Century England*, ed. by K. Sharpe and S. Zwicker, Berkeley, Los Angeles, and London: University of California Press, 1987, pp. 117–146; K. Sharpe, *Criticism and Compliment*, Cambridge: Cambridge University Press, 1988; and Malcolm Smuts, *Court Culture and the Origins of a Royalist Tradition in Early Stuart England*, Philadelphia: University of Pennsylvania Press, 1987, especially chapters 7, 9, and 10; the literature on the politics of the court masque is especially rich; see Stephen Orgel, *The Jonsonian Masque*, Cambridge, Mass.: Harvard University Press, 1965, *The Illusion of Power: Political Theater in the English Renaissance*, Berkeley and Los Angeles: University of California Press, 1975, and S. Orgel and R. Strong, *Inigo Jones, The Theatre of the Stuart Court*, 2 vols., Berkeley and Los Angeles: University of California Press, 1973, and the recent collection of essays, *The Court Masque*, ed. David Lindley, Manchester: University of Manchester Press, 1984.

4. See the language at the opening of Dryden's *Astraea Redux*, pp. 18–28; the Oxford panegyrics can be studied in *Britannia Rediviva*, Oxford, 1660, see especially W. Portman, 'We that of late were fill'd with fears,' A2^r; J. Ailmer's 'Wonder of Kings and men,' Bb2^v; and the verse by G.V., 'Our water laughs it self now into Wine, / Bacchus extends beyond his long line. / Fair May gave life, gives rule unto our King: / Needs must his future Reign be flourishing', Ff2^r.

5. See Derek Hirst and S. Zwicker, *The Culture of Partisanship*, 'Monarchy Restored', forthcoming, Berkeley and Los Angeles: University of California Press.

6. See the *Declaration of Breda, 1660*, with its emphasis on quiet and peaceable possession, ancient and fundamental rights, and liberty to tender consciences, *English Historical Documents, 1660–1714*, ed. by Andrew Browning, New York: Oxford University Press, 1953.

7. For this background, see Leah Marcus, *The Politics of Mirth: Jonson, Herrick, Milton, Marvell, and the Defense of Old Holiday Pastimes*, Chicago and London: University of Chicago Press, 1986; see also David Underdown on the use of popular rituals at the Restoration, *Revel, Riot and Rebellion: Popular Politics and Culture in England, 1603–1660*, Oxford: Oxford University Press, 1985, ch. 10.

8. *The Diary of John Evelyn*, ed. William Bray, 2 vols., Washington and London, 1901, I, pp. 332–333; cf. 'The Glory of these Nations', *Cavalier Songs and Ballads*, London: S. Austin and Sons, 1887, p.

222, 'The bells likewise did loudly ring, / Bonfires did burn and people sing; / London conduits did run with wine, / And all men do to Charles Incline'; but see Christopher Hill for a more sceptical account of the reception of the Restoration, *Some Intellectual Consequences of the English Revolution*, London: Weidenfeld and Nicolson, 1980, ch. 1.

9. Hirst and Zwicker, 'Monarch Restored', forthcoming in *The Culture of Partisanship*, Berkeley and Los Angeles: University of California Press.

10. See, for example, *To the Kings Most Excellent Majesty. The Humble Petitionary Poem of Edmond Dillon*, London, 1664, 'Much of these blessings now (like Manna) show'rs / On Albion, from Jehovah's azure Tow'rs / Dispens'd by You; since that auspicious time, / God made his Type, and lawful Steward climbe / The Widowed Throne; and in this Orphan-land, / Restor'd the Father's Soveraign Command,' A4^r.

11. See, for example, the closing prophecies of Dryden's *Astraea Redux* and *To His Sacred Majesty*; Henry Bold's 'To His Sacred Majesty Charles II. At His Happy Return', *Poems Lyrique*, London, 1664, p. 206; and as well the poems on the marriage of Charles and Catherine of Braganza in the Oxford volume, *Domiduca Oxoniensis*, Oxford, 1662.

12. See, for example, the verses to Henrietta Maria, *Horti Caroline Rosa Altera*, Oxford, 1640.

13. *The Eloquence of the British Senate*, ed. William Hazlett, 2 vols., London, 1808, I, p. 161.

14. On the Restoration settlement and returning cavaliers, see J.R. Jones, *Country and Court: England, 1658–1714*, Cambridge, Mass.: Harvard University Press, 1978, pp. 131–136; and Ronald Hutton, *The Restoration: A Political and Religious History of England and Wales, 1658–1667*, Oxford: Oxford University Press, 1985, Pt. 3, 'The Restoration Settlements'; cf. *An Humble Representation of the Sad Condition of many of the Kings Party, who since His Majesties Happy Restauration have no Relief, and but Languishing Hopes . . . .*, London, 1661; 'The Cavaleers Litany', March 1660, *Cavalier Songs and Ballads*, London: S. Austin and Sons, 1887, pp. 205–207; *An humble representation of the sad condition of many of the King's party*, London, 1661; cf. Pepys, '. . . it had been better for the poor Cavalier never to have come with the King into England again; for he that hath the impudence to deny obedience to the lawful magistrate, and to swear to the oath of allegiance, &c., was better treated now-a-days in Newgate, than a poor Royalist, that hath suffered all his life for the King, is at White Hall among his friends', *The Diary*,

March 7, 1662, ed. H.B. Wheatley, 6 vols., London, 1923, II, pp. 188–189.

15. See R.A. Beddard, 'The Restoration Church', in *The Restored Monarchy*, ed. J.R. Jones, London: Macmillan, 1979, especially pp. 164–165 and 169–170.

16. See the Lord Chancellor as early as 1661 on names, reproaches, and terms of distinction, in Cobbett, *Parliamentary History of England*, 36 vols., London, 1806–1820, IV, 127.

17. See R. Hutton, *The Restoration*, pp. 220–267.

18. See the proceedings in Achitell Grey, *Debates of the House of Commons from the Year 1667 to the Year 1694*, 10 vols., London, 1769, I, p. 21ff.

19. For a discussion and bibliography of the apocalyptic materials, see Michael McKeon, *Politics and Poetry in Restoration England: The Case of Dryden's Annus Mirabilis*, Cambridge, Mass.: Harvard University Press, 1975.

20. See J.H. Plumb, *The Growth of English Political Stability in England 1675–1725*, London: Macmillan, 1967; J.R. Jones, 'Parties and Parliament', in *The Restored Monarchy, 1660–1688*, ed. J.R. Jones, London: Macmillan, 1979, pp. 48–70.

21. A bibliography of the genre is provided by M.T. Osborne, *Advice-to-a-Painter Poems, 1633–1856. An Annotated Finding List*, Austin, Texas: University of Texas Press, 1949.

22. See Annabel M. Patterson, *Marvell and the Civic Crown*, Princeton: Princeton University Press, 1978, ch. 3, 'The Painter and the Poet Dare'.

23. Thomas Moore, *Fornication Condemned. ('Marriage is honourable in all, and the bed undefiled; but whoremongers and adulterers God will judge.')*, London, 1667.

24. See the sermons preached at Whitehall, before the King by Richard Allestree on Sunday Nov. 17, 1667, 'Resist the Devil, and he will flee from you', and on the last Wednesday in Lent, 1667/8, 'For many walk of whom I have told you often, and now tell you even weeping, that they are Enemies of the Cross of Christ', p. 244, 'But sensuality is most perfect opposition to this whole design; for it reverses that subordination without which there is no possibility of vertue as I shew'd you; and it puts that whether Lust or Passion in the Throne, which either constitution, conversation, or whatever accident, did give possession of our inclinations to; and makes the strangest prodigy of Creature where the Beast is uppermost and rides the man where the beast is God indeed. . . .'; cf. Hutton, *The Restoration*, pp. 185–190; and T. Harris, *London Crowds in the Reign of Charles II*, Cambridge: Cambridge University Press, 1987,

pp. 78–80, and the remarks on the bawdy house riots of 1668, pp. 82–91.

25. Hutton, *The Restoration*, pp. 281–284.

26. Citation is to the text in *Poems on Affairs of State: Augustan Satirical Verse, 1660–1714*, ed. George de F. Lord, et al. 7 vols., 1963–1975, New Haven and London: Yale University Press, I, pp. 21–33.

27. Citation is to the text in *Poems on Affairs of State*, I, 36–53; the controversy over Marvell's authorship of the various advice poems can be followed in Lord's volume of *Poems on Affairs of State*, in his edition of Marvell for Modern Library, *Andrew Marvell: Complete Poetry*, New York, 1968, in the Penguin edition by Elizabeth Story Donno, *Andrew Marvell: The Complete Poems*, Harmondsworth: Penguin Books, 1972, and in Legouis' revision of the Margoliouth text; see note 1.

28. The articles of impeachment drawn up against Clarendon can be found in Cobbett, *Parliamentary History*, IV, pp. 377–379; the harshness of the satiric attacks can be sampled in Marvell's *Clarendon's House-Warming*, *The Poems and Letters of Andrew Marvell*, I, pp. 143–147.

29. See 'The Second Advice to a Painter', lines 145–154, *Poems on Affairs of State*, I, p. 43.

30. 'The Third Advice to a Painter', lines 290–291, *Poems on Affairs of State*, I, p. 80.

31. See notes, *The Poems and Letters of Andrew Marvell*, I, p. 351.

32. *The Diary of Samuel Pepys*, ed. H.B. Wheatley, 6 vols., London, 1923, II, pp. 373–374, 'This day Mr. Moore told me that for certain the Queen Mother is married to my Lord St. Albans, and he is like to be made Lord Treasurer'.

33. Legouis denies the explicitly sexual content of the figure, but whether we see the line as a reference to Jermyn's work as 'pleasure salt' or to 'a Rabelaisian gird at the plenitude of the Ambassador's bottom', [*The Poems and Letters of Andrew Marvell*, I, pp. 351–352], the conflation of greed and physical appetite is clear enough.

34. John Wallace, *Destiny His Choice: The Loyalism of Andrew Marvell*, Cambridge: Cambridge University Press, 1968, pp. 163ff.

35. See notes, *The Poems and Letters of Andrew Marvell*, I, pp. 353–354; cf. Pepys, *The Diary*, V, pp. 139–140.

36. *The Poems and Letters of Andrew Marvell*, I, p. 352.

37. Wallace, *Destiny His Choice*, p. 146.

38. See John Dixon Hunt, *Andrew Marvell: His Life and Writings*, London: Paul Elek, 1978, p. 159; Rosalie Colie is especially good on Marvell's literary adaptations of Ovid; see *'My Ecchoing Song'*:

Andrew Marvell's Poetry of Criticism, Princeton: Princeton University Press, 1970, pp. 168ff.

39. See J.G.A. Pocock, *Virtue, Commerce, and History: Essays on Political Thought and History, Chiefly in the Eighteenth Century*, Cambridge: Cambridge University Press, 1985, chap. 2, 'Virtues, rights, and manners'.

40. Cf. Wallace, *Destiny His Choice*, p. 147; Dixon Hunt, *Andrew Marvell*, pp. 152–153, 162; John Kenyon, 'Andrew Marvell: Life and Times', in *Andrew Marvell: Essays on the Tercentenary of His Death*, ed. R.L. Brett, Oxford: Oxford University Press, 1979, pp. 21–22; but see the brief remarks of M.C. Bradbrook and M.G. Lloyd Thomas, *Andrew Marvell*, Cambridge: Cambridge University Press, 1961, pp. 88–89.

41. The preservation of the verse paragraph beginning at line 864 which includes the portrait of Turner and continues without break into the portrait of Charles II is especially important; the verse paragraph is so preserved in the Oxford edition but broken by Lord and Donno at line 885, 'Paint last the King . . .'

42. For the outline of this pursuit, see R. Hutton, *Charles II*, Oxford: Oxford University Press, 1989, p. 204; C.H. Hartmann, *La Belle Stuart*, London, 1924, p. 117.

43. See E.R. Ormond and M. Rogers, *Dictionary of British Portraiture*, 4 vols., New York: Oxford University Press, 1979, I, p. 117.

44. Hartmann, *La Belle Stuart*, p. 142; *The Diary of Samuel Pepys*, ed. R. Latham and W. Matthews, 10 vols., Berkeley and Los Angeles: University of California Press, 1970–1983, VIII, p. 83.

45. See H.M.C. Fleming, 46, Newsletter of March 30, 1667, 'Mrs. Steward, now the Duchess of Richmond, continued at Whitehall till yesterday morning, when the King first learned that she was married, and then she immediately returned to Somerset House.'

46. Hutton, *Charles II*, p. 251.

47. Both Bennet and Sir William Coventry are attacked in the second and third advice poems.

48. Wallace stresses the political continuity of Marvell's 'loyalist and constructive principles' by accepting as conviction Marvell's handling of the device of the King's evil ministers, *Destiny His Choice*, p. 163.

4   'I would not tell you any tales':[1] Marvell's Constituency Letters

N.H. Keeble

The sending of letters during the Restoration period was a hazardous business. All too easily might any letter find its way into the hands of a recipient other than its addressee, and one, moreover, eager to detect in it subversive senses which, if confirmed, could prove disastrous to its sender. In January 1661 Richard Baxter, one of those Puritan divines to whose aid Marvell would later come in *The Rehearsal Transpros'd* (1672),[2] having been by episcopal opposition driven from his Interregnum Kidderminster cure in Worcestershire, wrote to his step-mother from London a letter 'containing nothing but our usual matter' and some 'sharp Invectives' against Thomas Venner's recent uprising:

> By the means of Sir *John Packington*, or his Soldiers, the Post was searched, and my Letter intercepted, opened, and revised [misprint for *reviewed?*], and by Sir *John* sent up to *London* to the Bishop [Gilbert Sheldon] and the Lord Chancellour [Edward Hyde]: so that it was wonder that having read it, they were not ashamed to send it up: But joyful would they have been, could they but have found a word in it, which could possibly have been distorted to an evil sence, and Malice might have had its Prey. I went to the Lord Chancellour and complained of this usage, and that I had not the common liberty of

111

a subject, to converse by Letters with my own Family. He disowned it, and blamed Mens rashness, but excused it from the Distempers of the Times; and he and the Bishops confessed they had seen the Letter, and there was nothing in it but what was good and pious.[3]

By the 'Distempers of the Times' Clarendon referred particularly to Venner's Fifth Monarchist insurrection, but it was the temper of the times more generally to be in constant fear of distempers. The apparently effortless ease with which the revolution (in the seventeenth-century sense of that word) of 1660 had so unexpectedly occurred, when, in Abraham Cowley's representative view, royalists had not 'the least glympse of Hope'[4] of it, might be persuasive evidence of Providential intervention, as Cowley triumphantly asserted in his ode 'Upon his Majesty's Restoration',[5] but it also raised misgivings about the durability of that revolution and about the genuineness of protestations of loyalty to the new régime. That 'His present Majesties happy Restauration', as Marvell observed in 1672, 'did it self ... without any need of our officiousness'[6] testified to human inadequacy as well as to divine beneficence. Power so unexpectedly regained, despite rather than because of political and military attempts to retrieve it, could not be enjoyed with the easy confidence of secure and unchallenged hegemony.

To read Pepys's diary is to be made repeatedly aware just how nervously unstable the restored régime was, anxious to identify both its friends and its enemies, and to be appraised of their activities. The Court, he recorded on 27 October 1662, was subject to 'jealouses' of 'people's rising'; four days later, 'great plots are talked to be discovered'.[7] Although in August that year Pepys had been moved to pray 'God keep peace among us', he was himself generally sceptical about the reliability of reports of sedition and conspiracy.[8] Not so the government: it suspected plots to be the business of every gathering of friends, every meeting of old soldiers, every religious conventicle. Rumours of conspiracies, uprisings and rebellions from every part of the land gained ready credence in Whitehall. As the pages of the *Calendar of State Papers, Domestic Series* testify, they continued for the next thirty years to preoccupy the state's servants for many of their waking hours. The age was haunted by the ghost of the revolutionary trauma of the mid-century. Every apologist for the established order and every polemicist against its critics was prey to the fear, bred of insecurity, that the 1660s, or 1670s, or 1680s, might go the way of the 1640s. Watchfulness and wariness were demanded, lest all be lost.

It was this which made Baxter's such a common experience, for it was from intercepted letters that much of Whitehall's knowledge of the nation's doings was culled. Those in public offices of state were persistently curious about, and suspicious of, private correspondence exchanged between subjects of the realm, and they were entitled to be so. Private letters were officially recognized as a main source of the government's information. The rather ill-defined responsibilities of the Restoration Secretaries of State included the gathering of intelligence at home and abroad and the dissemination of news for public consumption. To these ends they had a monopoly of the publication of printed newspapers and of the circulation of handwritten newsletters; they operated an extensive spy network; and they controlled the post, with authority to open mail.[9] A condition of the lease of the office of Postmaster-General to Daniel O'Neill in 1663 was that he should allow the Secretaries of State 'to have the survey and inspection of all letters'.[10] It was not an empty condition: inspect them, and open them, they, and their agents, did.[11]

This was not, in itself, a new state of affairs. Cromwell's Secretary John Thurloe had exercised a similar power,[12] and Baxter himself had, in 1659, had a letter intercepted and sent to Sir Henry Vane in the hope of its revealing his complicity in royalist plotting.[13] What, however, the 1661 experience impressed upon him was that, in this respect at least, the Restoration had changed nothing: one had as much need under legitimate monarchy as under usurped authority to be self-protectively on one's guard. Thereafter, he dared not write to his Kidderminster people 'past once in a year, lest it should bring Suffering upon them . . . For had they but received a Letter from me, any displeasing thing that they had done, would have been imputed to that'.[14] In a letter written to Kidderminster, probably in 1681, he still recalled the shock of that interception and the fact that as a consequence 'I *many years forbore so much as to write any letters to you* because of the jealousys of Malice here [in London], which would have reported that I did it to disaffect you to the prelates or to the Government and Orders of the Church'.[15]

Such caution was well-advised, for it was not only those actively treacherous or rebellious who ran a risk by committing themselves to paper. Any merely critical sentiment might very well prove sufficient to incur a charge of sedition or libel. In 1664 Chief Justice Sir Robert Hyde declared that, 'by the course of the common law', for any person 'to publish that which is a reproach to the king, to the state, to his government, to the church, nay to a particular person, it is punishable as a misdemeanour'.[16] What constituted 'reproach' was understood very broadly. Restoration courts continued to act on the Star Chamber principle that any adverse reflection upon the sovereign, government, or established church was malicious and culpable since it fostered discontent, if not subversion and sedition.[17] This view prevailed into the next century: in 1704 Chief Justice Sir John Holt advised the jury in the trial of John Tutchin for seditious libel that to 'possess the people that the government is male-administered' is libellous since 'If the people should not be called to account for possessing the people with an ill opinion of the government, no government can subsist. For it is very necessary for all governments that the people should have a good opinion of it'.[18]

If such comprehensive legal rulings rendered the least critical observation actionable, equally, to be found guilty of having published such observations it was not necessary to have had them copied, by hand or by print, nor to have disseminated them publicly. The indictment of Algernon Sidney for high treason in 1683 quoted from 'a certain false, seditious and traitorous libel', namely, private papers discovered in his desk; upon these, his trial turned. The 'publication' for which the Seven Bishops were tried for seditious libel in 1688 was the single copy of their Petition presented to the King.[19] And in 1684 Sir Samuel Barnardiston was convicted for political opinions expressed in unsigned private letters, which were read to the court; this was the sole evidence adduced. Counsel for the defence, Sir William Williams, wondered how far 'sending to the post-house . . . can be a publishing of a libel', but the court, directed by the infamous Lord Chief Justice Jeffreys, was in no doubt.[20] Indeed, news itself, even without comment or opinion, and however transmitted, was a suspect commodity. The Restoration authorities were as fully persuaded as later tyrannies that the too easy availability of information was destabilizing, and it expended a good deal of effort upon stemming the flow, and controlling the content, of the news. Roger L'Estrange, whose Tory polemics in defence of the monarchical and episcopal authorities would include *An Account of the Growth of Knavery* (1678) in reply to Marvell's *An Account of the Growth of Popery* (1677), nicely epitomized the prevailing view of the Restoration establishment in the first editorial (31 August 1663) of his short-lived paper *The Intelligencer*:

> I do declare myself . . . that supposing the Press in order, the people in their right wits and news or no news to be the question, a Public mercury should never have my vote, because I think it makes the multitude too familiar with the actions and counsels of their superiors, too pragmatical and censorious, and gives them not only an itch but a kind of colourable right and license to be meddling with the Government . . .[21]

In a letter of June 1672 to his nephew William Popple, in which he had mentioned war with the Dutch, the death of Jan de Wit, and fears of France, Marvell himself observed that 'There was the other Day . . . a severe Proclamation issued out against all who shall vent false News, or discourse ill concerning Affairs of State. So that in writing to you I run the Risque of making a Breach in the Commandment' (328/1–4).

Marvell had, then, good reason to be careful in the letters which from 1660 till 1678 he sent, as its MP, to the corporation of Hull from London with news of Parliamentary debates and legislation. Throughout the correspondence there is an almost conspiratorial air. A cautious and a cautionary note is frequently struck as Marvell repeatedly warns the mayors and aldermen to whom he writes not to allow the matter of his letters to enter the public domain. He adjures them 'Let not my willingness to acquaint you with affairs be made too common or prejudiciall' (91/1–2). They are to be 'verie private' (10/34), not to be 'forward to Communicate' (156/25) what they read in his letters nor 'to speak much of it' (19/37–20/1). Having, in a letter of 8 November 1670, written in some detail of parliamentary debates on taxation, he concludes:

> These things I haue been thus carefull to giue you a plain account of, not thinking a perfunctory relation worthy your prudence but must in exchange desire you will not admit many inspectors into my letters. For I reckon your bench to be all but as one person: whereas others might chance either not to understand or to put an ill construction

upon this openesse of my writing & simplicity of my expression. This
perhaps is needlesse. (113/28–35)

Perhaps the caution is needless, but it is clearly with admonitory
force that in a later letter Marvell confides, 'neither will you I
know be forward to propagate the discourse' (162/17–18) of what
he communicates. Although in his letter of 21 October 1675 he
does not 'write deliberately any thing which I feare to haue
divulged yet seeing it is possible that in writing to assured friends
a man may giue his pen some liberty and the times are something
criticall', he desires 'that what I write down to you may not easily
or unnecessarily returne to a third hand at London' (166/16–22).
Nevertheless, two weeks later he finds that the subject of his letter
is known in London:

> I am very well satisfyd Gentlemen by your Letter that it was none
> of you: but it seems therefore that there is some sentinell set both
> upon you and me. And to know it therefore is sufficient caution. The
> best of it is that none of us I belieue either do say or write any thing
> but what we care not though it be publick although we do not desire
> it. (169/34–9)

The spirit of these wary cautions is not in the constituency letters
confined to Marvell's explicit admonitions to his correspondents.
Although he himself refers, in such passages, to the 'liberty' of
his pen, to the 'openesse' of his writing and to the 'simplicity' of
his expression when addressing 'assured friends', a reader of his
letters to Hull would be hard pressed to detect the indulgence of
any such familiar licence. The impression made by the letters is
rather one of closeness than of openness, of restraint than liberty.
It is an impression formed, in the first instance, by the restricted
range of Marvell's epistolary material. A careful selectivity ensures
that nothing casual, opinionative or reflective intrudes into what
are, essentially, parliamentary bulletins: 'It is a Tribute due from
one in my Station to your Prudence to informe you from time
to time of things that passe in Parliament' (181/8–9). And that is
all he will inform them of.[22] His constituency letters have almost
exclusively to do with parliamentary proceedings. Marvell reports
on the business of the House, the progress of debates and of
committee work, on the Bills in hand, those lost by prorogations,
those which receive the royal assent at the end of a session. Much
of the correspondence has the terse manner of minutes, often the

form simply of notes or lists. These tend to be most detailed on matters which bear closely upon Hull, particularly customs and excise, commerce and shipping, where Marvell provides, for example, exact specifications of proposed taxes to be levied (e.g. pp. 112–15, 118, 119, 135–6). He additionally keeps the Hull corporation informed by sending printed copies of Acts as soon as they are off the press (e.g. 15/18; 16/38; 54/13–14, 20; 108/4, 12–13), of proclamations (e.g. 17/15; 46/1; 55/33; 158/15) and even newsbooks (e.g. 18/3). He sends copies of Charles II's speeches opening parliamentary sessions (e.g. 96/22; 210/2), or summaries of them (e.g. 144/28ff; 201/30ff), as well as of royal messages to the Commons (e.g. 199/10–11) and of addresses from the Commons to the Crown (e.g. 211/9–20; 225/8–9; 233/6–7).

These indications that Marvell took seriously his responsibility to keep Hull informed are of a piece with his determination to maintain his correspondence with the Corporation. He sent regularly when the House was sitting, writing usually at the end of the day and developing the 'habit of writing euery Post' to Hull (186/2–3; cf. 153/3). The mails left London for provincial towns on Tuesdays, Thursdays and Saturdays, usually at midnight, or later:[23] these were Marvell's 'writing nights' (155/17). In composing his letters, he drew on notes made during the day, which, if need be, he was able to pass to another for writing up when prevented himself from so doing, as on 5 March 1670 he did to Hull's London 'Intelligencer' Robert Stockdale, 'who I doubt not will informe you particularly of what hath passed this week' (99/23–4; cf. 105/26–7). Often, he did find it difficult to maintain the correspondence. Explanatory apologies for brevity or belatedness are common (e.g. 100/3–4; 190/4; 216/24–5). He was frequently 'straitned in time for writing' (61/18–19), too 'busy' to write (65/11), his letters truncated as the post is 'upon going' (103/9–10). On 14 November 1667, he begins 'Really the businesse of the house hath been of late so earnest daily and so long, that I haue not had the time and scarse vigour left me by night to write to you' (59/29–31). The burden of such apologies is, however, his determination not to fail. On 2 May 1668, though ''Tis nine at night & we are but just now risen', Marvell writes 'these few words in the Post-house[24] for surenesse that my letter be not too late' (74/28–9). On 17 March 1677, he 'must beg your excuse for paper penn writing & euery thing' for he has 'by ill chance neither eat nor drunke from yesterday at noone till six a clock to night that the house rose' (189/12–14). Two-and-a-half weeks later, 'the House hauing sate to day without intermission till almost nine at night' he writes 'fasting' (195/18–19), but he will write: 'if I wanted my right hand yet I would scribble to you with my left rather then neglect your business' (28/7–8).

This impression of conscientious diligence is reinforced by the many dutiful expressions in these letters from the Corporation's 'most affectionate servant',[25] as Marvell signs himself. He 'intend[s] all things for your service' (2/22–3), takes 'great pleasure in writing to you, [but] more in serving you to my ability' (76/33–4), and has 'no greater delight then to be serviceable to you' (17/8). Indeed, he can (though this is in November 1660, early in the correspondence) aver '"Tis much refreshment to me after our long sittings daily to giue you account what we do' (6/7–8). Having been elected to serve in the Cavalier Parliament, Marvell, 'as in gratitude obliged', commits himself to continue, with 'constancy and vigour', 'to execute your commands & study your service' (23/2–4). He frequently desires precise instructions, and can grow exasperated when these are not plain, for he has 'in the things concerning your town no other sense or affection but what is yours as farr as I can understand it' (30/35–7), and would 'carefully conforme' to their instructions (177/9).

It is a measure of the authenticity of these protestations of service that the one personal sentiment to emerge clearly from the constituency letters is the writer's attachment to Hull. Mention of the town, uniquely, can tempt him from his factual record to reminiscence and to reflection. It alone invests the persona of the letters with a specific biography and a distinct selfhood. Marvell works always for 'our Interest at Hull' (265/4), and, when Parliament is not sitting, he entreats his correspondents 'during my continuance in Town' to use him 'as freely as formerly in any thing wherein I may be of service to your selfe to the Town or to any particular person there' (14/36–15/2). This commitment to Hull is inspired by concern about, and love for, the town. Four months after the Great Fire, the many fires 'here in the South' have made him 'almost superstitious', and, hearing of 'seuerall fires of late in your town', he implores his correspondents 'to haue a carefull ey against all such accidents' (55/16–24), repeating his concern in his next letter (56/22–6). His editors note as one of the very rare 'autobiographical touches' in the letters Marvell's recollection of those 'blessed days' when, he then 'a child', 'the youth of your own town were trained for your militia, and did methought become their arms much better then any soldiers that I haue seen there since' (2/14–17, with n. on p. 359). And, most engagingly, Marvell concludes one letter: 'It is hard for me to write short to you. It seems to me when I haue once begun that I am making a step to Hull & can not easily part from so good company' (17/31–3).

Nevertheless, though he may be diligent, conscientious, deferential, his sincere affection for Hull never prompts this 'affectionate servant' to be intimate or informal beyond these very few occasions (and even then his reflections upon the risk of fire are followed by an apology for his 'digression' (55/26–7)). Marvell's biographers owe no debt to these letters, in which Marvell hardly appears. We may recall Aubrey's observation that Marvell was 'in his conversation very modest, and of very few words', and that he 'had not a generall acquaintance'.[26] Nor, though in January 1660 he promises that '(for I doubt you are not so well served with intelligence) I shall as long as I continue here in Town furnish you weekly with what comes to my notice' (17/1–3), is there much 'intelligence' of a general sort to be gleaned from the letters to Hull. Whenever Marvell is in danger of straying into social inconsequentialities, rumour or gossip, he pulls himself back. Very occasionally, there is a snippet of news in the more popular sense: ''Tis two days news upon the Exchange that some French in the Bay of Canada haue discovered the long looked for Northwest passage to the East Indyes' (22/34–6); but Marvell much prefers matters of 'higher importance' (55/15).

An explanation for this exclusion of the personal from the letters might be formulated in terms of their recipients' expectations and the conventions governing such a correspondence. Marvell addresses not a close friend, or even a single person, but a corporation. Whatever their separate, individual interests and proclivities, and whatever their particular relationships with Marvell may have been, the mayors and aldermen of Hull would, in their role as public officers and as Marvell's correspondents, be possessed not of an individual's curiosity about personal experience but of a corporate concern about statutory changes which affected civic responsibilities and duties. Public, not private, affairs are their business, and the proper matter of any correspondence with them. However, it appears that this letter-writer is no more forthcoming when he is about what indisputably is his business. An extreme reticence, reluctant to stray from the enumeration of facts or to indulge in an explanatory gloss upon what is reported, is characteristic of the presentation of the governmental and parliamentary material which is the main burden of Marvell's constituency letters. As Isabel Rivers has remarked, Marvell has 'left very little in the way of autobiographical explanation of his political opinions',[27] least of all here, where it might be most expected. Indeed, the most elementary information concerning his political life is wanting from these exclusively political letters. Their writer seems hardly to have been a participant in parliamentary affairs at all.[28] It does not appear that he ever contributed to the debates which he reports,[29] nor, though he often gives the precise results of parliamentary divisions, does he reveal how he himself voted. He will mention parliamentary committees, but not his own membership of them (e.g. 43/14 with n. on p. 362). If the persona of these letters wants a personal history, equally, when he handles his matters of 'higher importance', he writes as an observer and a chronicler uninfluenced by personal involvement or political allegiance.

This characteristic manner is struck early in the correspondence. The Bill 'for making this declaration of his Majesty a Law in religious matters' is merely noted as 'proceeding' through the Convention (2/24–5), or as about to have its first reading (5/33), with no hint of its potentially momentous consequences for the Restoration religious settlement. The restriction of episcopal power and the concessions to the Presbyterian point of view in Charles II's Worcester House Declaration of October 1660[30] held out good promise of comprehending within the established church most of those subsequently ejected from their livings by the Act of Uniformity. It was an expression of precisely that royal policy of indulgence to tender consciences which Marvell would later defend in *The Rehearsal Transpros'd*. When the Bill is finally lost on 28 November 1660 by 183 votes to 157, Marvell's regret that 'there is an end of that bill and for those excellent things therein' (6/14) is considerably less pointed than the observation – perhaps Marvell's own – in the satiric couplet, 'So Bishops must revive, and all unfix / With discontent to content twenty six'.[31] Even so, it is a comment a good deal more specific and explicitly partisan than is usual in the correspondence. While it was tightening its grip on the organs of government, the restored régime considered it prudent to woo eminent Presbyterians with the offer of bishoprics: though on 27 November 1660 'It is said that on Sunday next Doctor [Edward] Reynolds shall be created Bishop of Norwich' (5/33–4), Marvell himself has nothing to say of the policy, or of Reynolds' decision to accept.[32] Eight days later, ''Tis thought' by persons unspecified (and whether or no including Marvell does not appear) 'that since our throwing out the bill of the kings declaration Mr. [Edmund] Calamy & other moderate men will be resolute in refusing of Bishopricks' (7/19–21). Nor can it be inferred from the report in that same letter of 4 December 1660 what (if anything) Marvell thought of the replenishment of the episcopal bench by a series of consecrations which, with attendant ceremonial and celebration, asserted in the capital a notion of the religious dignity and the political power of bishops quite contrary to that articulated in the Worcester House Declaration,[33] or to that held by the ridiculer of the episcopalian Samuel Parker, or by the man so appalled by the contrivances of 'the Episcopal Cavalier party' (341/29). And the celebrator of 'The First Anniversary of the Government under O. C.' and the elegist of 'A Poem upon the Death of O.C.' is seemingly undisturbed when ''tis ordered that the Carkasses & coffins' of Cromwell, John Bradshaw, Henry Ireton and Thomas Pride 'shall be drawn, with w^t expedition possible, upon an hurdle to Tyburn, there be hanged up for a while & then buryed under the gallows' (7/33–6).

It would be as vain to seek some sign of dissatisfaction with the penal legislation subsequently enacted against those who though, it seems, not Marvell's co-religionists were nevertheless those with whom in his prose works he expressed greatest sympathy.[34] The First Conventicle Bill is simply preparing 'many further remedyes against refractory persons' (37/7–8). Indeed, as that example indicates, Marvell's letters can assume the very tone of the legislation itself, sharing in the discourse of persecution: reporting the debates in 1669 on the Second Conventicle Bill, and the reaction of the House to yet another rumour that Edmund Ludlow was in England and plotting a rebellion,[35] Marvell writes that the Commons 'entered a resolution upon their books without putting it to the question that this House will adhere to his M^ty and the

Government of Church & State as now established against all its Enemyes' (92/4–7). This echo of the very words of the oaths imposed by the Act of Uniformity and the Five Mile Act[36] passes without remark. No more does Marvell comment when reporting that the Lords 'haue made very many materiall alterations in the Bill of Conventicles', including 'a reserving clause for his Majestyes ancient prerogative in all Ecclesiastical things' (104/33–6). It would, in *The Rehearsal Transpros'd*, be Marvell's own business to defend the exercise of that very prerogative,[37] yet this step to safeguard it wins no applause from him in these letters. Equally, the author of *An Account of the Growth of Popery and Arbitrary Government* does not even look askance at this collusion with tyranny. Certainly, there was precious little applause in the Commons. In its struggle with the Lords and the Crown to establish its dominance within the constitution, the Commons was nervously jealous of its own authority and suspiciously watchful of Charles's attempts to maintain as generous a conception of the royal prerogative as possible.[38] The Commons would quickly let it be known that it found intolerable a Declaration of Toleration issued not on its authority but upon that of the Crown, and would force Charles to withdraw it.[39] For Marvell to opine that in this matter the exercise of the royal will might be preferable to the exercise of parliamentary authority would be for him to break ranks. And that, in the constituency letters, he never does. Although in *The Rehearsal Transpros'd* Marvell would write in support of a policy designed to relieve nonconformists from the impositions and restraints of the Clarendon Code, in what he writes to Hull there is no hint of an attitude more liberal or tolerant than that of the legislators. The discourse of the letters is that of the Cavalier Parliament and of high episcopal divines, which construed nonconformist conventicles as potentially seditious 'unlawful meetings' threatening 'the peace of the nation' (67/30), and designated nonconformists themselves 'refractory persons' (37/7–8). No other language is admitted. The only voice heard in the constituency letters is the voice of prevailing opinion.

It follows that contentious or controversial matters do not in these letters engage the Marvell whose every Restoration poem and prose tract was contentious and controversial in nature. On the contrary, the persona he constructs for himself in the letters is expressly one 'free from Faction' (177/17). Indeed, so far is he

from factious partisanship that very rarely is any judgement passed
in the first person, and almost never an adverse one. More usually,
the appeal is to the common sense of 'all good Englishmen' who
'will be of the same mind', 'infinitely satisfyed with the Kings
prudence justice & kindnesse' (97/36–7). The 'most fixedly honorable & true' (31/19–20) Charles always receives such commendatory mention as one peculiarly favoured by Providential protection
'against all attempts of discontented persons or partyes' (15/21–3),
and the letters are generally well satisfied with the workings of
the constitution. On occasions of tension between the two Houses
of Parliament, Marvell retreats into a kind of bewildered agnosticism: 'The Contest between the Lords and Commons goes on
and I do not see the way out but hope the best' (157/6–7). The
writer of this letter, unlike the narrator of *The Growth of Popery*,
apparently holds no view on the issues which gave rise to this
'Contest', and, as becomes such a cautious reticence, he withholds
all expressions of sympathy from any discontented or refractory
persons whose critical views or subversive intent might be discovered. Marvell takes no view on the dispute whether, by its
fifteen-month prorogation from November 1675 to February
1677, the Cavalier Parliament was *de jure* dissolved (pp. 177–8),
but neither has he any comment to make on one particular consequence of that dispute which bore closely upon himself. The man
who, by March 1677, was a seasoned author of anonymous and
illegal satirical works with false imprints and a practised evader
of the pursuit of Roger L'Estrange, the Surveyor of the Press,
and his agents, in that month reports with factual dispassion the
examination by the Lords of Nicholas Carey, the ejected Vicar of
Monmouth now practising as a physician in London, for having
arranged the publication of Denzil Holles' anonymous and
unlicensed *Some Considerations upon the Question, Whether the
Parliament is Dissolved* (1676): 'he not satisfying them therein,
they therfore fined him a 1000^{li} & committed him close Pris'ner
to the Tower by a second warrant till he shall pay the fine'
(183/2–4).[40]

Marvell has, then, no distinctive voice, personal or political, in
the constituency letters, even on such matters of 'higher importance' as, in his verse satires and prose tracts, are the occasion of
indignation and outrage. He may occasionally express some
dismay when affairs appear 'very ill' (75/6), and pray 'God send

us moderation & agreement' (93/26–7), but he is never sufficiently master of their political circumstances to apportion blame, still less sufficiently sure of his own judgement to ridicule or to mock. Isabel Rivers identifies as the 'heroes' of *The Growth of Popery* 'the independent country members' who formed an opposition in the House of Commons,[41] but there is no hint here of approval for either independence or opposition. The discourse of the establishment prevails, unquestioned; the will of the legislature holds sway, unchallenged. The satirist's ironic individuality is exchanged for the safe anonymity of the majority's opinion. Authorial choice responding to the contingencies of adverse circumstances creates a correspondent observant but not percipient, diligent but not thoughtful, an altogether inoffensive spectator of the parliamentary scene. His letters may as a consequence make for rather dull and disappointing reading, with neither the acuity nor the wit of Marvell's other writings, but herein lies their textual security. They are quite unexceptionable; and if, being unexceptionable, they pass undisturbed about the world, so may their author.

Something of the degree to which this ingenuous, disinterested correspondent is a rhetorical construct, part of what John Dixon Hunt calls Marvell's 'studied epistolary style in communicating with the Mayor and Corporation',[42] can be gathered from a comparison of the constituency letters with Marvell's more personal correspondence with his nephew William Popple.[43] Where the former are incurious and characteristically non-committal, the latter is vital with indignant reflection upon motives, consequences and intentions. The full account of the provisions of the Second Conventicle Bill sent by Marvell to Mayor John Tripp contains no word of comment (pp. 101–2), but to Popple it is described as 'the terrible Bill . . . the Quintessence of arbitrary Malice' (314/33, 39). This Marvell is alert to the implications of constitutional moves which pass unremarked by the less curious MP: to Tripp, Marvell merely reports as 'most extraordinary' Charles's attendance at the Lords' debates in April 1670, for which the upper House tendered 'thanks for the honour he did them' (104/21–5); to Popple, this is presented as an action which, though it had precedent, 'it is now so old, that it is new, and so disused that at any other, but so bewitched a Time, as this, it would have been looked on as an high Usurpation, a Breach of Privilege' (316/23–6). Popple's correspondent can damn as 'a Piece of absolute universal Tyranny' (317/10) the attempt of the Lords to give statutory force to the royal prerogative, which the Hull correspondent passed over unremarked (104/33–6). Popple's correspondent is, clearly, an opinionative writer, and one who will disclose even politically dissident opinions:

> It is also my Opinion that the King was never since his coming in, nay, all Things considered, no King since the Conquest, so absolutely powerful at Home, as he is at present. Nor any Parliament, or Places, so certainly and constantly supplyed with Men of the same Temper. (315/31–5)

As such a generalization implies, for this correspondent neither King nor Commons comport themselves with that dignity or disinterested eye to the commonweal which characterizes their behaviour in the constituency letters. There is here an altogether darker awareness of the self-interested manoeuvres of realpolitik: 'The *Prince of Orange* here is made much of. The King owes Him a great Deal of Money' (318/36–7). To Popple, Marvell can admit what is never acknowledged to the Corporation of Hull, that Parliament meets because 'It seemed necessary for the King's Affairs, who always, but now more, wants Mony' (341/15–16). 'The King, though against many of his Council, would haue the Parliament sit this twenty fourth of October. He, and the Keeper [Sir Orlando Bridgeman], spoke of Nothing but to have Mony' (318/23–6). As for the Commons consequently assembled, 'We are all venal Cowards, except some few' (317/12–13), who may in this correspondence, as they do not in the constituency letters, grow 'odious to the People' (325/14).

If the personal correspondence reveals fears and enemies unsuspected by the constituency letters, equally, it introduces unexpected friends. Whereas in the letters to Hull only 'refractory persons' fall foul of the law, and Bushel's Case[44] appears a matter deserving of no especial notice (117/35–118/2), to Popple Marvell reveals not only his knowledge of a Quaker tract, *The Peoples Antient and Just Liberties Asserted* (1670), an account of the trial of William Penn and William Mead for perpetrating a riot, but also his sympathy with the point of view of the defendants and his dissatisfaction with the behaviour of the civil and judicial authorities:

> There is a Book out which relates all the Passages, which were very

pertinent, of the Prisoners, but prodigiously barbarous by the Mayor and Recorder. The Recorder, among the rest, commended the *Spanish* Inquisition, saying it would never be well till we had something like it. (318/12–16)

Just such an alienation from the régime whose activities were uncritically reported in the constituency letters and just such a sympathy with its victims inform Marvell's terse anecdote of Sir Giles Strangways, who, Marvell writes to Popple in July 1675, 'having been lately made Privy Counsellor, is dead, like a Fool':

He was gone into the Country, swoln with his new Honour, and with Venom against the Fanatics. He had set the Informers to work, and dyed suddenly, notwithstanding his Church's Letany, *From sudden Death, good Lord*, &c. He was their great Pillar in the House of Commons. Thus Holy Church goes to Wrack on all Sides. (343/3–8)

Here, it is Sir Giles, not the fanatics, who embodies the anarchic force of an irrational and pernicious enthusiasm out of control. This passage is disturbed by the grotesquely vindictive zeal of the law's upholder rather than by any threat posed by the fanatics who are outside the law. And its writer is, like them, an outsider, alienated from the Law (Sir Giles was about its business), the Commons (where he was a 'great Pillar'), and the established Church (whose prayers are so impotent). He, the provincial who retains his love for 'our town', belongs, like the despised 'Fanatics', in the country, a marginalized figure, far from the courtly centre of patronage and influence. It is the likes of the Privy Councillor Sir Giles who enjoys its confidence. This mocking, sceptical outsider, whose subversive irony situates him in a rhetorical and political 'country' beyond the pale of central authority and its discourse, is a far cry from the quietist observer encountered in the letters to Hull. His is the language not of objective reportage but of committed political opposition. The Marvell of the constituency letters, with what Barbara Everett has called his 'impersonal, flawless rectitude',[45] has no discernible identity, personal or political: his correspondence would give no Secretary of State cause for alarm. It would hardly be possible to argue from its authorship to the authorship of scurrilous libels. The Marvell of the correspondence with Popple, however, has a political identity which would have been all too readily recognizable: his indignation would all too distinctly recall the strains of the Good Old Cause and would reveal precisely the kind of disaffected intelligence which could produce *The Rehearsal Transpros'd*, *The Growth of Popery* and *Mr. Smirke*.[46]

Something of this prudential and self-protective strategy is acknowledged by the texts of the letters themselves: 'Many more particularityes I might insert concerning these matters' (162/16), but I choose to content myself with uncontentious generalities and indisputable facts. Such intimations of an authorial understanding and awareness more extensive than that of his texts can never, however, be allowed to challenge the adequacy or integrity of the texts he creates. The 'particularityes' which Marvell might have included are 'perhaps all better spared, neither will you I know be forward to propagate the discourse of them' (162/17–18) because what has not been said cannot incriminate. However, though the texts recognize this authorial power to select and to exclude, they cannot acknowledge further that its exercise in any way compromises the texts themselves. To concede that what is said is inadequate or partial by virtue of the author's selectivity would be to concede to the omissions from the text an authority equal to that of the texts themselves. It would be to admit that textual substance had been given not to the truth but only to a version of the truth. And that would raise very awkward questions about the alternative, marginalized, versions, which, if pursued, would subvert the whole enterprise: the ingenuous Marvell would begin to appear far too disingenuous.

And perhaps he does. Perhaps the innocuous epistolary Marvell is not to be understood merely as a contrivance to deal with the pressure of adverse contemporary circumstances, nor, perhaps, are his texts to be divorced from those of the elusively ambivalent lyrical Marvell or the ironically satiric Marvell. It was undoubtedly true that 'The times are something criticall', but, in a unique moment in the 1675 letter to Mayor William Shires in which Marvell made that remark, he goes on to add a reason for not divulging the matter of his letters which again calls to mind Aubrey's characterization: 'that I am naturally and now more by my Age inclined to keep my thoughts private' (166/19–20). Annabel Patterson has discerned in the cautionary passages in the constituency letters not merely prudence but also that 'Irony and detachment *about himself* generally characteristic of Marvell'.[47] It is a perception which raises the possibility that the constituency letters are as authentically a Marvellian creation as the other works in the canon, whatever the political circumstances which constrained their composition. After all, the man who made such rhetorical capital from Samuel Parker's 'skulking' anonymity, bestowing upon him, because he 'hath no Name or at least will not own it, though he himself writes under the greatest security', the mocking appellation 'Mr. Bayes',[48] was clearly fascinated by ironic masks, by the shifts of anonymity, by the perspectives to be achieved by distancing oneself from one's self, from one's own name and from one's own writing. His prose tracts had perforce to appear anonymously, but this seems to have been a matter rather of delight than of grievance to Marvell. A political constraint was transformed into an almost ludic creative strategy, with Marvell playing his part to the full. He wrote in a letter of 1 July 1676 to Sir Edward Harley that the anonymous *Mr. Smirke* 'said to be Marvels makes what shift it can in the world but the Author walks negligently up & down as unconcerned' (346/2–3). He professes that, in the 'Essay on General Councils' published with *Mr. Smirke*, 'Marvell, if it be he, has much staggered me in the busnesse of the Nicene & all Councils' (346/21–2). Even for his nephew, when writing of the recent anonymous publication of *The Growth of Popery*, he becomes, as Professor Patterson observes, 'a politic irony, a figure of speech', writing of himself, with 'as much irony . . . as caution',[49] in the third person:

> There have been great Rewards offered in private, and considerable in the Gazette, to any who could inform of the Author or Printer, but not yet discovered. Three or four printed Books since have described, as near as it was proper to go, the Man being a Member of Parliament, Mr. *Marvell* to have been the Author; but if he had, surely he should not have escaped being questioned in Parliament, or some other Place. (357/14–20)[50]

'Mr. Marvell', of course, was not the author; at least, not the 'Mr. Marvell' who signed himself the 'affectionate servant' of the Hull Corporation. The persona of the constituency letters would serve well the cause of so public a suspect; no incriminating evidence to be found there. Nevertheless, although Marvell may have wished to tell no tales in order to deliver no hostages to the critical times, the entire correspondence participates in the creation of the tale – the fiction – of the non-partisan member for Hull whose only will is that of the Corporation of Hull and whose only awareness is that of the House of Commons. Omission was as important to the construction of this persona as inclusion: he is defined by the tales he did not, or could not, tell. However, if only some statements could be admitted to (and admitted by) the letters of this correspondent, as some are 'only proper within the walls of the Parl^t house' (164/36–165/1), then, in other places – other genres – what here could not be said might be uttered with propriety. Few writers are as sensitive to generic decorum as the lyrical Marvell, or as alert as he to the conditionality of their texts, to the ways in which what is said is gainsaid both by what has been said before elsewhere and by what is left unsaid. It is their self-reflective awareness of the way texts are situated within, and take their meanings from, a cultural context, which gives to Marvell's poems of the 1650s their endlessly suggestive inconclusiveness. The crux of Marvell criticism is, of course, how this dense intertextuality, these ambivalently suspended meanings, could be forgone for the partisan directness of the later satires. Perhaps the single-minded commitment, demanded by Marvell's parliamentarianism, of the later poetry can be accommodated to our sense of Marvell's creative nature by remembering his simultaneous composition of the letters to Hull. The mutually contradictory tales of, on the one hand, satires and tracts, and, on the other, constituency letters, concurrently composed, may have answered not, or not only, to political circumstances, but to Marvell's need for a medium in which both to say and to unsay. Marvell the parliamentarian and Marvell the MP, each in his proper way and neither telling any tales, contrived to create texts which exist as ironically subversive commentaries upon each other.[51] Truth – even political truth – is in Marvell rarely single; there is always another tale which might be told, or not, as the case may be.

Notes

1. *The Poems and Letters of Andrew Marvell*, ed. H.M. Margoliouth, rev. Pierre Legouis and E.E. Duncan-Jones, 2 vols., 3rd edn., Oxford: Clarendon Press, 1971, ii.28, 1. 11. Subsequent parenthetical references in the text are to the pages of volume ii of this edition, with the line numbers given after an oblique stroke. References in

the notes are to *Poems and Letters*, followed by volume and page numbers.

2. Cf. Richard Baxter, *Reliquiae Baxterianae* (1696), Bk. III, p. 102, §
    221: 'There came out a Posthumous Book of A[rch] Bishop [John]
    Bromhall's [*i.e.* Bramhall's *Vindication of Himself and the Episcopal
    Clergy from the Presbyterian Charge of Popery* (1672)], against my
    Book, called, *The Grotian Religion* [(1658)] . . . And before the
    Book was a long Preface of Mr. [Samuel] *Parker*'s, most vehement
    against Dr. [John] *Owen*, and some-what against my self: To which
    Mr. *Andrew Marvel* . . . did Publish an Answer [*The Rehearsal
    Transpros'd* (1672)] so exceeding Jocular, as thereby procured abun-
    dance of Readers, and Pardon to the author'.
3. Baxter, *Reliquiae*, II.302, § 159, and appendix iv, p. 106.
4. Abraham Cowley, *The Essays and Other Prose Writings*, ed. Alfred
    B. Gough, Oxford: Clarendon Press, 1915, p. 87.
5. G.A.E. Parfitt (ed.), *Silver Poets of the Seventeenth Century*,
    London: Dent, 1974, p. 228, lines 124–44.
6. Andrew Marvell, *The Rehearsal Transpros'd and The Rehearsal
    Transpros'd. The Second Part*, ed. D.I.B. Smith, Oxford: Clarendon
    Press, 1971, p. 135.
7. *The Diary of Samuel Pepys*, ed. Robert Latham and William Mat-
    thews, 11 vols., London: Bell, 1970–83, iii.237, 245.
8. Pepys, *Diary*, iii.169, and, for his disbelief, ii.204, 225, iii.236.
9. See Peter Fraser, *The Intelligence of the Secretaries of State . . .
    1660–1688*, Cambridge: Cambridge University Press, 1956, pp. 1–2,
    9, 20–34; Mark A. Thomson, *The Secretaries of State 1681–1782*,
    Oxford: Clarendon Press, 1932, pp. 2–3.
10. Fraser, p. 21.
11. For other examples of intercepted letters see N.H. Keeble, *The
     Literary Culture of Nonconformity in later seventeenth-century
     England*, Leicester: Leicester University Press, 1987, pp. 78–82, and
     Richard L. Greaves, *Deliver Us From Evil: The Radical Under-
     ground in Britain 1660–1663*, New York: Oxford University Press,
     1986, *passim*. See also Fraser, pp. 23, 24–6, and the *Calendar of
     State Papers, Domestic Series, passim*.
12. Fraser, p. 24.
13. Baxter, *Reliquiae*, II.206–7, § 65.
14. Baxter, *Reliquiae*, II.376, § 254.
15. Frederick J. Powicke, *A Life of the Reverend Richard Baxter
     1615–1691*, London: Cape, 1924, appendix ix, p. 315.
16. William Cobbett (ed.), *A Complete Collection of State Trials*, cont.
     T.B. and T.J. Howell, 33 vols., London: Longman, 1809–26, vi.564.
17. The law in this respect is discussed in Sir William Holdworth, *A
     History of English Law*, 17 vols., London: Methuen, 1903–72; vols.

i-iii, 3rd edn., 1922–3, v.208–9. viii.333–78, and in Frederick S. Siebert, *Freedom of the Press in England 1476–1776*, Urbana, Ill.: University of Illinois Press, 1952, pp. 116–26, 269–75.

18. Cobbett (ed.), *State Trials*, xiv.1128 (quoted in Holdsworth, viii.341, and in Siebert, p. 271).
19. Cobbett (ed.), *State Trials*, ix.819, 833, 839–40, 854–60, xii.278–9.
20. Cobbett (ed.), *State Trials*, ix.1333–58.
21. Quoted in George Kitchin, *Sir Roger L'Estrange*, London: Kegan Paul, 1913, pp. 142–3, and in James Sutherland, *The Restoration Newspaper and its Development*, Cambridge: Cambridge University Press, 1986, p. 97.
22. Cf. J.P. Kenyon, in R.L. Brett (ed.), *Andrew Marvell: Essays on the tercentenary of his death*, Oxford: Clarendon Press, 1981, p. 1: Marvell's letters 'to relatives or friends tell us little about Marvell himself, and his letters to Hull Corporation are little more than formal newsletters'.
23. J.C. Hemmeon, *The History of the British Post Office*, Cam., Mass.: Harvard University Press, 1912, p. 27; Herbert Joyce, *The History of the Post Office*, London: Bentley, 1893, p. 46.
24. The General Post Office was in Lombard Street, but the receiving stations whence letters were taken to the Post Office for sorting included one at Westminster (Hemmeon, p. 27).
25. To the subscription 'Your most affect. ffreinds' to a letter of 11 December 1660 written by his fellow MP John Ramsden, Marvell added in his own hand 'and servants' (*Poems and Letters*, ii.11/36, with n. on p. 359).
26. *Aubrey's Brief Lives*, ed. Oliver Lawson Dick, Harmondsworth: Penguin Books, 1972, pp. 356, 357.
27. Isabel Rivers, *The Poetry of Conservatism 1600–1745*, Cambridge: Rivers Press, 1973, p. 101. Dr. Rivers adds that the little evidence that is available is 'chiefly' in Marvell's letters to William Popple, which are discussed later in this paper.
28. Cf. Annabel Patterson, *Marvell and the Civic Crown*, Princeton, NJ: Princeton University Press, 1978, p. 12: in these letters 'Marvell went out of his way to give only the most objective accounts of all debates in Parliament, and to avoid both value judgements and any indication of his own participatory role'.
29. For a summary of what is known of Marvell's parliamentary career, see Patterson, pp. 29–49, and, more at large, John Dixon Hunt, *Andrew Marvell: His Life and Writings*, London: Elek, 1978, chapters viii and ix.
30. The original draft of the Declaration is printed in *Reliquiae*, II.259–64, and the final version in Andrew Browning (ed.), *English Historical Documents 1660–1714*, London: Eyre Spottiswoode, 1966,

pp. 365–70. The discussions surrounding it are detailed in *Reliquiae*, II.265–79, §§ 106–115, and in Robert S. Bosher, *The Making of the Restoration Settlement*, London: Dacre Press, 1951, pp. 184–90.

31. 'Third Advice to a Painter', 11. 239–40, in *The Complete Poetry of Andrew Marvell*, ed. George de F. Lord, London: Dent, 1984, p. 137.

32. Bishoprics were offered also to Richard Baxter and to Edmund Calamy (with Deaneries to Thomas Manton and William Bates): see *Reliquiae*, II.281–4, §§ 118–27; Bosher, pp. 193–4; I.M. Green, *The Re-Establishment of the Church of England*, Oxford: Clarendon Press, 1978, pp. 83–8. Only Reynolds accepted.

33. For an example of the fervour and height of episcopal sentiments at this time, see John Sudbury, *A Sermon Preached at the Consecration of the right Reverend Fathers in God* ... , 1660, discussed in Norman Sykes, *From Sheldon to Secker*, Cambridge: Cambridge University Press, 1959, pp. 6–8, and cf. Bosher, pp. 179–84.

34. As far as is known, Marvell was not a member of any nonconformist church. There is, nevertheless, no doubt where the sympathies of the defender of Milton, Baxter, John Owen and John Howe lie. In *The Rehearsal Transpros'd*, p. 186, when he denies that he is a nonconformist, Marvell adds the parenthetical explanation, 'not that I fly it as a reproach, but rather honour the most scrupulous', and, acknowledging that his father was 'a Conformist to the established Rites of the Church of *England*', he adds 'though none of the most over-running or eager of them' (ibid., p. 204). See further Warren Chernaik, *The Poet's Time*, Cambridge: Cambridge University Press, 1983, pp. 121–4; Caroline Robbins, 'Marvell's Religion', *Journal of the History of Ideas*, xxiii, 2 (1962), pp. 268–72.

35. For a summary account of these rumours, see Keeble, pp. 70–2.

36. See Browning, pp. 379, 383.

37. Marvell, *The Rehearsal Transpros'd*, esp. pp. 43–61, 111–13, 278–9 (the editor summarizes Marvell's case in this respect on pp. xv–xvii).

38. See on this struggle during the period of Marvell's membership of the Commons Clayton Roberts, *The Growth of Responsible Government in Stuart England*, Cambridge: Cambridge University Press, 1966, and J.R. Tanner, *English Constitutional Conflicts of the Seventeenth Century*, Cambridge: Cambridge University Press, 1961.

39. See Browning, pp. 77–81.

40. For details of this episode, see *Calendar of State Papers, Domestic Series 1675–6*, p. 547; *1676–7*, pp. 543, 544, 550, 555, 565; *1677–8*, pp. 1, 3, 47, 135, 188. See also A.G. Matthews, *Calamy Revised*, Oxford: Clarendon Press, 1934, *s.v.* Cary.

41. Rivers, p. 123.

42. Hunt, p. 143.

43. This point is made in Christopher Hill, *Writing and Revolution in 17th. Century England*, Brighton: Harvester Press, 1984, pp. 51, 170, and in Keeble, pp. 80–1, which is drawn on in what follows. For Popple, see Caroline Robbins, 'Absolute Liberty: the life and thought of William Popple 1638–1708', *William and Mary Quarterly*, 3rd ser., xxiv, 2 (1967), pp. 190–223. He was from 1670 resident in Bordeaux.

44. The plea of Edward Bushel, foreman of the jury imprisoned for contempt for having acquitted the Quakers William Penn and William Mead contrary to the direction of the judge, that he had properly fulfilled his duty as a juryman by returning a verdict in accordance with what he had inferred from the evidence, was in this case upheld. On the legal significance of the ruling, which recognized the right of juries to judge facts and whose implications were fully appreciated at the time, see Holdsworth, i.344–7, and William C. Braithwaite, *The Second Period of Quakerism*, rev. Henry J. Cadbury, 2nd edn., 1961; reprinted York: Sessions, 1979, pp. 71–3.

45. Barbara Everett in Brett (ed.), p. 68. Kenyon, in ibid., p. 20, similarly speaks of 'the busy, dutiful, rather pedestrian' MP who appears in the constituency letters.

46. Assessments of Marvell's precise political opinions and their history differ, but no one doubts that, in the late 1660s and 1670s, he was, in the words of Michael Foot, 'swimming against the tide and at loggerheads with the authorities' (in Brett (ed.), p. 119), nor that he was 'identified clearly with the opposition' (Hunt, p. 162), 'a leading figure in the Country Party' (Chernaik, pp. 66–7) and 'a notable member of Shaftesbury's Country Party' (K.H.D. Haley, *William of Orange and the English Opposition 1672–4*, Oxford: Clarendon Press, 1953, p. 58). There is also a majority opinion that his satires express 'the country point of view' (Rivers, p. 124), and that his later writings were part of a concerted opposition campaign (Haley, pp. 57–8; Patterson, pp. 33, 43), but see Wallace, pp. 212–13, for a contrary view, and cf. Conal Condren, 'Andrew Marvell as Polemicist', p. 157ff below.

47. Patterson, pp. 10–12.

48. Marvell, *The Rehearsal Transpros'd*, pp. 9, 166. Mr. Bayes, a caricature of John Dryden, is the hero of Buckingham's burlesque play *The Rehearsal*, to I.1.80–92 of which Marvell's title refers. This, and the satiric strategy of *The Rehearsal Transpros'd*, are discussed in Chernaik, pp. 182–94, and in Patterson, pp. 175–210. Parker wrote in the 'greatest security' because, as chaplain to the Archbishop of Canterbury, Gilbert Sheldon, he was himself a licenser of the press.

134 The Political Identity of Andrew Marvell

His exercise of a partisan censorship is one of Marvell's targets in *The Rehearsal Transpros'd* (see, for example, pp. 166, 196–8, 205).

49. Patterson, pp. 48, 11.

50. The *London Gazette* in March 1678 offered rewards of £50 for the discovery of the printer and of £100 for 'the hander ... to the Press' of *The Growth of Popery* (Kitchin, p. 228, note 1). In his reply to *The Growth of Popery*, L'Estrange, pointed to Marvell as its author (*An Account of the Growth of Knavery*, 1672, pp. 6, 27, 34). Cf. Conal Condren, 'Andrew Marvell as Polemicist', p. 157ff below.

51. If the 'Mock Speech from the Throne' (M.C. Bradbrook & G. Lloyd Thomas, *Andrew Marvell*, Cambridge: Cambridge University Press, 1940, pp. 125–7) is by Marvell, it burlesques directly his report of Charles's speech in his letter of 13 April 1675 (*Poems and Letters*, ii.144–5), and there are many other cases where the same matter is handled by letter and by satire, but the point is one rather of literary persona and tone generally than of exact parody.

5   The Religion of Andrew Marvell: Locating the 'Bloody Horse'

William Lamont

> You praise the firm restraint with which they write –
> I'm with you there, of course;
> They use the snaffle and the curb all right,
> But where's the bloody horse?
>
> (Roy Campbell)

With Andrew Marvell there *is* no bloody horse; there *is* only snaffle and curb. This is not a limiting of his artistic achievement, as it might be with lesser writers, but a precondition of its success. Thus a recent essay on Marvell is entitled 'The aesthetics of inconclusiveness'.[1] Inconclusiveness is his secret weapon; it even infects those who write about him. Is his 'Horatian Ode' Cromwellian or anti-Cromwellian? Blair Worden, sensitively relating the poem to its historical context, replies: 'It is both, and it is neither, and yet we know not.' His article sustains that balance almost right up to the end, when it seems to be moving to a conclusion after all, and one which is pro-Cromwellian. Then Worden rights himself, and restores inconclusiveness with this conclusion:

> Reading the poem through once more, we think that Marvell has declared a commitment after all. Then we see the shadows moving in.[2]

It is one thing, in 1650, to see the shadows moving in; another, to claim that they overcast the rest of his political career. The servant of two Cromwells, Oliver and Richard, after all becomes after the Restoration the patriotic Protestant MP, fearlessly exposing the Court's intrigues with Papist France. Inconclusiveness has turned into commitment, it would appear. But if so, it is an odd kind of commitment. In his celebrated study of Marvell in the 1650s, Professor J.M. Wallace, it is true, showed that charges of time-serving against Marvell would not stick, but he saw 'loyalism' as the governing theme of his political activities.[3] After the Restoration there is, on the other hand, a parliamentary record of opposition to Court politics, but it is a spotty one. It is spasmodically heroic. There are the set-pieces: Marvell bravely speaking out in defence of Milton in December 1660; his attacks on the Cabal, and in particular, Arlington, on his return to the Commons between 1665 and 1668; his defence of James Hayes, a victim of the Conventicles Act, in 1670 and his attack on Danby's Bill for 'Securing the Protestant Religion' in 1677. But against this there are the explained and the unexplained absences, both between 1662 and 1665 and earlier during the Civil War itself; the silence in the Commons apart from these two debating occasions; the taunt of his enemy, Samuel Parker, that he was 'fearful of speaking';[4] his own self-reproach to his nephew William Popple in 1670, 'We are all veneal cowards, except some few';[5] and his personal apologia: 'not to write at all is much the safer course of life'.[6] And it is impossible, once one has read Aubrey's description of the lonely bachelor tippler, who wouldn't drink in company for fear of letting the mask slip,[7] to banish this image from the mind when one moves from the inconclusiveness of the 'Horatian Ode' to the de facto loyalism of the Protectorate and on to the vacillations between action and inaction after the Restoration.

Nevertheless – as Annabel Patterson has noted, the characteristic Marvellian stylistic device[8] – he did write, even if it was much the unsafer course of life. He covered his tracks, of course, and so successfully that we are still in doubt, for instance, about how many of the satirical 'Portrait' verses really are his. But we are in no doubt about the prose. It comes in a cluster, as we know, in the 1670s, in the form of four works. Two of these are justly famous: The Rehearsal Transpros'd I and II and An Account of the Growth of Popery; they form the basis of Marvell's literary reputation, after all, until T.S. Eliot's recovery of his *poetic* stature in 1921. They are anything but inconclusive: the critic who urged us to respect 'the aesthetics of inconclusiveness' was careful to exempt Marvell's late prose pamphlets from the categorization. The error which he, and others, warn against is any single-minded attempt *to read back* the later conclusiveness to earlier times. Marvell struck out boldly at an insufferable cleric and a wrong-headed foreign policy. These were responses to immediate provocations, rather than the unfolding of a coherent policy throughout a political life. On this point, at least, critics can agree. Annabel Patterson, who devoted much of her valuable analysis of Marvell's prose to these two particular pamphlets, nevertheless says: 'It has not seemed possible to make a completely whole man out of the poet with too many personae, as Rosalind Colie called him.'[9] According to Barbara Everett: 'He is not at all an easy writer to see whole.'[10] Isabel Rivers argues that, 'unlike the revolutionary Milton or the conservative Dryden, Marvell had no commitment to the idea of political life'.[11] Worryingly, Muriel Bradbrook – sharing their scepticism of this 'whole' Marvell, committed to political life – wrote a witty essay in which she projected her personal nightmare of a future when some eager-beaver researcher would try to make Marvell's earlier career 'chime completely with the later one'.[12] I say 'worryingly', for that is not a bad description of what I shall try to do in the rest of this essay. I will try to do it, however, by concentrating on the two Marvell prose works which critics normally touch upon glancingly, if they touch at all. One pamphlet, *Mr. Smirke* (1676), defends Herbert Croft, (1603–1691) Bishop of Hereford, against an Anglican critic; the other, *Remarks upon a Late Disingenuous Discourse* (1677), defends one Nonconformist minister, John Howe (1630–1705) against another, Thomas Danson. In Annabel Patterson's comprehensive discussion of the later Marvell, which runs to two-hundred-and-fifty pages, these two works occupy between them a mere ten pages, most of which are taken up with the examination of stylistic echoes from other writings. What do we gain in an understanding of Marvell by giving greater attention to these works?

One modest gain can be claimed instantly: we can learn what Marvell's religion is. This would not, at first sight, appear to be in dispute. Yet so all-conquering has been the theme of inconclusiveness that it has extended even to Marvell's religious beliefs.

Thus J.P. Kenyon warns: 'It would be unwise to assume from this [his opposition to the Conventicles Act] that he was a Non-conformist himself'.[13] Pierre Legouis, author of the standard biography of Marvell, goes much further:

> We can tell more easily what he attacks than what he approves. Let us limit ourselves to his religious beliefs. His hostility to the Roman Church is beyond all doubt, but when it comes to defining the irredeemable opposition between Protestants and Catholics, he mostly tells us in what it does not consist.

His questioning continues:

> But does it make him a Dissenter? Some of his biographers affirm it; others deny it with equal confidence. We shall nonsuit both parties; for a layman of his generation, a bachelor especially, the Act of Uniformity entailed no necessity of choice, provoked no certain tests of orthodoxy ... Does he not hold out his hand to the Deists?[14]

Marvell's two neglected prose works not only establish him firmly as a Dissenter, and hold out no hand to the Deists.[15] They are able to tell us precisely what sort of nonconformist he was, and the exact position he occupied in the spectrum of the controversial beliefs of his day.

I want to establish this point, but I want to do more with these two Marvell works. There seems to me at least three significant further points to be made. First, in *Mr. Smirke* what begins as another polemical knock-about, a feebler imitation of the first part of *The Rehearsal Transpros'd*, ends in a long and surprising essay on Church Councils. Annabel Patterson rightly commented: 'it is easy to forget how much research he did into the opinions of the medieval Church fathers and early ecclesiastical historians'.[16] But why did he do so, and why did he produce such a heavyweight historical contribution at the time that he did? Second, in *Remarks* he defends Arminian doctrine against Calvinist determinism: what is the significance of taking such a stand at such a time? Third, what is the significance of defending, in the latter work, a man as well as a doctrine, and that man, John Howe? The answers to all three questions not only will, I hope, show where Marvell stood in the controversies of 1676 and 1677. They will do that certainly, but they will also reveal *continuities of concerns* stretching back particularly to the years of Oliver Cromwell's Protectorate, and, even more forcibly, to the brief Protectorate of his son. The argument which will emerge is often no more than circumstantial, and indeed is predicated on the methodology abhorred by Muriel Bradbrook, of reading back from the later period to the earlier. Even bearing in mind these limitations, it is possible, I will argue, to construct a convincing alternative to the inconclusive Marvell of 'the snaffle and the curb'.

That task has been made easier by the recent publication of a landmark in Marvell studies: *Apocalyptic Marvell* by Margarita Stocker.[17] The title tells us the story she wants to tell. She offers new readings of many Marvell poems, in particular his 'Horatian Ode', 'Upon Appleton House' and 'To His Coy Mistress', in the light of new understandings of the importance to Marvell of Protestant apocalyptic beliefs.[18] Between this 'apocalyptic' Marvell and the 'loyalist' Marvell of J.M. Wallace there would seem to be an insurmountable gap. This is not so. It is a difference of emphasis, not substance. It is true that Wallace rooted Marvell's acceptance of the powers that be in the *de facto* controversies of the early 1650s. Yet, even with reference to 'The Horatian Ode', Wallace acknowledged how 'the new wave of millenarianism, with which all parties were touched, had revived the hopes of a protestant alliance and a united onslaught against the forces of Papal Rome', and went on: 'the peroration looks forward with a controlled millenarian emotion to England's success under her new leader'. And Wallace acknowledges millenarianism as 'the obsessive theme' of *The First Anniversary*, though he disarmingly concedes that had not been his first reaction to the poem: 'arguments I lost with my student' had changed his mind. So the Marvell of the 1650s displayed 'a sober millenarian hopefulness that rejected the dramatic excess of fervent chiliasts'. On the other hand, he is clear about the decisive break with the Restoration: 'the millenarian possibility had disappeared forever' and 'thereafter Marvell toiled with all the patience he could muster to preserve the constitution from collapse'.[19] On this view Marvell's later anti-Catholic activities – in Parliamentary speeches, conspiracies abroad, the verse of the 1660s and the prose of the 1670s – are to be seen as responses to specific political provocations, which themselves have to be reconciled with the *de facto* loyalism which characterized Marvell's career (apart from the atypical millenarian flurry of interest in the late 1650s) and not as expressions of a consistent overall apocalyptic commitment.

Two popular assumptions merge here. The first assumption is that, come 1660, 'the millenarian possibility' has indeed disappeared forever. I made just such a bold claim at the end of one book, and had to spend the whole of my next book in retracting it.[20] The second assumption, more specific to Marvell studies, is that 1660 is a watershed for his personal development. For Christopher Hill, the radical republican became 'a public servant' for whom the Restoration brought 'new complications' and 'the great poetry ceases'; for Legouis it meant the abandonment of 'the intellectual delicacy which was his greatest strength' and for Carey 'the abandonment of poetry for politics'.[21] Stocker's apocalyptic reinterpretation of his verse, important as it is, is not extended to his Restoration prose. One scholar who is concerned with continuities, and runs against the critical stream on this, is Annabel Patterson. Like Wallace, and unlike Stocker, she picks up millenarianism only as *one* of the themes of early Marvell, rather than as the controlling principle, but unlike Wallace she emphasizes the significance of a lengthy passage in Marvell's *Rehearsal Transpros'd* defending the idea of 'Christian Empire', and then makes the relevant connection: 'we find ourselves back with the millennial aspirations of *The First Anniversary*'.[22]

I find this insight very illuminating. It was a commitment to the idea of 'Christian Empire', across the artificial divide of the Restoration, which I found to be the key to the political philosophy of Richard Baxter. From the recovery of secret manuscripts on the Apocalypse which Baxter had composed in prison in 1686 – and which led to my chastened toning down of earlier claims that millenarianism went out of fashion with the Restoration – I went back, in his career, to his writings in the 1650s and most particularly to the brief period of Richard Cromwell's Protectorate. Although, as we have already noted, Patterson is sparing in her use of *Mr. Smirke* and *Remarks upon a Late Disingenuous Discourse*, she does note that they give the lie to Legouis's suggestion that Marvell was moving under rationalist influence to Deism[23] – a similar, and equally groundless, claim to that which has been made about Baxter's evolution at this period.[24] But we shall now see that a closer look at these two pamphlets brings out even more significant affinities between the two men.

The religious tensions – unlike the political disputes – at the Cromwellian court have not yet found their historian. But two different philosophies competed for the Protector's support, within the broad spectrum of Protestant nonconformity. The first was represented by John Owen (1616–1683).[25] He was the man in the ascendant for most of the 1650s. Not only was he chaplain to Oliver Cromwell, he was Vice-Chancellor of Oxford University and regarded by some as Cromwell's 'Pope'. The second strand was represented by Richard Baxter (1615–1691). He was very much not in the ascendant in the early years of the Protectorate. He had even argued against taking the Engagement Oath to the Commonwealth.[26] The process by which he came in from the cold is a tortuous one, and has been told elsewhere.[27] But a catalyst in that development was John Howe.[28]

It is a matter of great regret that Howe's private papers were destroyed at his death. We have, in part-compensation, however, the rich documentation of the Baxter Archive, and the biographical memoirs of Edmund Calamy (1671–1732), as the basis – along with many printed works – for reconstructing some of the religious disputes of this period. Howe came to London from his ministry in Devon on a chance visit, and was talent-spotted by Oliver Cromwell. Asked to preach sermon after sermon before the insatiable Protector, he was at last prevailed upon to become Cromwell's household chaplain and lecturer at St. Margaret's Church, Westminster. He was thus in a good strategic position to advance the policies of his friend and fellow minister, Richard Baxter.[29] Their correspondence throws fascinating light on their closeness to one another, their tactics to engage the Protector's sympathies, and their frustration with the spoiling activities (as they saw it) of the faction around their rival, Owen, who had maintained vital links with Cromwell's son-in-law Fleetwood. These tensions came even more to the surface in the brief period of Richard Cromwell's Protectorate: Baxter and Howe blamed the fall of Richard (on whom they placed enhanced hopes – he did not even have the regicide taint of his father) upon 'Dr. Owen and his assistants'.[30]

There were three main areas of dispute between the two branches of Nonconformity. The first was on doctrine. Baxter had daringly, as early as 1649, reclaimed Arminianism for the Protestant cause with his *Aphorismes of Justification*.[31] Owen in response had sternly reasserted the old Calvinist truths which had been good enough for his forebears. The second was on organization. Baxter began his Worcestershire Association, and this was followed by Brotherly Associations in other counties on the same basis, on the principle of a wide admission of communicants to the Lord's Supper. The 'deeper discoverie' asked for by Owen – and confirmed by the Declaration of Independent ministers at the Savoy Conference on 12 October 1658 – made nonsense of such hopes. 'How low then hath this laid our hopes of Reconciliation' records Baxter, in an unhappy manuscript note at this time.[32] The third was on politics, and behind the politics, history. Even at the height of Owen's influence with Oliver Cromwell – and at its height, it *was* high – he never allowed the political convenience of serving a compliant magistrate to remove old sectarian suspicions of the civil power. Owen's history was Milton's: the Church was at its best in its first three hundred years, when it was being persecuted; with the Emperor Constantine, the rot set in.[33] No view could have been less attractive to Baxter. 'Christian Empire' was the heart of his political philosophy: his imagination quickened at the prospect of Oliver, and after him Richard, taking on that Constantine role which had been given as a model to English rulers in the apocalyptic writings of John Foxe (1516–1587).[34] That philosophy found its public testament in his *Holy Commonwealth* of 1659. The private dedication to magistracy was no less emphatic in a letter which Baxter wrote to Howe a year earlier, in which he urged that reproofs to rulers should only be made to them personally, and never given a public airing.[35]

For Baxter, Howe and Marvell, Richard Cromwell's Protectorate presented a unique opportunity. The apocalyptic expectations of the father ('The Lord Protector is noted as a man of a Catholic spiritt, desirous of the unity and peace of all the servants of Christ', wrote Baxter to Howe in April 1658[36]), traced by Stocker in Marvell's three poems about Cromwell, 'An Horatian Ode', *The First Anniversary* and *The Elegy*, were now transferred to the son. Calamy noted: 'When Oliver died, his son Richard succeeded him as Protector, and Mr. Howe stood in the same relation to the son, as he had done to the father'. Howe could be made angry, in later years, by any statements which implied that Richard had been a weak man. He would recall the opposition to the Protector of the Army and Fleetwood, and how, with only Thurloe to aid him, he stood out all night against his Council of State in the bid to avoid Parliament being dissolved.[37] That Parliament had marked the beginning of Marvell's public career, as representative for Hull. He began it with the conviction that Richard could defeat his enemies: 'it is to be hoped that our justice our affection and our number which is at least two thirds will weare them out at the long runne', he wrote in February 1658 to Downing.[38] Those hopes were dashed. Baxter's bitterness at Owen's part in Richard's downfall was expressed in a whole paragraph which was expunged by Sylvester from his published edition of *Reliquiae Baxterianae*[39], but which survives in the original manuscript. When Howe was dying in 1705, Richard Cromwell stepped briefly out of retirement to pay a courtesy call on his old domestic chaplain.[40] Wallace noted parallels in the political stance of Marvell and Baxter in 1659, but saw them in the casuist formulations in Baxter's *Holy Commonwealth* about the conferring and transferring of power, rather than in apocalyptic hymns to a Christian Magistrate.[41] On the other hand, Margoliouth in the definitive edition of Marvell's *Poems and Letters* footnotes the conclusion of Marvell's *Elegy*:

> Cease now our griefs, calm peace succeeds a war,
> Rainbows to storms, Richard to Oliver

with a direct comparison with Baxter's address to Richard Cromwell, with its millennial expectations that 'you have been strangely kept from participating in any of our late bloody contentions, that God might make you the healer of our breaches'.[42]

Pace Wallace, this 'millenarian possibility' had not 'disappeared forever'; after 1660, without Richard, however, it had to be recast drastically. For most of the decade after the Restoration, Baxter and Owen, Presbyterian and Independent, were driven together as victims of a persecuting Anglicanism. But old wounds did not heal easily. In 1668 negotiations, centering around the ecumenical figure of Bishop Wilkins (1614–1672), foundered on Owen's desire for toleration as against Baxter's desire for comprehension. At least that was the perception of Baxter and his allies. We see it surfacing in an undated letter from Thomas Manton (1620–1677), fellow Nonconformist minister, to Baxter, which is clearly written at this time, and which speaks of their common frustration at the way in which Owen's proposals for toleration cut across their own hopes for comprehension.[43] It is notable that when Marvell, a few years later, writes to defend Howe's Arminian theology against Thomas Danson's Owen-like Calvinist dogma, he takes particular exception to Danson's bringing Manton in on *his* side of the argument. It is with an insider's authority that Marvell claims that Manton had 'consulted with Howe on this point'.[44]

Owen was a useful scapegoat for breakdown, but it is doubtful whether the basis really existed for union between Wilkins on the one hand and Baxter and Howe on the other. They could agree, against the sectarianism of Owen, on the value of a 'National Church', and could mean it. But the *latitude* which led men like Wilkins to embrace Nonconformists in their vision of Church government was not easily reconcilable with the *disciplinary* requirements of men who had not given up on their visions of a 'Holy Commonwealth' (under Constantine in a remote past, under the Cromwells in a more recent one).[45] Thus we have the interesting reported exchange of views between Wilkins and Howe:

> The Doctor asked him whether it was the *discipline* of the church, that was the thing from whence he drew his chief objection? To which Mr. Howe replied, that he could not by any means be fond of a child, that in reality had no *discipline* at all, and he thought that a very considerable objection against the establishment.[46]

For Owen, this dialogue would have been meaningless. It was precisely because discipline and a National Church *were* incompatible that an answer had to be found outside an imposed national framework. We have seen that he held no brief for the overrated Constantine: Christianity was best in the catacombs, in the three hundred years before a Christian magistrate. And if Christian magistracy *were* such a constructive force, why was its name being invoked by the very bishops who persecuted dissidents?

The Protestant imperialist had an answer, and it was to be found in history. Constantine was not to be written off, but a closer scrutiny of the limits of his achievement was required than had been given in the sixteenth century by even the revered John Foxe. A search into history revealed that the enemy were bishops, even in Constantine's day, who exalted Church Councils above Emperors, as well as Popes, as part of a master-design. There were worrying historical parallels with persecuting prelates of the seventeenth century. Baxter had begun his diagnosis early, in the middle–1650s. He identified Grotius as the architect of a plan to advance Popery, not the conventional 'Italian' way by exalting Popes, but the 'French' way by exalting Councils.[47] The key English figure was Peter Heylyn (1600–1662), who was ostensibly Protestant in denouncing the Pope, but who was really impugning 'Italian' Catholicism to advance 'French' Catholicism. The persecuting Anglicanism of the Clarendon Code was the logical extension of principles which had been nurtured in the years before the Restoration.

Heylyn's posthumous biography of Laud, *Cyprianus Anglicus*, was not published until 1668. Its effect upon Baxter was traumatic. Here was the authentication of the fears which Baxter had voiced earlier in pamphlets and letters – once bizarrely to Heylyn himself[48] – and which revealed the coherence of the 'Grotian' masterplot.[49] Up to this point, Baxter had written very little about Laud. There was not much controversial literature to bite upon: Laud had written very little. His Arminianism could hardly offend the man who had himself, in 1649, broken the Puritan consensus on doctrine. But now, so it appeared to Baxter and others, the master spoke through the pen of the pupil. Whether he did so is another matter.[50] The point is that Baxter believed that he did. The choice of title told all: Laud had referred admiringly to the third-century martyr/saint as one who held 'no great opinion of the Roman infallibility'. Here then was the basis for Church union, as Grotius had contemplated it: not the 'Italian' way, with its emphasis on Papal primacy, but the 'French' way, with its emphasis on conciliar power. The historical investigation of this conciliar power had led to an agonizing reappraisal of the powers of the Christian Empire, and specifically of its first ruler, Constantine.

And so we come to Marvell's two little-noticed public interventions. In 1676 he wrote in defence of the well-meaning, if intellectually low-powered, Herbert Croft (1603–1691), Bishop of Hereford, against Francis Turner (1638–1700). The point-by-point rebuttal of Turner, similar to, if less effective than, his earlier demolition of Samuel Parker (1640–1688) in *The Rehearsal Transpros'd*, gives way abruptly on page 43:

> But the Printer calls: the Press is in danger. I am weary of such stuff, both mine own and his. I will rather give him this following Essay of mine own to busie him.

Then follows, in very different tone, the erudite and searching investigation, *The Historical Essay Touching General Councils.* At every point the diagnosis chimes with that of Baxter's. The good-natured Constantine had let himself be imposed upon, and realized his mistake too late; through Councils, bishops asserted themselves, not through support of Papal infallibility:

> the good Constantine brought them [the Bishops] the Fiddles. But it appear'd likewise how soon he was weary of the Ball, and towards his latter end, as Princes often do upon too late experience, would have redressed all, and returned to his natural temper.

The culprits are clearly named:

> ... the true and single cause then was the Bishops. And they were the cause against Reason.[51]

Baxter puts the point similarly:

> all cometh but to this, that the Italians are Papists, who would have the Pope rule Arbitrarily, as above Councils; but the French are no Papists, who would have the Pope rule only by the Canons or Church Parliament, and to be *singulis Maior, at universis Minor.* This is the true Repeal of Church-Government, in which the English should (by them) agree.

He went on to draw the implications for foreign policy of such thinking:

> Get but the poor trick of calling nothing Popery but the Pope's Arbitrary Absolute Power, and do but tie him to Rule by the Consent and Laws of Church-Parliaments, that is, set up the Church French Government, and then they are no Papists. Do not the French Protestants deserve all their sufferings for calling the Church or Bishops then *Papists*, and separating from so Excellent a Government.

Marvell's pamphlet of 1677, *An Account of the Growth of Popery and Arbitrary Government in England*, with its political account of the attempts of Parliament to resist the designs of Louis XIV, has never been linked closely enough to the parallel historical effort in *An Essay Concerning General Councils* to recover the intellectual basis for 'French' Popery (see below, p. 159). It should not be overlooked that Oliver Cromwell's justification to his Parliament in 1656 in not having to do 'with any Popish state except France' was because 'in that country it is true that they do not think themselves under such a tie to the Pope': a distinction trounced by both Baxter and Marvell in 1677.[52]

What of Marvell's second neglected foray, this time into Church doctrine? The defence of John Howe's views against Danson's on predestination seems innocuous enough. Marvell tries, at one stage in the argument, to pass it off as such: his aim, he says, was to 'hinder one Divine from offering violence to another'.[53] But the stakes are high, and of this Marvell is well aware. The doctrinal differences between Baxter and Owen lurked below the surface during the abortive negotiations between the two men in the 1660s. They surfaced again in 1673, after the Declaration of Indulgence. Baxter and Owen were two of six Presbyterian and Congregational lecturers appointed to preach each Tuesday at Pinner's Hall. As early as 1674 Baxter was arousing opposition there by his Arminian doctrinal views, foreshadowing the final break in 1694, with the secession of Arminian Presbyterian lecturers to Sadler's Hall under the leadership of John Howe (Baxter having died three years earlier). Danson's great crime in Marvell's eyes was to call Howe a Papist because he spoke kindly of Free Will: 'to represent him under a Popish Vizard'. And Marvell stresses:

> For although we live under a rationall jealousie alwaies of Popery, yet whatever is said by any Author of that persuasion, is not forthwith therefore to be clamorously rejected.[54]

For men grappling with a Popish conspiracy, it was reprehensible to see one Protestant slagging off another with that epithet. And the damage ran deeper still. These same 'French' Catholics, bent on their bogus reunion, as Baxter pointed out, when they 'preach and write against the Calvinists, they render them odious as holding that men are necessitated to sin and be damned, and that it is long of Gods Decree which cannot be resisted':[55] the very doctrine which both Howe and Marvell were contesting in what they wrote against Danson.

There are two points, in the two more celebrated works of Marvell which have not received much attention and should now be pressed into the argument. The mocking tone of *The Rehearsal Transpros'd* gives way, at one point, to a moving personal statement of belief:

> Indeed although Christ did not assume an earthly and visible Kingdome, yet he by the Gospel gave Law to Princes and Subjects ... And he knew very well that without dethroning the Princes of the World at present, yet by the constant preaching of that benevolous

and amicable Doctrine, by the assimilating and charitable Love of the first Christians, and by the signal patience under all their sufferings and torments, all opposition would be worne out, and all Princes should make place for Christian Empire.

This was the passage in which Annabel Patterson rightly saw overlaps 'with the millenarian aspirations of The First Anniversary', but with this difference: the imperial ideal, it was recognized in the later work, could be betrayed from within – 'when once Christianity had in this regular and direct way obtained the sovereignty, Ecclesiastical persons in whose keeping the counterparts of Church Doctrine, and example are most properly deposited, began exceedingly to degenerate'.[56]

Finally, in Marvell's *Account of the Growth of Popery*, Louis XIV's machinations are put in a wider historical context:

> In the time of his late Majesty, King Charles the first (besides what they contributed to the Civil War in England) the Rebellion and horrid Massacre in Ireland, and which was even worse than that, they pretending it was done by the King's Commission, and vouching the Broad Seal for the Authority.[57]

The reference here is to the popular belief that Charles I had engaged the Irish rebels to take up arms – the famous Antrim Commission – as the prelude to, and indeed part-explanation for, the coming of the English Civil War.[58] I have argued elsewhere for the importance of the Antrim Commission to Baxter, although even in 1696, when his *Reliquiae Baxterianae* was posthumously published, the manuscript references made by Baxter to this issue had to be deleted from the text (as did his references, as we have already noted, to the part played in toppling Richard Cromwell). For both Baxter and Marvell, the Irish Rebellion was a logical, not merely chronological, prelude to the English Civil War.

One critic has found Marvell anything but inconclusive. Christopher Hill has made three relevant points towards a reassessment of Marvell. The first, made ten years before Stocker's study appeared, was this prophetic comment: 'scholars are just beginning to realize how much millenarianism there is in Marvell'.[59] The second, a consistent theme in Hill's writings, is to emphasize the swingeing, if erratic, punishments seventeenth-century governments could impose on their dissidents. The literary scholar praised the subtleties of the opaque presentation; the historian warned of the penalties of a transparent one. Hill made, for instance, telling use of this insight in discussing the absence of Unitarian ideas in *Paradise Lost*. The third point he made was to emphasize Marvell's covert republicanism. Marvell's cautious letters to his Hull constituents no more indicate a lack of engagement in political issues – contrast them with the lively indiscretion of his correspondence with his nephew, William Popple – than his praise of Charles II in contemporary pamphlets speaks for his royalism. When it mattered (defending Milton, attacking Louis XIV) he *did* speak out, at considerable personal risk (even if, by his own standards, he should have spoken out more). It is on such occasions that the authentic Marvell speaks. Armed with this insight, Hill makes sense of Marvell's earlier silences or ambiguities. His 'Horatian Ode' is not so finely balanced as critics have supposed. The personal virtues of Charles I are honoured, it is true, but since Cromwell personifies 'historical determinism' the scales are weighted in his favour. 'Upon Appleton House' does not celebrate retirement and action equally; Fairfax and Nature bow out to daughter Mary and 'the brute external force of the Mower'. The tensions in Marvell, which Hill does not deny and which, on the contrary, he believes, produced the great Commonwealth poetry, are resolved in one direction, and that a radical, republican one. Hill believes that 'by the time of *The First Anniversary* and *On Blake's Victory over the Spaniards* all Marvell's problems are resolved'. The end of 'the great poetry' did not quite coincide with the end of the tensions; however, 'the inward assurance Marvell had so hardly won in the fifties was never lost', and the 'polished and sophisticated wit of his Restoration prose' related both to the earlier tensions *and* to their resolution.[60]

Hill's first two points – Marvell's millenarianism, and the *necessity*, not the *aesthetics*, of his imposed inconclusiveness – seem to me valid, and they are at the core of the argument advanced in this essay. The third point does not, however, follow logically from the first two. There is no real evidence that Marvell ever was a republican; though, as we have seen, there is much evidence that he was a *Cromwellian*. Hill argues Marvell's republicanism largely from his association with Milton and Harrington; there is nothing Marvell wrote to support this reading. It is true that what Hill calls his 'urbane flattery' of Charles II in *The Rehearsal Transpros'd* doesn't argue much for his royalism either.[61] But to dismiss it merely as cant is to miss the change in Marvell's attitude to the King a few years later in *An Account of the Growth of Popery*. It is the difference in approach to a King who, however suspect his motives, seemed to be offering to his subjects, with the Declaration of Indulgence, an advance in religious freedom (Constantine returning to his natural temper, to the dismay of his bishops?), and on the other hand to a King who, *because of* the exposure of those motives, now seemed to offer to his subjects – by way of the secret Treaty of Dover – nothing less than 'French' tyranny. This very difference in approach casts a curious light on Marvell's 'republicanism'. Margarita Stocker is correct, therefore, when she argues:

> In effect, Marvell's problem was to experience the reigns of two Kings who were less than sensitive to constitutional restraints, and to see in Cromwell a statesman who, while lacking dynastic right, seemed fitted for the English form of government.[62]

In the light of this essay, her argument could be reworded:

> Marvell's problem was to experience the reigns of two Kings who betrayed their imperial role, and to see in two Cromwells statesmen who, while lacking dynastic right, had been marked out by Providence to fulfil it.

Hill is also wrong to say that 'like Milton, Marvell saw Constantine as the villain of the early history of Christianity'.[63] That was Owen's view as well as Milton's: *Antichrist* came in with Constantine. Baxter and Marvell saw it very differently. Antichrist had been dealt seemingly a mortal blow when Constantine became Christian Emperor. The villains of the early history of Christianity, however, were the insufferable bishops who exploited the *innocence* of the magistrate. Baxter and Marvell looked for new (perhaps more street-wise?) Constantines, and found them in the Protectorates of the two Cromwells. The Restoration marked for neither man the terminus of that search, but for both the 1670s were the low point: – Charles II selling out to Popish interests as his father had done in Ireland in October 1641;[64] Heylyn, Bramhall (1594–1663), Thorndike (1598–1672), Dodwell (1641–1711), Gunning (1614–1684), Pearson (1613–1686) and other Anglican divines reviving Grotius's dream of 'French' Popery via conciliar power. By his death in 1678 Marvell missed an even lower point, the reign of James II, and escaped the fate of Baxter in 1686, locked up in his prison cell and dreaming there his millenarian dreams. But he also missed the high point – the coming to power of Dutch William – which meant for Baxter (as it surely would have done for Marvell)[65] the millenarian dreams becoming reality, the revival of an apocalyptic 'National Church', the subjugation of Popery. The Cromwellian 'Holy Commonwealth' was back on the drawing board.

There are enough gaps in the Marvell story without our trying to pursue them beyond the grave (even if it is not unreasonable to guess at the sort of reception which Marvell would have given William III). This short essay has tried to fill one of these gaps – Marvell's religious beliefs – around which unnecessary mysteries have been created. As we have seen, he wrote very little, but what he did is so revealing that this is one area where the 'inconclusive' label will not stick. That he should defend, of all Protestant ministers, John Howe; that the defence should rest on the reasonableness of Arminian doctrine; that the prelates whom he disliked were those who magnified Church Councils above Emperors and who then thought that *that* did not make them Papists: all this places Marvell in a very clearly defined wing of Protestant nonconformity, once we have put these public positions into their historical context of the mid-seventies.

To be 'conclusive' in one sphere (religion) does not, of course, mean that Marvell was necessarily conclusive in others, but Margarita Stocker is one literary critic who has shown us that we do gain in understanding Marvell's earlier poems when we recognize the strength of these religious convictions. That recognition, neither in her book nor in this essay, is meant to cancel out all ambiguities in Marvell; to refer all the ambivalences, which have continually teased the reader, to some fixed set of religious beliefs would indeed be a crude reductionism. Better the openness of the best of the literary critics, of John Carey, with his understanding of Marvell's 'reversals transposed' or of Christopher Ricks, of Marvell's 'self-inwoven similes'. The dew dropping seen as a tear weeping by itself; lovers, like strands of a rope, pulled together by being turned away from each other; little TC naming the wild flowers and thereby destroying them; the Mower (*pace* Hill) not a 'brutal external force', but 'a creature of contradictions' – these, and other reversals, leading Carey to the conviction that an hour's silence would be the best tribute to the poet, or 'silent marvel-ling'.[66]

Which, in turn, is what Marvell himself was to say: 'not to write at all is much the safer course of life'.[67] The fact that he failed to follow his own good advice, in four prose works in the last decade of his own life, of unequal literary merit but not – we have argued here – of unequal historical interest, has been the historian's excuse to break the silence. The reconstruction of Marvell's religious milieu dispels some literary ambiguities, leaves others untouched, and creates new ambiguities for the historian to worry at. For what I hope even this brief sketch has shown for Marvell, as for Baxter and Howe, and maybe for many more of like mind once we have fuller documentation, is that the late 1650s lived on into the 1670s in England in ways which we do not yet fully understand. One clue to the problem is provided by a letter which Baxter wrote to Cromwell's agent, John Durie (1596–1680), that inveterate pursuer of Church unity, as early as November 1652. Baxter then saw the way forward as the con-vening by Cromwell of a consultative assembly of clergymen, 'as Constantine did'. In the same letter he referred to 'the Late King's Designe (for I strongly conjecture he was much of Grotius' mind)' as pursuing union the wrong way, by persecuting the godly.[68] And Marvell and Howe would have subscribed to both these principles then. But in the late 1670s, what do all three witness in the reign of his successor but the hideous perversion of a noble ideal, of Emperor being ruled *by* Council instead of ruling *through* Council? And what was that but Grotianism revived?

Marvell will go on being read, primarily for his use of snaffle and curb, but that doesn't mean that we give up entirely on the search for his bloody horse.

Notes

1. Balachandra Ravan, 'Andrew Marvell: The aesthetics of inconclusive-ness', in *Approaches to Marvell*, ed. C.A. Patrides, London: Rout-ledge and Kegan Paul, 1978, pp. 155–173.
2. Blair Worden, 'The Politics of Marvell's Horatian Ode', *Historical Journal*, 27, 1984, pp. 539, 547.
3. J.M. Wallace, *Destiny his Choice: The Loyalism of Andrew Marvell*,

Cambridge: Cambridge University Press, 1968. For a cautionary comment on the implications of 'loyalism' see, in this volume, Conal Condren, 'Andrew Marvell as Polemicist: his *Account of The Growth of Popery and Arbitrary Government*', note 30.

4. Samuel Parker, *A Reproof to the Rehearsal Transprosed*, London, 1673, pp. 521–526.
5. *The Poems and Letters of Andrew Marvell*, ed. H.M. Margoliouth, 11, *Letters*, Oxford: Oxford University Press, 1971, p. 317.
6. Marvell, *The Rehearsal Transpros'd and The Rehearsal Transpros'd: The Second Part*, ed. D.I.B. Smith, Oxford: Oxford University Press, 1971, pp. 159–160.
7. John Aubrey, *Brief Lives*, ed. O.L. Dick, Harmondsworth: Penguin Books, 1949, p. 356.
8. Annabel M. Patterson, *Marvell and the Civic Crown*, Princeton: Princeton University Press, 1978, p. 4.
9. Ibid., p. 3. Her reference is to: Rosalie Colie, *'My Ecchoing Song': Andrew Marvell's Poetry of Criticism*, Princeton: Princeton University Press, 1970, p. 3, note 2.
10. Barbara Everett, 'The Shooting of the Bears: Poetry and Politics in Andrew Marvell', in *Andrew Marvell: Essays on the tercentenary of his death*, ed. R.L. Brett, Oxford: Oxford University Press, 1979, p. 62.
11. Isabel Rivers, *The Poetry of Conservatism 1660–1745*, Cambridge: Cambridge University Press, 1973, p. 108.
12. Muriel Bradbrook, 'Marvell our Contemporary', in R.L. Brett, ed., op.cit., p. 114.
13. J.P. Kenyon, 'Andrew Marvell: Life and Times', in R.L. Brett, ed., op.cit., p. 23.
14. Pierre Legouis, *Andrew Marvell: Poet Puritan Patriot*, Oxford: Oxford University Press, 1965, pp. 221–222.
15. Patterson, op.cit., p. 213, is rightly sceptical of such a claim.
16. Ibid., p. 176.
17. Margarita Stocker, *Apocalyptic Marvell*, Sussex: Harvester Press, 1986. For an assessment of its critical importance to Marvell studies, see: David Norbrook, 'Coy Mistress Uncovered', *London Review of Books*, 19 May 1988, pp. 20–21.
18. These were wholly compatible with the scepticism of Fifth Monarchist pretensions which Marvell shows in 'The First Anniversary'; the same, we shall see, is true of Richard Baxter, whose views are discussed later.
19. Wallace, op.cit., pp. 94, 101, 109, 138, 229.
20. Cf. W. Lamont, *Godly Rule*, London: Macmillan, 1969, p. 158: 'Men no longer believed in a Millennium' with W. Lamont, in

Richard Baxter and the Millennium, London: Croom Helm, 1979, *passim*.

21.   Christopher Hill, 'Society and Andrew Marvell', in *Puritanism and Revolution*, London: Mercury Books, 1965, pp. 365–366; Patterson, op.cit., p. 5 (commentary on Legouis's critical divide at the Restoration); John Carey, 'Reversals transposed: An aspect of Marvell's imagination', in *Approaches to Marvell*, p. 153.

22.   Patterson, op.cit., p. 205.

23.   Ibid., p. 213; Legouis, op.cit., p. 222.

24.   W.K. Jordan, *The Development of Religious Toleration in England*, Harvard: Harvard University Press, 1965, iii, p. 343.

25.   The best recent study of Owen is: P. Toon, *God's Statesman: The Life and Work of John Owen*, Exeter: The Paternoster Press, 1971. But see Blair Worden, 'Toleration and the Cromwellian Protectorate', *Studies in Church History*, 21, 1984, ed. W.J. Sheils, pp. 199–233, for some excellent comments on Owen's influence on Cromwell.

26.   (Doctor Williams' Library) *Baxter Correspondence*, ii, f. 15v, 24v.

27.   See the third chapter of my *Richard Baxter and the Millennium*, pp. 124–209.

28.   There is no good recent study of Howe. But see the introductory memoir by Edmund Calamy to the first volume of John Howe, *Works . . . with memoir of his Life by Edmund Calamy*, New York, 1938.

29.   Ibid., pp. 4–5.

30.   (Doctor Williams' Library) *Baxter Correspondence*, iii, f. 196, 198, 200; vi, f. 231, 232; G.F. Nuttall, 'Richard Baxter's Apology, its occasion and composition', *Journal of Ecclesiastical History*, iv, 1, 1953.

31.   Lamont, *Richard Baxter and the Millennium*, pp. 134–155.

32.   (Doctor Williams' Library) *Baxter Treatises*, vi, f. 203.

33.   John Owen, *Animadversions on a Treatise Intituled Fiat Lux*, London, 1662, p. 253.

34.   Lamont, *Richard Baxter and the Millennium*, passim.

35.   (Doctor Williams' Library) *Baxter Correspondence*, iii, f. 200.

36.   Idem.

37.   Howe, *Works*, i, p. vi.

38.   *The Poems and Letters of Andrew Marvell*, ii, p. 308.

39.   See documentation in note 30 above.

40.   Howe, *Works*, i, p. xlviii.

41.   Wallace, op.cit., p. 141.

42.   *The Poems and Letters of Andrew Marvell*, i, p. 335.

43.   (Doctor Williams' Library) *Baxter Correspondence*, ii, f. 273–273v.

44. Marvell, *Remarks Upon A Late Disingenuous Discourse*, London, 1678, p. 96.
45. This difference becomes clear in the disputes in the last year of Richard Baxter's life, in 1691, with his old friend, John Humfrey, about the meaning of a 'National Church'. Both approved of it, but meant different things by it. Humfrey actually suggested the title of Baxter's work, *Of Nationall Churches in order to a Comprehension*, with the words: 'this will make the book sell': (Doctor Williams' Library) *Baxter Correspondence*, i, f. 72. But compare the very different concepts in: Humfrey, *Union Pursued*, London, 1691, with Baxter's 'A Political Primer for Nationall Church-makers', (Doctor Williams' Library) *Baxter Treatises*, vi, f. 296–302.
46. Howe, *Works*, i, p. vii.
47. This theme runs through three Baxter pamphlets between 1658 and 1659: – *The Grotian Religion Discovered*, *A Key for Catholicks*, and *A Holy Commonwealth*.
48. (Doctor Williams' Library) *Baxter Correspondence*, ii, f. 268: in this letter of 20th October 1658 Baxter had expressed his pleasure that Heylyn was denying any attachment to the 'Grotian Religion'.
49. Baxter, *The True History of Councils*, London, 1682, p. 49.
50. Royce MacGillivray, *Restoration Historians and the English Civil War*, The Hague, 1974, pp. 31–32, has some scepticism on this point.
51. Marvell, *Mr. Smirke*, London, 1676, pp. 43, 71. Compare this with Baxter's revised view of Constantine at this time: he 'foresaw not the evils that afterwards would follow ... The Emperor also being a Christian, worldly men are mostly of the Religion of the Prince or highest powers': Baxter, *Church-History of the Government of Bishops, and their Councils*, London, 1681, p. 15.
52. Baxter, *The True History of Councils*, preface, p. 49. Oliver Cromwell, *Letters and Speeches*, ed. T. Carlyle, London, 1897, iii, p. 274.
53. Marvell, *Remarks Upon a Late Disingenuous Discourse*, London 1678, p. 155.
54. Ibid., p. 142. Baxter notes how unfair it is that Howe, not himself, should be the anti-Arminian target, although he does not specifically mention Marvell's defence of Howe: notes, 10 May, 1679 Baxter Treatises, (Dr. Williams' Library) 18, fol. 73.
55. Baxter, *The True History of Councils*, p. 53.
56. Marvell, *The Rehearsal Transpros'd and The Rehearsal Transpros'd: The Second Part*, Oxford: Oxford University Press, 1971, ed. D.I.B. Smith, p. 236; Patterson, op.cit., p. 205.
57. Marvell, *An Account of the Growth of Popery and Arbitrary Government in England*, Amsterdam, 1677, p. 12.

58. Conrad Russell, 'The British Background to the Irish Rebellion of 1641', *Historical Research*, 61, 145, June 1988, pp. 166–182, exposes the shallow historical base for this belief. But for its important *mythical* quality, see my *Richard Baxter and the Millennium*, pp. 76–123, 330–332 and Caroline Hibbard, *Charles I and the Popish Plot*, Chapel Hill: NC, 1983, *passim*.

59. Christopher Hill, 'Milton and Marvell', in *Approaches to Marvell*, p. 18.

60. Christopher Hill, 'Society and Andrew Marvell', in *Puritanism and Revolution*, pp. 337–366.

61. Christopher Hill, 'Milton and Marvell', in *Approaches to Marvell*, p. 14.

62. Stocker, op.cit., p. 25.

63. Christopher Hill, 'Milton and Marvell', in *Approaches to Marvell*, p. 17. The same point of view will be found in: Warren L. Chernaik, *The Poet's Time*, Cambridge: Cambridge University Press, 1983, p. 140. He claims (ibid., p. 121) of Marvell that '. . . a church to him, as to Milton and other left-wing Independants [sic] and sectaries of the 1640s and 1650s was a voluntary organisation of Church believers, members of the body of Christ'. I have made clear in this essay my reasons for disagreeing with this interpretation: on the other hand I share his scepticism of the 'loyalist' Marvell of John M. Wallace (ibid., pp. 10–11).

64. Baxter, *The True History of Councils*, p. 221: 'who sinned more? The Irish for murdering 200,000 or Sir John Temple, Dr. Henry Jones, the Earl of Orrery, for recording and reporting what they did?'

65. K.H.D. Haley, *William of Orange and the English Opposition 1672–4*, Oxford: Oxford University Press, 1953, pp. 57–59, for Marvell's role among a group of pro-Dutch activists operating under Peter du Moulin. On Peter du Moulin's correspondence with Baxter on his proposed history of the Papacy, see (Doctor Williams' Library) *Baxter Correspondence*, iii, f. 127. Like Baxter and Marvell, du Moulin knew the Papist complicity in the coming of the Civil War: 'the late rebellion was raised and fostered by the arts of the Court of Rome', Peter du Moulin, *A Vindication of the Sincerity of the Protestant Religion*, London, 1664, p. 58.

66. Christopher Ricks, 'Its own resemblance'; John Carey, 'Reversals transposed. An aspect of Marvell's imagination', in *Approaches to Marvell*, respectively, pp. 108–136, 136–155.

67. Marvell, *The Rehearsal Transpros'd and The Rehearsal Transpros'd: The Second Part*, pp. 159–160.

68. (Doctor Williams' Library) *Baxter Correspondence*, vi, f. 89.

6 Andrew Marvell as Polemicist: his Account of the Growth of Popery, and Arbitrary Government

Conal Condren

Andrew Marvell died quite suddenly of a fever on 18 August, 1678 – all for the want of some Peruvian bark, the 'Jesuit's bark' no less.[1] Had he lived, he could hardly have escaped either owning or disowning his *Account of the Growth of Popery and Arbitrary Government*.[2] His name had been tied to the tract almost since the government had first offered a reward to anyone who could inform on author and printer. A pro-government pamphlet had then referred to 'Andrew' 'a shrewd man against popery';[3] and in his own last letter Marvell alludes to his public association with the work in a typically distancing and ironic manner.[4] A little information goes a long way, but not far enough really to suggest innocence of authorship.[5] He had not been dead a week before the secretary of State, Sir Joseph Williamson received information that Marvell was indeed guilty of authorship;[6] and thus for the government's enemies he was fit for posthumous praise.

> 'Twas he th' approach of Rome did first explore,
> And the grim monster, arbitrary pow'r[7]

In the dénoument of his life we have all that needs teasing out of his final masterly political statement: an apparently ambivalent

public involvement; an authorial distancing from the text; ingenuity of argumentation; an oblique and disingenuous style masking
a firm political commitment; a breadth of political vision and a
potency of imagery through which the central concern is
developed. One could almost be writing of the Cromwellian
poems. All this however, is capped by a twist of personal *fortuna*
which could have appealed to Machiavelli (though not in the
circumstances to Marvell himself). His sudden death has added a
resonance to the text which has prompted some critics to ponder
just where Marvell would have stood when the sordid confusions
of Charles II's reign culminated in the tragi-comedy of the Popish
and Rye House plots, The Monmouth Rebellion and the Bloody
Assize;[8] odd questions superficially, given the difficulty of grasp-
ing Marvell's political identity when he was alive, though in death
one needs at last be still. 'To His Coy Mistress' had made the
point to perfection. And in this case, I believe we can disengage
an uncompromisingly activist illocutionary force from the embrace
of a protective disingenuousness.[9] We can be fairly sure where
Marvell would have stood in the confusions that ushered in the
reign of James II. Indeed, given Marx's famous aphorism about
Christianity being the opiate of the masses, there is a gruesome
Marvellian irony in the fact that his final piece of deliberative
rhetoric was unambiguously a Christian incitement, and its author
ended with an opiate.

Previous accounts of the work have suggested more or less
converging images for which the label 'Christian incitement' is
intended as a partial corrective. The predominant image of the
poet as measured, subtle, arcane and urbane might suggest that
the *Account* be seen in similar terms. Perchance such epithets have
been thought appropriate to the 18th century 'whig' ethos to
which Marvell and the other dissidents of Charles II's final years
have been appropriated.[10] Whether or not Marvell was close to
being Shaftsbury's hired pen in 1677,[11] Marvell has certainly been
tied to the coat-tails of a somewhat elusive 'whig party' riding
'time's winged chariot' into the 'long eighteenth century'.[12] It is
a century which in turn has been a staging post for railroading
emblematic figures into the Liberal Tradition of the twentieth.
Until relatively recently such unlikely characters as John Milton
and Algernon Sidney have been deemed liberal, even left-wing,
and for Chernaik at least, they still keep company with Marvell.

Meanwhile, back in the seventeenth century, the very insubstantiality of a Whig Party in 1677 has made it difficult to be sure of Marvell's allegiance to it; thus by a deftly circular motion, the aloof and balanced nature of Marvell's own commitments may seem confirmed and his elevation as a Whig hero marked by Whig virtues, becomes easy.

If continuity in his thought has been sought, it has been in the fittingly whiggish or liberal terms of constitutionalism, balance, a trimming sceptical moderation, agnosticism, and patriotism.[13] If discontinuity has been claimed, it has been in terms of political opportunism – the distaff side of judicious proto-whig trimming.[14] In a sense this has been appropriate, not because Marvell was really the moderate constitutional Whig, or a mere chance-luck and trimmer; but simply because his circumstantial shiftiness at the end was a fitting epitaph. The whole incident of authorship and death was as decorous a finale to his manner of juggling the demands of epideictic and deliberative rhetoric, as Tom May's death was for him.[15] The only trimming evident in the *Account* is that which is necessary to establish the narrator's credentials of balance and moderation. So, Marvell presents a moderate aspect, much as the stones of 'Appleton House' were made to express the moderation of its owner (see above, pp. 55–9). Indeed such virtues as moderation, balance and modesty were, generally speaking, important rhetorical credentials throughout seventeenth century England and they had an added resonance in a time of ferocious censorship;[16] for Marvell they were vital precisely because of the shrill extremity of his message. It is a message that does not look forward to the still waters of the eighteenth century, even to the relatively quiet 'revolution' of 1688, but (contra Wallace) back to the Civil War and Reformation, to the Good Old Cause and violence.[17] The only ambiguity is protective, as befitted a man ever conscious of the consequences of public praise and blame.[18]

The difficulties of Marvell's position may be indicated at this stage by comparing the *Account* with what might be called its companion piece, *A Short Historical Essay Touching General Councils, Creeds and Imposition in Religions*, 1676. The works are in important respects at one; they share a concern for Christian liberty, the role of established churches and the function of the magistrate with respect to religion. Each text is also a narrative.

But precisely because the *Essay Touching Councils* explicitly concerns distant times rather than the immediately echoing past in which Marvell was involved, his need for protecting and distancing devices is altogether less evident. The *Essay* deals with early Christianity up to the establishment of the Nicene Creed. Christianity, it argues, was never a threat to the magistrate, and a number of pagan magistrates realized this and left good Christians in peace (*Essay*, 95–100). Ironically, it was as Christianity became more powerful and hierarchically established, that life became systematically more distressing for Christians (*Essay*, 146). Specifically, it was the ambition of bishops, the development of bishoprics and then the alliance between bishops and (effectively duped) magistrates that caused Christians to suffer (*Essay*, 146–54). As Marvell focuses on the Arian Heresy and the Nicene Creed, the bishops attacked are those who were to germinate into the mighty hierarchies of the medieval Catholic church. Consequently, the target was easy and safe. The force of the *Essay*, however, was by historical analogy to turn attention to the plight of innocent Protestants in what Marvell saw as a rigid, oppressive and bishop-ridden Church of England (*Essay* e.g. 118–119, 123, 126–7, 154: see Lamont, above). This, too, was protected by, and in alliance with a relatively innocent magistrate.

In contrast, as will become clear, the *Account* is fastidious in by-passing the real target, Charles II, who probably seemed less innocent by 1677 than at any time since his Restoration. The result is a highly-wrought narrative which, by allusion, authorial distancing, ironic inversion and the suggestiveness of a sustained metaphorical structure, conveys by the contexture of its words a good deal more than a quick reading might suggest. Wallace's injunction to read the *Account* 'straight' seems quite inappropriate and fails to explain why there should have been such a hue and cry when the work appeared. As my argument should make clear, I believe the recent views of Klause (Marvell was a sceptical agnostic) and Smith (a firm believer in royal prerogative) are also wide of the mark – at least if we take the *Account* seriously.[19] With respect to the *Account*, the revisionism of Chernaik and Stocker seems more plausible. That Stocker's thesis may force the poetry into too procrustian a bed does not detract from the fact that the sheets of her thesis wind very snugly around the body of Marvell's last work.[20] Chernaik's complementary emphasis on

Christian liberty is also salutary – despite being dressed in the terminology best suited to slipping Marvell into the pages of the Liberal's Own Book of Heroes.[21] What in all this literature has been lacking, in short, is a detailed exposition of the *Account* as something other than an addendum to the poetry (and if Marvell makes himself clear, a disappointing one at that); or a prolegomenon to a world Marvell never lived to see.

The overall structure of the *Account* is at least straightforward; it is divided into an introductory section specifying the conspiracy and threat to England; a central narrative section; and, there is a short conclusion in which the narrator reiterates his honourable intentions, his wish to be proved wrong and appeals to his Majesty to remedy the evil.

The introduction could hardly start more bluntly: there is a conspiracy afoot to change the government to an 'absolute tyranny' and 'down right popery', (248). The bluntness is not, however, without an arresting subtlety. The redundancy of 'absolute' as a predicate for tyranny plays on the notion of absolute monarchy and in conjunction with 'down right' suggests that both tyranny and popery are partially established. Marvell hastens to indicate that the governmental system under threat, is a mixed and limited monarchy, in which the people share through Parliament (249).

Marvell then spends several pages specifying the ultimate enemy to both church and state: 'popery'. It can hardly be called a religion. Unlike Judaism and 'Turkerey' (250) it has no 'bona fides' (ibid), being based on the 'counterfeit donation of Constantine, and wresting another donation from our Saviour' (256). The bishopric of Rome has been so improved by good management that all of 'Romish perswasion' are now obliged to rebel at the Pope's pleasure (257). It is remarkable that any Prince should tolerate it, yet many in Europe do (257) and having alluded to its omnipresence, Marvell catalogues its sins in English history; in Mary's reign papists made 'fewel of protestants' (258); and thereafter English monarchs might have counted their reigns in papal plots (259). Popery's introduction would affect every aspect of life, even threatening a redistribution of property (260). All Englishmen will lose by the change of religion.[22] As it is treason to make Britain a commonwealth, so from the same principle it is treason to make the country absolute (261). So popery and arbitrary power are merged by Marvell into one.

It is at this point, immediately prior to the central illustrative narration, that Marvell is obliged to anticipate scepticism; to display his credentials of disinterested fairness and moderation; and somewhat protectively, to identify himself in all good will with a potentially hostile audience. Who, he asks, could possibly be involved in such a conspiracy? Certainly not old cavaliers who, though loyal to King Charles I and his memory, are too wise and too good as subjects. They have not mistaken 'this Long Parliament also for rebels' (262). Certainly those exposed by the Test Act are not the conspirators; their resignations of public office were the signs of honourable men (261–2) and his Majesty treated them with great magnanimity (262).[23] Instead, he continues, the conspirators turned to France. Marvell turns away from answering the question recently posed as to who they are. Danby is unmentioned in the whole essay. Instead he reiterates his purely public-spirited intentions to present a 'naked narrative' concerning the conspiracy's development and the nation's present danger.

In this opening section of the argument we can already see the principal intellectual characteristics of the work: anonymity and reference to the author as a 'narrator' (later he will call himself simply a relator of events and information) distance him from the text. His statements of modest intention; his disarming praise of old cavaliers and recusants and veneration of the King leave a markedly disingenuous air, embedded as they are in an unrelenting hostility, even to a tolerance of papacy around which Charles had been manoeuvring for most of his reign. Marvell's allusions to Europe indicate that his perspective is more than insular; his hostility to France is less parochial xenophobia than a hatred of the vanguard of the Roman advance.[24] As Samuel Parker remarked of the last years of Charles's reign, during these times the 'inchanting terms' Popery and The French Interest, were by their pronouncement likely to turn men into beasts.[25] Marvell is no mere pronunciator but a relentless Circe. Penultimately, the opening section shows very well that Marvell must confront the possibility that present events were leading to a re-play of the old Civil War; negotiating the hopes and fears attendant upon its mythology was a very large part of any polemicist's armoury in the late seventeenth century.[26] Finally, the permeating monetary and gaming imagery has already been introduced by the play on 'donation' and of the Pope's improving his bishopric. Its cumulative effect is to suggest a passion in counterpoint to the studied narrative blandness.

Immediately however, Marvell turns to the business of his narration. This, in fact, takes up nearly 90 per cent of the tract with about 22 per cent of this being direct quotation from the King or from parliamentary debates or proposed legislation. By a different means this somewhat 'thick' description creates an ambience of objectivity and authorial distance, and with remarkable acuity lets the King's machinations and Parliament's faltering but stalwart defence of national and Protestant interest, seem to speak for themselves.

He begins the central narrative section with an Ariadnean thread for 'so intriguing a labyrinth' (264) as the conspiracy provides; this thread ties England and the conspiracy against her governmental form to the plight of international Protestantism. After a period of wars and uneasy peace with Holland, Charles II formed a Triple Alliance with Holland and Sweden in 1668 against the threatening expansion of France. For this Marvell has nothing but praise; it was entirely the King's work, and excellent, as it always is when the King is able to follow his own good judgement (265). Yet from 1670 the alliance was nullified by secret agreements with France, whilst the King enjoyed what Marvell calls a 'triple supply' to support the 'Triple League' (273).[27] This having been given, Parliament was prorogued until February 1672 (273); and the conspirators were thus provided with the ideal environment in which to bring war between the allies Holland and England, from which only the French and the Catholic cause could hope to gain. Marvell spends considerable space on the attempts to manoeuvre Holland into war, emphasizing how difficult a task it was as the Dutch acted with such honourable fastidiousness. Finally, the outbreak of war was orchestrated then declared (282) in March 1672. In the meantime, non-conformity with the Church of England was persecuted.[28]

> . . . [Instead] of squaring their governments by the rule of Christianity, [men] have shaped Christianity by the measures of their government, have reduced that straight line by the crooked, and bungling divine

and humane things together, have been always hacking and hewing one another, to frame an irregular figure of political incongruity. (281)

This architectural image of a malformed Sion almost an abridgement of the *Essay on Councils* is not offered as a criticism of Charles; but it is a commentary on the policies of Charles's reign (not always his) which might have come from the non-conforming pens of men such as Humfrey, Bagshaw, Baxter or Owen more obviously than from the quill of a conforming MP. According to Marvell, however, the greatest incongruity during this time is the encouragement of Catholicism which, it was planned, should come 'to pass like current money over the nation' (282). Domestic and foreign policies are linked by quoting Charles's demand that the Dutch re-establish Catholicism, its churches and the stipends of its clergy (285–6). Yet throughout by a deft use of anaphora, only 'they' are to blame. All those actually named are excused, exonerated or considered pawns. Finally, at this twist of the labyrinth, it is 'by the conspirators' good leave that Parliament was allowed to sit again in February 1672 (291). So, by implication, the King is a pawn or a conspirator.

For a short time thereafter, the conspirators tried to further their aims through Parliament, attempting to damage English trade in the interests of France and promoting the Declaration of Indulgence; whilst Parliament itself gave more money for the war against her true Protestant ally. The nation became suspicious, and so the Parliament was dismissed amongst mounting consternation about James Duke of York and his marriage to the Catholic Mary of Modena. Such marriages, relates our relator, were believed always 'to have increased Popery, and encouraged priests and Jesuits to pervert his Majesty's subjects' (296).[29]

Yet, despite a capacity to determine parliamentary sittings and the general direction of hostilities in the interests of France, by 1674 the conspirators had failed in their designs. A peace had been declared with Holland; land forces disbanded; and future Catholic marriages had been precluded for the Royal Family. Above all, continuing royal impoverishment insured that Parliament was still a force to be reckoned with (301). The conspirators, however, continued to work on two fronts. By encouraging the maintenance of British regiments in French service, they prepared them for use at home; and at home they appealed to 'the old

Cavalier party' (303) to regenerate fears of 1641 and of damage to Church and State '(How truly said! but meant, how falsely!)' (303). By April 1675 they had still met with inadequate success and were now confronted with the possibility of a test, an oath to flush out Catholics from office. The matter of even tighter provisions against Catholics was fought out in the Lords, a brave minority fighting in favour (309), of whom Marvell singles out Shaftsbury and Buckingham, not, he claims because they were pre-eminent but to balance the reproach that has been cast upon them (309). Controversies over privilege (fanned by the conspirators) distracted Parliament from the vital issue and, amidst mounting inter-House rivalry, the King prorogued Parliament (310).

When Parliament re-sat the King asked for continuity of supply to build ships; in return Parliament moved more strongly against papists at home and the French abroad (321). The bickering between the Houses continued; Parliament was duly prorogued until February 1676 (313–314). Meanwhile, as Marvell intimates, the increased hostility to the French was justified by two years in which French privateers had harassed British merchantmen and damaged commerce without hindrance (317–318).

'Thus we are at length arrived at this much controverted, and as much expected Session' (319). The King 'demanded of the Parliament' supply for ships (319); Parliament was hostile, some members still smarting from the prorogation: The Duke of Buckingham, 'who usually saith what he thinks', claiming it to be null. This is about as close Marvell gets to relating the aggressive hostility to Charles and his 'demands'. Buckingham, Wharton and the Earls of Salisbury and Shaftsbury were committed to the Tower 'under the notion of contempt . . . Thus a prorogation without precedent was to be warranted by an imprisonment without example' (322).

At this point, effectively pacing the mounting tension, Marvell changes voice to explain why the Commons was so ineffective; he does so according to post-Machiavellian interest theory.[30] He claims that about one third of the members are directly dependent upon the King as they hold office. Honourable though they may be, it is thus in their interests to promote his. About a third is excluded from office and seeks it; thus it is prepared to voice the concerns of the nation until elected and attracts attention thereafter only to be bought off (323–7). The final third, divided as light

and darkness, consists of the best and the worst; the latter profli-
gate and ill-mannered are considered 'necessary men . . . whose
votes will go furthest' (328). The best who alone can stop the
body from putrification, by doing duty to God, Prince and Nation
are such 'a scantling in number' that they are hardly accounted
more than a quorum (329). Here, Marvell, who no doubt would
be wished to be counted amongst such impeccably credentialled
critics, affects a disinterested balance by reporting what is said of
them. Of the other two thirds plus, he had spoken directly as if
his indictments were simple facts. At all events, he explains, the
House has lost its ancient authority, cannot counsel, debate and
persuade by reason, and sensible of its shortcomings, 'dare not
adventure, as heretofore, the impeaching of any man before the
Lords' – thus the conspirators have gone unpunished (331). The
envious glance back to the impeaching proclivities of the Long
Parliament needs no labouring, and Marvell has come close to
insinuating that outright defiance of Charles's policies is a criterion
of political integrity.

Returning to the narrative, he relates that with four of the most
defiant Lords in the Tower, the mood of the Upper House was
markedly different. Amongst other things, Dr. Cary was brought
before the bar of the House and questioned concerning a book,
criticizing the prorogation 'which it seems he had carried to be
printed' (333). The King got plentiful supply for his ships with
ease (336), Parliament thereby hoping to purchase its own continuance (336); and Bills came down from the Lords, which despite
their titles, were against the religious interests of the nation; and
L'Estrange's authority to control the press and search for dubious
papers, was much enhanced (338ff). The Bill for the more effective
prosecution of recusants was thrown out of the House with little
ado; but that for the securing of Protestantism by the education
of royal children got as far as a second reading. Marvell quotes
this 'notorious bill' (352) in full and concludes comment on both
with 'thus let these perish like unseasonable and monstrous births,
but the legitimate issue of the conspirators . . .' (353).

The House responded by reminding Charles at some length of
the danger of the power of France, pressing him to make further
alliances against Louis, though opinions differed as to whether
this would promote peace or war. The conflicting views are given
in measured and cautious terms which show great deference to

the King, after which Marvell quotes a reply from Charles which in its very brevity makes the monarch seem impatient and discourteous. He reminds Parliament that it is his job to look after such matters, and if Parliament wishes to sit longer, it should now adjourn for Easter (361). Marvell uses this reply and a much longer and exasperated one dated 28th May, 1677 to frame the disintegration of trust between the Commons and the King; relating the ebb and flow of arguments within the House in a uniformly even third person impersonal, he conveys the increasing tension and brinkmanship with a remarkable air of coolness and objectivity (362–80). Individual figures almost disappear from the narrative; instead we have 'it was argued', 'it was objected', 'it was replied'. Emotion and lack of balance return only through Charles's own heated words in reply to the House's communications through its Speaker.

The issues are seen simply enough. On the one hand, Charles requires supply for defence – especially for building ships; but he will not be constrained in his foreign policies. A degree of secrecy and freedom of manoeuvre are essential in foreign affairs. Is he no longer trusted? On the other, Parliament will only give supply if it knows what is going on and if Charles makes clear that he is confronting the real enemy: expanding France. If he needs more money, why can't he withdraw the British troops aiding the French King? (364). Why doesn't he strengthen the alliance with beleaguered Holland? (376). Supply, His Majesty is reminded, is not normally given towards the end of the session, although provision could be made to allow the King to borrow a little. In any case, the members have started to go home and the matters are too weighty for anything but the full representative of the people to consider (371–2). His Majesty is assured that the recess will only be a short one. In the end, without an earnest of good faith in the form of a conspicuous change of policy, Parliament, in terms of the greatest respect, would only agree to increased credit for specific purposes.

Throughout, Marvell relies upon a rhetoric of trust to convey its opposite. It is trust reported and only a reported trust. The King is assured that he may always trust the people (366); he is trusted in return, although not all his ministers (365). Allowing him extra credit is but an earnest of what is intended (369). The French seem to be trusted with knowledge of the King's foreign policy 'why is it concealed from his Parliament. Why this darkness towards us?' (379).

Parliament was eventually summoned to Whitehall and told by Charles that he wished to rectify 'those mistakes and distrusts which I find some are ready to make ... I assure you on the word of a King that you shall not repent any trust you repose in me ...' He continued that, although he would not break credit, he would not inform them further, that he could not pursue any policy for the protection of the realm without money and if it were not forthcoming Parliament would be to blame for insufficiency of security (380).

The House withdrew to consider the speech and Marvell withdraws to the impersonal idiom which effectively has become that of Parliament. The assurances failed to sway the House, which continued to press for a strengthened alliance with Holland because of its increasing fear of France. 'It is a plain case, unless the power of France be lowred we cannot be safe' (385).

This is communicated to the King in the most deferential of terms (389–93). The King is then quoted as reiterating his urgent need for money to build ships (394). Again Marvell abbreviates the ensuing Parliamentary debates – those supporting the King now seeing the matter clearly as an invasion of his prerogative; those hostile denying this. Parliament, it is claimed, is only advising on the matter of alliances (397). The terms of debate have significantly altered.

Prerogative and arbitrary power were, rhetorically speaking, two sides of the same coin and the new emphasis on prerogative represents a hardening of attitudes – for, where the governmental form was seen as a mixed monarchy, either encroachment of royal prerogative, or a rise of arbitrary power was itself seen as destructive of the polity, irrespective of the more distant threat of French invasion. The supporters of Charles are thus depicted as trying to escalate the controversy from financial on to constitutional terrain, in order to put his opposition seriously in the wrong. This of course, is precisely what Marvell is doing by steering, through his fear of Catholicism, the reader to the second part of his title. Structurally, the conspirators are no longer needed, the deliberations having attained a momentum of their own. The scene is set also for the King's final blistering eruption into the narrative through his speech of 28th May 1677: Parliament is meddling; his prerogative has been 'dangerously invaded' (404); should he 'suffer this fundamental power of making peace and war to be . . . invaded . . . no prince or state would any longer believe that the sovereignty of England rests in the Crown' (404); he would believe himself to be no more than the 'empty sound of a King' (404). The House, reports Marvell, is said to have been 'greatly appalled' (405), and amid consternation, the Speaker adjourned until 16th of July (405). When Parliament reassembled, writes Marvell, his Majesty made it plain he wanted a further adjournment, thus the Speaker would allow nothing to proceed 'And went forth (trampling upon, and treading under foot, I had almost said, the privileges and usage of Parliament . . .)' (408). Parliament, rounds off Marvell, whatever it be called and however irregular some of its proceedings, had stood firm against popery (406); and all despite being 'kickt from adjournment to adjournment' and if such unconstitutional and improper behaviour cannot 'dissolve them, this Parliament is indeed immortal' (410).

Meanwhile, back in the Tower, the four Lords languished, though all except Shaftsbury managed to petition the King for release; and with Mr Speaker Seymour's last kick at a Parliament 'having no mind yet to *go out of doors*' (410) Marvell closes the narrative of events, wondering if the next act will take place in Rome or Paris, whilst idle spectators continue to give money to their own tragedy; and claiming to have revealed the conspiracy (as he adds, it seems to be) against religion and country, though hoping to be proved wrong and trusting in his Majesty's 'healing touch to apply the remedy' (414). This final remark itself has a touching irony as by the end of the *Account* there is precious little trust, and Marvell probably believed in the literal efficacy of the Royal Touch no more than did Charles. Superficial naivety is the narrator's last defence.

Although the narrative is divided into three principal parts, the central narrative has a clear interlace structure, direct quotation within indirect reportage; this is used not just to tell the story, but to show how the deterioration of trust within the governmental structure augments the issues involved to the extent that the very constitution of England is threatened. And, as I have suggested, despite several strategies that distance the author from the text (indirect reportage, description, quotation and ironic inversion) the force of the argument is clear enough, and we are now almost in a position to specify and contextualize Marvell's political identity in the months before his death. Immediately before doing so, however, a few words on the plausibility of his case; after all, his adopted persona and style invite an assessment of historical accuracy; he even hopes he has been wrong.

It is true that in religious terms England and Holland were natural allies – there had even been talk of some formal political union between them; yet economically they were just as much natural enemies, and this dimension of their relationship is quite ignored by Marvell. It is true also that France was likely to be the principal beneficiary from any conflict between England and Holland. This had manifestly been the case with the Second Dutch War (1665–7). Yet, Louis XIV, rather than consistently fomenting discord between the Protestant rivals, had mediated and attempted to bring them to peace – a difficult task as in both countries the wars had strong support.[31] This, too, is by-passed by Marvell, as is the irony to which I have already alluded, that Louis's France could be more tolerant of Protestants than could England.

Moreover, Marvell does give a wrong impression as to the principal source of hostility to dissent. Charles had initially favoured toleration and was rarely fully behind persecution; Clarendon, whose reputation has been the long standing victim of the Clarendon Code, was always against persecution; and the House of Lords, despite the Bishops, showed a noticeable degree of tolerance towards dissenters. It was the Lower House, in conjunction with Archbishop Sheldon and his clerical supporters, who showed the most consistent enthusiasm in the matter.[32]

Marvell exaggerates the cohesion of a court party and the strength of Louis's long financial arm in the House of Commons. In this way Marvell has played a part in bringing the eighteenth century into the seventeenth. With respect to all these silences or distortions, however, one must consider the polemical purpose which explains them. Marvell's was a conspiracy theory, and with all such theories simplicity of causation must be maintained; either the conspiratorial *explanans* must be rendered sufficiently amorphous and ubiquitous to encompass a vast diversity of events; or else events must be tailored to fit. Marvell adopted the second of these courses.

Notwithstanding Marvell's austere economy of relevant fact, the *Account* was, overall, a remarkably prescient conspiracy theory.

Charles was effectively in the pocket of Louis XIV. He had fled
the frying pan of parliamentary financial restrictions to play with
the fires of Catholic aid and as a result was committed to the
promotion more than the simple toleration of Catholicism in
England. How far Charles would really have gone is a moot point,
but suffering an invasion by his own and French troops was not
beyond the bounds of possibility. As England and Holland were
effectively just about all that was left of the Protestant Reformation, it was well within the bounds of fear. Further, the reforms
of the Long Parliament and the Interregnum had all but been
undone after the Second Settlement of 1662. Whatever the latitude
of the notion of a mixed monarchy (see below) Charles gave it
but grudging lip-service and would have preferred to rule as his
father had tried to and as Louis managed to, as an absolute
monarch. He also believed that Catholicism was the religion best
suited to such a form of rule. There is in short, enough truth in
the drift of Marvell's argument and the yoking of Catholicism to
arbitrary rule for Marvell to have scored a palpable hit and to
have encouraged deeply-felt prejudices. It is little wonder that the
author of the *Account* had a price on his head.

Where then, politically, does Marvell stand in the months before
his death?

First to some red herrings in a barrel of constitutional form.
Marvell's claim, of course, is that England enjoys a mixed constitution, a system in which Parliament shares power with the Monarchy. This, however, really tells us very little; certainly it does
not reveal much in the way of underlying political loyalties.[33] As
Weston and Greenberg have argued, from 1660 a belief in a mixed
form of government was increasingly popular and orthodox and
had behind it the dubious and protean authority of Charles I's
Answer To the Nineteen Propositions.[34] We should, however, see
mixed monarchy theory less as a doctrine or as a guiding ideology
than as a portable rhetoric which could be embraced or understood quite differently. It could refer either to a corporate and
indivisible sovereign,[35] or, more commonly, to a shared or divided
sovereignty. It is in the second sense that Marvell adheres to it.[36]
Yet in this second sense there was considerable latitude as to
which powers were held by whom, how their limits might be

specified and their integrity guaranteed. Mixed monarchy was, in truth, a phrase purporting to describe the English system which covered fundamental differences as to what that system was or should be. Affirmations about mixed monarchy could be made by republicans as well as by monarchists of differing propensities towards absolutism.[37] By the same token, then, the attribution of a republican commitment to Marvell is similarly unhelpful. It is true that Marvell had kept republican company in the egregious form of John Milton, but as Lamont notes, there had been little that is in this sense Miltonic in Marvell's prose. It is true also that he sounds somewhat like the republican Henry Neville, but this is more with respect to his anti-catholicism than anything else, and even Neville praises legitimate kings (see above, n. 22). Firmly republican sympathies were not easily enunciated in the latter part of Charles II's reign. The real barrier to discovering such a constitutional commitment lies in the very indeterminancy of 'mixed government' which could embrace anything from Stuart England to the *governo misto* of fifteenth century Florence.

Further, as Charles insists, and Marvell never denies, Monarchy, or the monarchical element of a *gonfaloniere* within such a system, required prerogative right; yet as Marvell is at pains to suggest, Parliament must have a share. It is in this way that prerogative may be seen as arbitrary power; parliamentary advice, however deferential, as meddling. The appeal of mixed monarchy theory was not that it answered any constitutional questions at all, but that it was close to a theoretical cipher. It can be seen then as part of that propensity to amphibolous generalization and public dissimulation that Zwicker has seen as characteristic of Restoration political discourse.[38] We must look elsewhere for Marvell's loyalties.

The specific issues upon which Marvell focuses: Catholicism, the Protestant succession, fear of France, and the mewing up of monarchy, place him as all have recognized, close to Shaftesbury; and if Shaftesbury has taken over from Thomas Aquinas as the first Whig, it might be concluded that the same label will do for Marvell.[39] What he says on these issues however, would align him just as well with Algernon Sidney, who was certainly no Whig or a part of Shaftesbury's political entourage.[40] The country Whig fear of standing armies is itself not a major issue;[41] what is, throughout is the Protestant cause. (See Lamont, above.) The

Account is almost as pro-Dutch as anything else, and protective of parliamentary independence, threatened above all by the very powers of prorogation and adjournment that made Charles a king. The irony to which Marvell himself pointed was that the policy of prorogation itself created a 'long parliament' literally, and figuratively, just as the religious policies of Charles I had, in many eyes, created the Long Parliament which had destroyed him. More specifically, Marvell's objection to the King's policies for which prorogation was but an instrument, concerned their religious direction at home and abroad; and this suggests that, as his enemy L'Estrange insists, we look backwards to the Civil War for Marvell's political loyalties.

There are clues enough as to where we should look in the absence of the sort of direct affirmation of commitment that would destroy the authority bestowed by naked narration.[42] Indeed, the apparently simple narrative casts the events and the actors into the scenes and roles of the Civil War. Marvell plays upon its memory establishing documents like 'The Grand Remonstrance' and 'Protestation' of 1641 as pre-texts for an agenda of debate that would dominate the remainder of Charles's reign. Leaving aside reference to the Long Parliament and to Charles I, Marvell accuses the conspirators of trying to stir up Civil War memory and of trying to manipulate the old Cavalier party (which is precisely what he is doing through the medium of accusation). Against a Civil War backdrop, his use of conspiracy theory stands directly analogous to the strategies used indirectly to attack Charles I in the Long Parliament; the Duke of York's marriage stands analogous to Charles I's; and the complexity of the King's demand for supply is nearly always presented synecdochally as a demand for building ships – for ship money.

In this way too, one may see a clear play throughout with literal and symbolic meanings: supply for ships and Ship Money; a long parliament and the Long Parliament; mistrust and trusting in the royal touch. Marvell's cause in 1678 is close to being the Good Old Cause which, if it was not overtly republican, was focused on Christian Liberty, the continuation of the European Reformation and the extirpation of Catholicism. Unfortunately, much beyond this point the notion of a Good Old Cause has its limitations. Richard Baxter in *A Holy Commonwealth* had claimed to be supporting the Good Old Cause; as had Henry Stubbe in

An Essay in Defence of the Good Old Cause – a scathing attack on Baxter's work; and neither sounds much like *A Coffin for the Good Old Cause*, or Milton's *Readie and Easie Way*, all printed in 1659. Against a background of such contestability, Marvell's frustratingly ironic remark in *The Rehearsal Transpros'd*, that the Good Old Cause was too good to be fought for, ties him down less than one might think. Hill rather briskly concludes that if Marvell thought the cause that good, fighting against it was even worse. The 'it' remains elusive and Marvell is clearly evoking intricate issues raised by writers such as Hyde and Lawson concerning casuistry and the relationship between means and ends rather than insinuating a precise commitment. A propos of this, if Marvell did at some stage think the cause too good to be fought for, it opens a wider gap between him and Milton than Hill is prepared to accept and *a fortiori* raises a question mark over Hill's and Chernaik's propensity to fill in lacunae in Marvell's thought with quotations from Milton.[43] Yet this being said, such a putative gap was narrowing as Marvell's life came to a close, and England seemed to drift ever nearer to France and Rome. If Marvell's views were hardening, the mythology surrounding Charles I's reign, which Milton himself had helped fashion, provided the mould into which they flowed.

Traditionally the English monarchy had assumed a leading role in matters of religion. It was when, and insofar as it was seen to be undoing the matter of reformation and protestant liberty, that the role or even existence of the monarchy was questioned. Once the issues had shifted from political to religious ones, resistance could be contemplated and a potent Reformation rhetoric of justification could be called upon. Tom May had made these points clearly enough. Under Elizabeth the cause of religion and the interest of her state were so closely entangled, he claims, that to alter one was to risk ruining the other. This was no longer the case under Charles I.[44] Parliament 'whensoever they charged the corrupt Statesmen of injustice and Tyranny, would put Popery, or a suspicion of it, into the first place . . .'[45] May considered this strategy counter-productive. Such charges levelled against the King whilst he still claimed to be a Protestant prince were too amorphous (they constituted merely 'the peoples' reason) and distracted attention from specific arbitrary acts.[46] The rhetorical options, however, were not that simple. Shared terminology was always apt to erode distinction between religious, political and legal fields of discourse; and the King's conception of and justification for his rule had insured that dispute always be fought with at least one foot on the high ground of religious intransigence. Clear choices between rhetorics were not easily made on any side. Marvell's *Account* can be seen as learning from May's critique of the rhetoric of parliamentary accusation without at the same time (as May seemed naïvely to wish) sacrificing the suggestive potency of the peoples' reason – the fear of 'popery'. Marvell does this by joining religious and constitutional idioms of accusation. In this way, his work exemplifies the continuing and potent fluidity of religious and political discursive realms. Against such a Civil War background and Civil War argumentative strategies, his *Account* is manifestly designed to make an escalating shift of salient issues, yet without sacrificing the authoritative ethos of disinterest which overt employment of an ominous rhetoric of violence would have entailed, and of which no one needed reminding.[47]

The catalyst which was seen to justify or promise such violence, despite the memory of Civil War, was not the Restoration of the Monarchy in 1660, though for recalcitrant republicans such as Milton this was bound to lead to disaster. If one can specify abrupt points of alteration, the catalyst came first with the re-establishment of the Church of England and then after the fall of Clarendon in 1667.[48] The Church of England was re-established in such a way as to make it difficult for many to conform; and of those who did, many must have felt pangs of conscience and sympathy for those now more or less excluded from an official English Church. As there were traditionally such high hopes vested in the royal executive, especially between 1660–1662, so royal policy, somewhat unfairly, was held ultimately to blame, first for harsh measures against people who saw themselves still as in the vanguard of the Reformation, and then even worse (for a little persecution served to brace saintly resilience) through moves to ease the disadvantages of Catholics.[49] As Marvell was clearly aware, both of these policies had an increasingly ominous international dimension in the attitudes to Holland and France respectively. After Clarendon's fall Charles was able to move in directions, both at home and abroad which his old advisors had made more difficult. As a result, it is not hard to find men increasingly uneasy with their society and their monarch, just as, concomitantly there were those who believed non-conformity had to be tainted with 'rebellion'.[50]

More specifically it is not hard to find men who seem to have taken a common intellectual journey from the Civil War and, whatever their initial attitudes to it, never escaped its shadow.[51] Lamont has shown how Baxter, a politically quiescent man with naïvely high hopes of a Godly Prince in 1659, was alienated from society and suffered agonies of conscience when confronted with a monarchy moving ever closer to Rome. A similar story could be told of the increasingly politically active John Humfrey, who was re-ordained in the Church of England at its re-establishment in 1662, tore up his papers and who thereafter ran his own church and attended his parish church on a regular basis.[52] The theme of all his writings from 1662 was both the need for the Church of England to comprehend all good Protestants and to stand firm against Catholicism.[53] Affirming his loyalty to the Crown with noticeable regularity, he seems also to have been dangerously close to the doomed circle of that inveterate conspirator Colonel John Wildman.[54] John Locke, too, in 1660 was enunciating Erastian views which showed unquestioned faith in a Protestant sovereign and fear of the consequences of tolerating sectaries and most pressingly, Quakers.[55] By 1683 his views had turned about; at the end he would control all monarchs and tolerate all Protestants.

Marvell's intellectual journey, I suggest, was much like these. In the end his political location would not have been too far from Locke. More precisely, his public circumspection and ecclesiological location are close to John Humfrey's at the soft and suspicious edges of the Church of England.

In sum, we may say that the Civil War had been fought around the issues of reformation and tyranny. It was only the orchestration of these two catch cries that had mobilized sufficient hostility to Charles to make war possible. The Interregnum had been tolerated or actively supported because, although failing to settle the nation, it continued or made safe the Reformation; the Restoration had been welcomed because it was not thought to be undoing the Reformation or re-introducing tyranny; the policies after 1662 made numbers of people change their minds; increasingly it was seen as a spurious restoration.[56] Marvell was amongst them and, by 1678, recourse to petitions and prayers was thought an inadequate protection. Ten years later, that was the view of the most powerful. Parker's 'inchanting terms' 'Popery' and the 'French Interest' were echoes of the persuasive rhetoric of the 1640s and had proved 'inchanting' for that reason. Faith in the Godly Prince of the English Reformation had been destroyed and this affected the role and conception of monarchy in a way from which it was never to recover. In this context the character of the Parliament of which Marvell was a part was crucially important, providing an unheeded note of warning for James, the last of England's Godly Princes. Overall, writes Whitcombe of the Cavalier Parliament, 'the central mass followed their own line, combining loyalty to crown with suspicion of crown servants and with a determined adherence to the Anglican Church'.[57] Marvell was sufficiently close to this configuration of attitude to exploit it. In the end, suggests Whitcombe, that House was more loyal to its Church than to its King, but precisely because Charles was prepared to back down on religious issues, religion did not become the burning issue that it had been in the past and was shortly to be in the future.[58]

In this light, Marvell's precise exploitation of Cavalier prejudice was to make religion the issue whilst at the same time deflecting attention from the Dissenters who had been seen as far more of a threat to the established church than the Catholics. It was a well-timed disruptive move at the end of an uncharacteristic lull in the sequence of plots, risings and disturbances which had marked English politics since 1640. Breaking the nexus of confidence between Church and King as Marvell correctly saw, was the crucial thing, and I believe this was simply because Marvell had lost all faith in the government and its direction. He captures the transition between faith in petitioning a Godly Prince and the lack of faith that promises resistance once more. This is epitomized in the disingenuous appeal to Charles with which he ends the *Account*. One of the tragedies of Charles's reign is that at the beginning the faith would have been justified, by the end it was not, and it was partly Marvell's own Parliament that was responsible.

The full scope of the argument, however, can be seen by looking at the *Account*'s monetary imagery which provides a figurative coherence sufficient to sustain the force of the message. Clearly the theme of money is central; it is the only hold that Parliament has over Charles, a Parliament later called the Pension Parliament

because of its indebtedness to Louis XIV; as had been long suspected Charles himself was the chief pensioner, formally committed to fostering Catholicism and eventually returning England to
the fold; conversely lack of money tied Charles to his Parliament
as his father had been and he tried similarly extreme measures to
free himself so that he should be more than 'the empty sound of
a King'. Added to this, concern for trade and commerce and the
shared, if uneasy interest with Holland surface clearly enough, as
does the fear that if England is reconverted property will be
redistributed.

   This literal concern with money, then, provides a particularly
decorous area of figurative expansion for structuring the argument:
– The Pope is the clerk of the spiritual market place, (cf *Essay*
143, 133) who buys and sells Christ's body daily; he sets a rate
on all crimes, so the poorer the Christian one is the better the
customer – thus he is a traitor to Christianity whereas the Jews
are open enemies. In this way Papacy and Jewry stand analogous
to conspirators and France respectively (252–6). Reference has
already been made to the pun on the 'Donation of Constantine'
(256) and the Pope's improvement of his bishopric by good management (256; cf *Essay* 144). Ship money and Peter's pence drain
away the kingdom (260); the Declaration of Indulgence is an
attempt to defraud our religion, which has been dearly bought
(279); we ought to have been reimbursed, a bargain has been
broken (280). The Declaration might further enable popery to
pass like 'current money over the nation' (282). The King of
France is the great and lucky gamester, who pays off the conspirators with a quarrel for his money (287). They had sold all to him
for those 'two pearls of price, the True Worship and the True
government' (289). England suffers a lottery for all offices (304);
whilst a large proportion of parliamentarians can be bought and
sold, only their number makes them cheaper and they let slip
their own market by over evaluation (328 also 407; *Essay* 131).
Then, picking up the subordinate gaming imagery again, Marvell
remarks that where the cards are so well known, their benefit is
only for a cheat (331). Parliament hedges, and purchases it own
continuance (336). The jibe once levelled at Tom May is echoed
when Marvell refers to a pamphleteer being paid by the sheet;
and as good money goes out of the country, Catholicism comes
in (383) and we, like idle spectators sit giving money to our own

tragedy (412). This image may perhaps allude to the structure of the *Account* much of which is set in dramatic scenes punctuated by the King as chorus. More obviously, however, the imagery at this point in the peroration brings together the sense of loss, exclusion, and artificiality of the political process that were evident, though expressed with less bitterness in the theatrical scaffold imagery of the first of the Cromwell poems.[59] Finally, the currency image is implicitly evoked in Marvell's own concluding reiteration of his integrity. He writes to inform, not as an informer; his narrative is thus a gift carrying no price.

The dominant force of the imagery is to create an ambience of corruption; it was well chosen and heavily patinated. Money imagery traditionally associated with the communication of beliefs and ideas was, when used to convey religious beliefs, associated with evil and corruption.[60] Thus this well-worn field of figurative expansion drew on strongly entrenched spiritual prejudices; whilst the associated sub-fields of gaming and playing, even play acting evoked equally conventionally the fortunes and machinations associated with the *arcana imperii*.[61] In a way, it was thus appropriate for Marvell to conclude with an appeal to the King for he, being at the centre of the game, is alone in being able to do anything about the cheats – Parliament has been denied its role. But there is an added resonance that reveals the disingenuousness of Marvell's concluding appeal. The issue of coinage was one of the hallmarks of sovereignty and was exchanged on trust;[62] the corruption of coinage speaks both of a collapse of legitimate sovereignty and of trust; and, to risk a familiar gaming image from a later time, the concluding appeal to the King is little short of reminding the reader of where the 'buck' had to stop. It was exactly such an attitude that brought about the First Civil War. It was fear of another Civil War which hampered concerted action against the King and Papacy after Marvell's death, but for want of his dying, more than his trying.

Notes

1. Pierre Legouis, *Andrew Marvell: Poet, Puritan, Patriot*, Oxford: Clarendon Press, 1965, p. 162; and *André Marvell, Poète, Puritan,*

Patriote, Paris, 1928, reprinted and corrected, New York: Russell and Russell, 1965, pp. 297–8.

2. All page numbers in the text are to the *Account* as printed in Grossart, *The Complete Works of Andrew Marvell*, privately printed, 1875, reprinted, New York: A.M.S. Press, 1966, vol. 4, pp. 248–414; or to the *Short Historical Essay Touching General Councils, Creeds and Imposition in Religion*, 1676, cited as *Essay* in Grossart, ibid., pp. 91–163.

3. Legouis, *Andrew Marvell*, p. 160; *André Marvell*, pp. 294–5.

4. *The Poems and Letters of Andrew Marvell*, ed. H.M. Margoliouth, 3rd edn., revised by Pierre Legouis and E.E. Duncan-Jones, Oxford: Clarendon Press, 1971, vol. 2. Misc. Letters, 44, To William Popple, June 10th, 1678, p. 357. 'There have been great rewards offered in private, and considerable in the Gazett ... Three of four printed books since have described as near as it was proper to go, the Man being a Member of Parliament, Mr. *Marvell* to have been the Author; but if he had, surely he should not have escaped being questioned in Parliament, or some other Place. My good Wishes attend you'.

5. Legouis, *Andrew Marvell*, p. 160; *André Marvell*, p. 295 reads this not as a denial of authorship but as an expression of security.

6. Legouis, *Andrew Marvell*, ibid.

7. *Poems on Affairs of State*, ed. G. de F. Lord, New Haven: Yale University Press, 1963, vol. 1, 1660–1678, p. 436. Shortly after, the less than sympathetic John Nalson seems to be alluding to Marvell or his success in claiming that recently the catch-cry 'arbitrary government' had been elevated to the status of a religious principle and was being taken by some to be the mark of true Protestantism. Yet he continues, it is the most arbitrary (the Presbyterians) who make the cry, those responsible for the death of Charles I. See Nalson, *The Complaint of Liberty and Property Against Arbitrary Government*, in *Political and Religious Tracts*, 1681, p. 1–2.

8. Cf. Legouis, *Andrew Marvell*, p. 158; *André Marvell*, p. 292; John Wallace, *Destiny His Choice: The Loyalism of Andrew Marvell*, Cambridge: Cambridge University Press, 1968, p. 230. Warren Chernaik, *The Poet's Time: Politics and Religion in the Work of Andrew Marvell*, Cambridge: Cambridge University Press, 1983, p. 96.

9. *Contra*, Wallace, also, John Dixon Hunt, *Andrew Marvell: His Life and Writings*, Ithaca, N.Y.: Cornell University Press, 1978, p. 182.

10. Legouis, *Andrew Marvell*, p. 159; *André Marvell*, p. 292–3 for an appropriate caution, although he seems to imply that the difference is simply a practical one, not a matter of theoretical perspective. J.G.A. Pocock, *The Machiavellian Moment*, Princeton, Princeton

University Press, 1975, pp. 406–8 for Marvell's appropriation to the Whig canon, through the energies of John Toland. Chernaik, *The Poet's Time*, places Marvell in 'the classical liberal tradition', and somewhat strangely seems to invoke Pocock's authority for doing so, p. 100.

11. Wallace, *Destiny his Choice*, thinks he was not; Legouis, *Andrew Marvell*, suspects he was. Chernaik, *The Poet's Time*, is altogether confident he was, p. 95.

12. Jonathan Scott, 'England's Troubles: Exhuming the Popish Plot' in *Liberty and Authority: The Politics of Religion in Restoration England*, ed., T. Harris, M. Goldie and P. Seaward, Oxford: Oxford University Press, 1989, for comment on the propensity to project the eighteenth century into the seventeenth century.

13. See at length Wallace, *Destiny His Choice*; Legouis, *Andrew Marvell*. John Klause, *The Unfortunate Fall; Theodicy and the Moral Imagination of Andrew Marvell*, Connecticut: Archon, 1983, p. 145.

14. Lawrence W. Hyman, *Andrew Marvell*, New York: Twayne, 1964, p. 92; Wallace, *Destiny His Choice* also associated Marvell with the arch trimmer George Savil, Marquis of Halifax, p. 230. Klause, *The Unfortunate Fall*, pp. 146–7 for a careful comparison with Halifax, and p. 145 for the claims that Marvell's association with the Country Party was a matter of convenience.

15. Hyman, *Andrew Marvell*, p. 91.

16. Annabel Patterson, *Marvell and the Civic Crown*, Princeton: Princeton University Press, 1978, pp. 183, 214 on the importance of the modesty topos in reference to Marvell.

17. Wallace, *Destiny His Choice*, p. 224 '. . . he desired reform without disturbance, and sought to achieve his end without raising thoughts of 1641'. See Scott, 'England's Troubles' for the context that makes such an assessment implausible, and below, an analysis of the text which contradicts it.

18. For further comment on the notion of protective ambiguity, see C. Condren, *The Status and Appraisal of Classic Texts*, Princeton: Princeton University Press, 1985, chap. 8; on the strategic difficulties of epideictic rhetoric and Marvell's habits of dealing with them, Patterson, *Marvell and the Civic Crown*, at length.

19. Klause, *The Unfortunate Fall*, p. 140f; Donald Smith, 'The Political Beliefs of Andrew Marvell', *University of Toronto Quarterly*, 1966, p. 55f.

20. M. Stocker, *Apocalyptic Marvell*, Sussex: Harvester Press, 1986. *The Account* gets no systematic treatment, for Stocker could well argue that Revelation is a pretext in the context of which the *Account* assumes great urgency. Of interest also in this context is Donald Bouchard's unpublished thesis, 'Andrew Marvell and the Millenium',

182   The Political Identity of Andrew Marvell

State University of New York 1969, esp. chap. 7 and for balance, Klause's warnings against seeing Marvell as a man in full control of his intellectual world.

21. Chernaik, *The Poet's Time*, a valuable work which in part seems elaborated from a perceptive essay by Christopher Hill, 'Milton and Marvell' in C.A. Patrides, ed., *Approaches to Marvell*, London: Routledge, 1978; but Chernaik does seem to simplify and I suspect mislocate Marvell's particular brand of partial non-conformity, rendering him more Miltonic than the evidence warrants and all sorts of people more 'radical', 'conservative', 'libertarian', 'liberal', or 'left wing' than *any* seventeenth century evidence can establish.

22. These are all standard accusations and were widely voiced by the most energetic dissidents at the time the *Account* was written. Marvell's phrasing is at times strikingly similar to that of the republican Henry Neville who attached Machiavelli to the protestant cause. See his *Nicholas Machiavel's Letter to Zanobius Buondelmontius in Vindication of Himself and his Writings* in *The Works of the Most Famous Nicholas Machiavel, Citizen and Secretary of Florence*, London, 1675 (no page numbers). For further instances of this sort of anti-papal accusation see for example Scott, 'England's Troubles': Hill, 'Milton and Marvell' notes the similarity of expression between Milton, Marvell and William Dell, p. 12; N. Wood, *John Locke and Agrarian Capitalism*, Los Angeles: University of California Press, 1984, suggests that the fear of property redistribution lay behind Locke's *Two Treatises*.

23. In the context of the *Account* even this is a barbed compliment, as it comes after the earlier expression of incomprehension that European monarchs actually tolerate Catholics. It is unclear whether Marvell is hostile to toleration *per se*, or to toleration of Catholics in any public capacity. Earlier he had been sympathetic to the Declaration of Indulgence. Despite the specificity of terms like 'catholic' and 'papist', 'popery' could be slippery.

24. Hence the whole emphasis of Legouis on Marvell as Francophobe seems to be misleading as it focuses on symptom rather than cause.

25. Cited in J.R. Tanner, *English Constitutional Conflicts of the Seventeenth Century*, 1603–1689, Cambridge: Cambridge University Press, 1961 edn., p. 239.

26. C. Condren, *George Lawson's Politica and the English Revolution*, Cambridge: Cambridge University Press, 1989, chaps. 10, 13; Scott, 'England's Troubles'. See also Hill's perceptive comments on Milton's *True Religion, Heresy, Schism, Toleration: and what may be used against the Growth of Popery* (1673) and its analogous treatment of the present with the 1630s, 'Milton and Marvell', p. 12. Conversely, defenders of the monarchy could exploit Civil War

mythology for their own ends. Roger L'Estrange replied to Marvell with *An Account of the Growth of Knavery*, 1678, in which he claimed that the libels of the present echoed those of 1641. See N.H. Keeble, *The Literary Culture of Non-Conformity*, Leicester: Leicester University Press, 1987, pp. 103–4.

27. Rumours of Charles's involvement with Louis had been current for some time, some of these included well founded suspicions of the secret treaty of Dover. 'Upon his Majesty's being made free of the City' (attrib. Marvell) in *Poems on Affairs of State*, vol. 1, p. 242, verse 20 is a good example of general insinuation.

28. Cf. *Essay on Councils*, pp. 146, 152; See Mark Goldie, 'The Huguenot Experience and the Problem of Toleration in Restoration England' in *The Huguenots and Ireland: Anatomy of an Emigration*, ed. C.E.J. Caldicott, H. Gough and J.P. Pittion, Dublin: Glendale, 1987, p. 175f for a reassessment of Charles II's policies in the light of the greater toleration enjoyed by many Protestants in France than in England.

29. The past tense tars Mary with the same brush as Henrietta Maria, whose public parading of her religious coterie had caused so much damage to Charles I.

30. Interest theory provided a dominant motif of Dutch and French political thought in the seventeenth century. Its principal representatives were de la Court and the Duc du Rohan. In England it is noticeable in the writings of Lord Halifax. It is found in Anthony Ascham and Marchemont Nedham in an earlier generation and has an almost universal point of reference in the *Discourses* of Machiavelli. For a recent and valuable discussion see Jonathan Scott, *Algernon Sidney and the English Republic 1623–1677*, Cambridge: Cambridge University Press, 1988, chap. 13.

31. Ronald Hutton, *The Restoration: A Political and Religious History of England and Wales, 1658–1667*, Oxford: Oxford University Press, 1984, p. 240. Hill following Legouis, suggests that Marvell may even have been associated with pro-Dutch plotting centred on Pierre du Moulin, 'Milton and Marvell', pp. 9–10; see also Klause, *The Unfortunate Fall*; but according to Kenyon, Marvell's name on a couple of lists of potential sympathizers amounts to little. His name is found on a similar list of those possibly sympathetic to James Duke of York. See J.P. Kenyon, 'Andrew Marvell: Life and Times' in R.L. Brett, ed., *Andrew Marvell: Essays on the Tercentenary of his Death*, Oxford: Oxford University Press, 1979, p. 25.

32. Hutton, ibid., p. 220f.

33. In this respect Wallace misunderstands the nature, or the full dimension of Marvell's loyalism which is not principally a constitutionalism, *Destiny his Choice*, p. 2. He is right to see a resemblance

184 The Political Identity of Andrew Marvell

between Marvell and Hyde, but is surprised at this because he assumes constitutionalism to have been more discriminate a notion than it really was.

34. C.C. Weston and J.R. Greenberg, *Subjects and Sovereigns: The Grand Controversy over Legal Sovereignty in Stuart England*, Cambridge: Cambridge University Press, 1981 at length. *The King's Answer* was written by Sir John Culpepper and Lucius Cary (Lord Falkland) and is a pre-text for much else besides Marvell's *Account*. But the protean nature of the document, arising in part from diplomatic comprise and ameliorating rhetoric, makes it very difficult to draw conclusions about ideological agreement from its use.

35. George Lawson, *Politica Sacra et Civilis*, 1660, chapter 4.

36. This is the only sense in which Weston and Greenberg understand the expression, *Subjects and Sovereigns* at length.

37. J.G.A. Pocock, *The Ancient Constitution and the Feudal Law: A Re-Issue with a Retrospect*, Cambridge: Cambridge University Press, 1987, e.g. pp. 309–10. After all, amongst the authoritative texts behind notions of mixed monarchy was Machiavelli's *Discourses* in which the monarchical element is found in the institution of elected consuls.

38. Steven Zwicker, *The Language of Politics in the Age of Dryden*, Princeton: Princeton University Press, 1984.

39. Richard Ashcraft, *Revolutionary Politics and Locke's Two Treatises of Government*, Princeton: Princeton University Press, 1987, at length; Shaftesbury seems to come complete with eighteenth century party organization, though convincing evidence is now thin on the ground. See also J.R. Jones, *The First Whigs: the Politics of the Exclusion Crisis, 1679–83*, Oxford: Oxford University Press, 1970.

40. Scott, *Algernon Sidney*, at length.

41. Pocock, *The Ancient Constitution*, p. 342 seems to imply that it is.

42. Cf. also *Essay on Councils*, p. 156. At the risk of labouring the point that the naked narration is nothing of the sort, passing reference can be made to Marvell's letters. The *Account* conveys no sense of the variety and quantity of business confronting Parliament. In the letters issues which dominate the *Account's* relation of business to the exclusion of all else, get passing mention only. (See letter to Mayor Foxley, March 1676/7.) There is also a double difference in tone. The letters do convey a sense of heated disagreement at times in marked contrast to the cooling paraphrases of the *Account*. At the same time, fewer judgements are passed. In contrast to the vitriol poured on the Bill to modify the Test Act (one of the 'unreasonable and monstrous births' of the *Account*) Marvell remarks, in a letter to Mayor Maister that the House 'threw out . . . a Bill . . . it seeming to relax something of the former vigour in taking' the Test. *Letters*,

2.217. The comment is preceded by a brief reference to a Bill against the growth of popery and a noticeably longer reference to increased penalties 'upon those that do not bury in Flannel' ibid., 2.216–7. The letters chronicle, the *Account* is a history. See N.H. Keeble, above.

43. Hill, 'Milton and Marvell', p. 16; Chernaik, *The Poet's Time*, esp. chap. 4. For a fine account of Marvell's handling of the theoretically unstable relationship between means and end see Klause, *The Unfortunate Fall*, chaps. 3 and 5; it was only such an ultimate goal as the continuation of Protestant Reformation that would have lead one such as Marvell to overlook what he and many believed, that dubious means destroyed just ends. Men such as Milton and Sidney and Parker as Klause shows, had fewer qualms or a firmer faith in the rhetorics of casuistry.

44. Tom May, *A History of the Parliament of England*, 1647, Bk. 1, pp. 2–3.

45. May, ibid., pp. 115–16.

46. May, ibid., pp. 115–16.

47. In this light Annabel Patterson's conclusion that Marvell is obviously most interested in the problem of arbitrary government, seems wrong. *Marvell and the Civic Crown*, p. 221.

48. Ronald Hutton, *The Restoration*, esp. Conclusions.

49. For discussions of the increasing unease and politicization of Independents and especially Nonconformists and occasional Conformists, see Hutton, ibid; Richard Ashcraft, *Revolutionary Politics*, Pt. 1; Douglas R. Lacey, *Dissent and Parliamentary Politics in England, 1661–1689*, New Jersey: Rutgers University Press, 1969, chap. 4.

50. John Nalson, *The Countermine*, and *The Complaint*, see above note 7. cf. *An Essay Touching General Councils*, pp. 95–100. The literary consequences of this strong association between rebellion and nonconformity are finely discussed in N.H. Keeble, *The Literary Culture of Non-Conformity*, at length.

51. Wallace, *Destiny his Choice*, p. 5 makes the point well but the character of the change and the company Marvell kept in making it can be given more precision. Chernaik, *The Poet's Time*, and Ashcraft, *Revolutionary Politics*, have both helped considerably here, and see also Lamont, above.

52. On Baxter see W. Lamont, *Richard Baxter and the Millennium*, London: Croom Helm, 1979. For some sense of Humfrey's agonizing see John Humfrey, *A Second Discourse About Reordination* 1662; R.A., *A Letter to a Friend; Tending to Prove that Valid Ordination Ought not to be Repeated*, 1661.

53. Humfrey wrote extensively throughout the Restoration and well into the 18th century. For a remarkable continuity of concern see

The Political Identity of Andrew Marvell

The Obligation to Human Laws Discussed, 1670/1; *A Plain, Honest, Easy and Brief Determination of the Late Controversy Concerning non Resistance to the Higher Powers* . . . 1689.

54. For discussions of tracts attributable to Wildman and/or Humfrey, see C. Condren, *George Lawson's Politica*, chap. 13.

55. John Locke, *Two Tracts on Government*, ed. Philip Abrams, Cambridge: Cambridge University Press, 1969.

56. Hutton, *The Restoration*, p. 1 remarks that nobody doubts that the Restoration was a culmination of the English Revolution. It was certainly doubted at the time, and is being doubted again now. See for example Scott, *Algernon Sidney*; but one did not have to be a Sidney or a Milton to see the Restoration as spurious and insecure. Satirical literature is evidence enough. It was precisely hindsight which contemporaries lacked, just as we have lost sight of how ominous and destabilizing the Civil War remained. Its potential, almost as contemporary history, was being re-worked well into the 18th century. See Debbie Stephan, 'The Early Eighteenth Century Reviews its Seventeenth-Century Past', Sydney University unpublished Ph.D thesis, 1986.

57. D.T. Whitcombe, *Charles II and The Cavalier House of Commons, 1663–74*, Manchester: Manchester University Press, 1966, p. 178.

58. Whitcombe, ibid., p. 172.

59. 'And thence the royale actor borne, / The tragic scaffold might adorn', 'An Horatian Ode Upon Cromwell's Return From Ireland'. The pun on scaffold had been prefigured by Thomas More in his *History of King Richard III* where he had sardonically remarked on the danger attending those who mounted the scaffold to play king's games. Marvell takes it further, providing a sense of audience, with the applause of the armed bands, in the following lines, and with the ambiguity of the remark about Charles's behaviour on 'that memorable scene'. Theatre imagery was pervasive in accounts of the execution. See the interesting paper by Nancy Klein Maguire, 'The Theatrical Mask/Masque of Politics: The Case of Charles I', *The Journal of British Studies* 28, (1989), pp. 1–22.

60. The Franciscan movement was predicated on the belief in the contaminating effects of money. The association of money with spiritual or moral corruption was so widespread (to be found in Machiavelli as well as the *fraticelli*) that seeking a precise derivation for Marvell's imagery is pointless. The imagery is much more fully sustained in the *Account* than in the *Essay* where it is used only on the few occasions noted above. Much earlier Marvell turned such imagery against the Dutch. 'Hence Amsterdam, Turk-Christian-Pagan-Jew, / Staple of Sects and mint of schism grew, / That bank of conscience,

where not one so strange, / Opinion but finds credit, and exchange'. 'The Character of Holland' (1653?) lines 70–4.

61. Henry Neville, *A Game of Picquet*, 1659 uses a card game as a sustained allegory for Interregnum politics. The last word is given to a Catholic who remarks, that if they play their hands like this, he will win out in the end.

62. See e.g. Lawson, *Politica; An Examination of the Political Part of Mr. Hobbs, His Leviathan*, 1657; and Thomas Hobbes, *Leviathan*. Before post-Bodinian notions of sovereignty linked money and sovereignty, the link between rule and patronage had been clear enough, for example in Fortescue's *Governance of England*, c. 1471, published 1714.

7   Miscellaneous Marvell?

Annabel Patterson

'Tis not, what once it was, the World,
But a rude heap together hurl'd;

Your lesser World contains the same,
But in more decent Order tame;

Speaking with the dead, a desire that has always been implicit in
historicist criticism from Petrarch onwards, must equally have
been, from those earliest endeavours *in* the Renaissance to recover
the texts of antiquity for then-modern apprehension, an imperative
in editorial practice. In contemporary study *of* the Renaissance,
the desire to speak with the dead has acquired a new cachet.[1] But
it has not yet had much impact on our assessment of the now-
modern editions on which we usually depend for access to those
English Renaissance writers who have received the canonical *impri-
matur* of a great press, or, still better from a marketable stand-
point, paperback circulation. I raise the question here of how
we should regard Marvell's *Miscellaneous Poems*, the posthumous
selection of his works published in 1681 and the only source for
most of his pre-Restoration poetry; in particular, what can we
learn from this early presentation of his writings that may have

been obscured in otherwise helpful, even invaluable, modern editions? And to what extent does the concept of the posthumous itself (speaking with the recently dead) inform and motivate the volume?

There are two questions to be asked of any posthumous collection of poems by a single author: is the arrangement authoritative? And what, if anything, does it signify? In the seventeenth century these questions are both difficult to answer with certainty and peculiarly demanding of inquiry. The poems of Donne, Herbert, Jonson's *Under-wood* and Marvell's *Miscellaneous Poems* were all published posthumously. Yet there is as much evidence of ordering in these volumes as in those of their contemporaries who saw to the publication of their own work, like Herrick or Milton; and from all indications the concept of significant order was culturally available, something that writers could count on intelligent readers to look for.

Such ordering was not necessarily authorial. In the case of Donne a principle of generic categorization (begun in the manuscript tradition and only partly Donne's own)[2] combined with bowdlerization. No doubt misled by its title, 'The Progresse of the Soule', Donne's first editor placed this incomplete and scatological satire first, followed by the devotional sonnets. 'It is no surprise', wrote Arthur Marotti, 'that the collected verse of the recently deceased Dean of St. Paul's would begin with poems signaling their author's interest in the spiritual life'. The most obviously bawdy poems, 'To his Mistris Going to Bed', 'Love's Progresse', and 'Love's Warre', which were, as Marotti points out, 'circulating freely in manuscript and ... especially popular in university students' manuscript anthologies' were completely censored. The love poems most valued today were placed discreetly towards the back of the volume; but the poems classified as epigrams and elegies, however erotic, could more safely precede them as exercises in classical imitation.[3] But when Donne's poems were re-collected in 1635, this tactical and ethical construction was replaced by a strict generical reclassification, and the love-poems took pride of place at the beginning of the volume, under a section heading, 'Songs and Sonets', that deliberately recalled one of the most famous early collections of English lyrics. For what is now usually referred to as *Tottel's Miscellany* was originally published by Richard Tottel in 1557 as *Songes and Sonettes*, *written by the ryght honorable Lorde Henry Haward late Earle of Surrey, and other.*

Jonson's *Under-wood*, published under the supervision of Sir Kenelm Digby, invoked a different miscellany tradition. Or rather, it invoked two different contradictory principles of arrangement, one asserted by the author, one by the text. That asserted by the author was a published note 'To the Reader' in the posthumous 1640 edition of Jonson's *Works*, which has nevertheless been taken as evidence that toward the end of his life Jonson himself had begun to arrange his so-far unpublished poems:

> With the same leave, the Ancients call'd that kind of body Sylva, or γλη, in which there were workes of divers nature, and matter congested; as the multitude call Timber-trees, promiscuously growing, a Wood or Forrest: so am I bold to entitle these lesser Poems, of later growth, by this of Under-wood, out of the Analogie they hold to the Forrest, in my former booke, and no otherwise.
>
> Ben Io[h]nson[4]

In other words, in relating *The Under-wood* to his first collection of lyrics and verse epistles, published in 1616 under the title of *The Forrest*, Jonson both explained his governing tree-metaphor in terms of the classical *sylva*, and suggested a deliberate indiscrimination, in which variety ('workes of divers nature') is attested not by the separation of genres but by their promiscuity, a term which still (and still more strongly than the comparable 'miscellany' or 'miscellaneous') carried its Latin meaning of *disorderly* mixture. If, as seems to be the case, Jonson here exaggerated the variousness of the classical *sylva* into actual disarray, his note 'To the Reader' certainly misleads; for in fact *The Under-wood*, though set in a frame of Christian and classical poems on death, eternity, grace and the quiet life, consists largely of occasional poems arranged in a roughly chronological order, with some ostentatious datings in the titles of poems or the margins of the page. With this discovery, *Under-wood* becomes intelligible as an autobiographical act, a form of recollection that is also inevitably a form of history-writing. As Jonson recorded his experiences with the state, the stage, friends, patrons, politicians, other men's publications, he told the story of James's reign from 1614, when Sir Walter Ralegh's *History of the World* was published and promptly suppressed by the King, and that of Charles I through

1635. Admitting as he went his own role as a poet 'Mendicant' in a patronage culture, Jonson may have attempted, through recollecting his occasional poems and making them speak to the larger issues of clientage, to reclaim the integrity he had lost by writing them.

When Marvell's *Miscellaneous Poems* appeared in the spring of 1681, about two and a half years after his death, this volume too carried a note 'To the Reader'. If Jonson's was disingenuous, this has been called a downright lie:

> These are to Certifie every Ingenious Reader, that all these Poems, as also the other things in this book contained, are Printed according to the exact Copies of my late dear Husband, under his own Hand-Writing, being found since his Death among his other Papers, Witness my Hand this 15th day of October, 1680.

> Mary Marvell

In 1726 Thomas Cooke stated that the volume was 'published with no other than a mercenary View; and indeed not at all to the Honour of the deceased, by a Woman with whom he lodged, who hoped by this Strategem, to share in what he left behind him. He was never married'.[5] In 1938 F.S. Tupper declared that Mary Palmer's claim to Marvell's name was indeed a fiction, part of a ploy involving Marvell's business associates, and discovered rival claims on a bond for £500 that was tied up in his estate.[6] It was merely an inference, however, that the publication of the poems was motivated by greed, a 'mere move in the game of obtaining credence for the widowhood'.[7] And there seems to have been a further inference derogatory to Mary Palmer, that because those who quarrelled with her over money described her as a person 'of mean condition' and no education, it was not only incredible that Marvell should have married her[8] but likely that the arrangement of the volume was unreliable. H.M. Margoliouth, Marvell's first great modern editor, therefore felt free to restructure the collection, on what it must be admitted are inconsistent principles. On the one hand, he worked by genre, trying to get the pastoral dialogues together, moving four prose epitaphs to the end of the volume and the single letter to the second volume, with the rest of Marvell's correspondence; on the other, 'satirical, commendatory and political poems' were 'collected together and arranged in chronological order'.[9]

We do not, however, need to go this route. Whether Mary Palmer 'Marvell' carried to the printer a single manuscript or a bundle of papers, someone not without intelligence arranged the contents of the *Miscellaneous Poems* in a way that belies their title. And there are other facts about the volume and the circumstances in which it appeared that deserve reconsideration. Prime among these is the extraordinary fact that the 'Cromwell poems' – 'An Horatian Ode upon Cromwell's Return from Ireland', 'The First Anniversary of the Government under O.C.' and 'A Poem upon the Death of O.C.' – were cancelled while the volume was actually in press, surviving only in two known copies. Even in those copies, the second half of the elegy (lines 185–324) for Cromwell was missing and may never have been set, perhaps indicating with some precision the point at which the publisher lost his nerve. The motives for publication and for cancellation cannot be entirely unconnected; between lies the question of the volume's arrangement and its possible significance.

There are two connected points of emphasis in the volume's front matter. One is the reminder, on the title page, that the author was 'Late Member of the Honourable House of Commons'; the other is Mary 'Marvell's' specification of the date: 15 October 1680. What links them is the recent history of the English Parliament in its struggles to survive as an institution, as a constitutional force, against the will of Charles II, who would have much preferred to rule without its interference. In that conflict Marvell had played a part, by publishing in the winter of 1676–77 his *Account of the Growth of Popery and Arbitrary Government*,[10] which, though published anonymously, was widely suspected to be his. In a letter written to his nephew William Popple on 10 June 1678 Marvell ironically described the reception of the *Account* as if he were speaking of someone else: 'Three or four printed Books since have described, *as near as it was proper to go*, the Man being a Member of Parliament, Mr. Marvell to have been the Author; but if he had, surely he should not have escaped being questioned in Parliament, or some other Place'.[11] This displacement of the self from the authorial position, the place of accountability, is both another device for maintaining anonymity (something which Marvell seems to have incorporated at a deeper psychic level than political prudence alone required) and inseparable from a pride in the role ('the Man being a Member of Parliament'). And we can perhaps best understand this pride by remembering not Marvell's near silence in debate, nor even his painstaking but colourless reports to his Hull constituency, but by his defence of the most famous or notorious of the Caroline Parliaments. In the second part of the *Rehearsal Transpros'd*, Marvell had responded to Samuel Parker's charge that the 1628 Parliament were 'notorious Rebels'; whereas, wrote Marvell, it had been described to him by 'unprejudiced men' as:

> an Assembly of the most Loyal, Prudent, and Upright English spirits that any age could have produced. Their actions are upon Record, and by them ... will posterity judge concerning them. And if we had not other effects and Laws from them but *the Petition of Right*, it were sufficient to eternize their memory among all men that wear an English heart in their bosome.[12]

Sir Roger L'Estrange, the indefatigable Surveyor of the Press,[13] who had failed to suppress the first *Rehearsal Transpros'd* because Charles II had himself intervened in its favour,[14] subsequently focused his efforts on the *Account*. Having offered a fifty-pound reward for information as to the *Account*'s printer, publisher or author, he published his own refutation, *An Account of the Growth of Knavery*, and hinted at the author's identity by calling him a 'Merry Andrew'.[15] L'Estrange did imprison Marvell's printer; but on August 23, 1678, just after Marvell died, he indicated defeat. Writing to Sir Joseph Williamson, Secretary of State, L'Estrange complained:

> with much difficulty I have found out the Widow Brewsters Lodging. I can prove against her, the bringing of Three Libells to the Presse in Manuscript: ... upon which Accompt, she hath so long conceld her selfe. She is in the House of a person formerly an officer under Cromwell: one that writes three or foure very good Hands ... From which Circumstances one may fayrly presume that all those Delicate Copyes, which Brewster carried to the Presse, were written by Brewsters Land Lord, and Copyed by him, from the Authour. Beside that it is very probable, that the late Libells concerning the Growth of Popery, and the List of the Members of Parliament past through the same hands. ... If she be questiond, probably shee will cast the whole, upon Mr Marvell, who is lately dead; and there the enquiry ends.[16]

This letter tells an important story about the activities of the opposition press during L'Estrange's tenure, and especially about his belief that the personnel engaged in surreptitious printing were Commonwealthmen, with a direct personal link backwards to the governmental and civil service structure under Cromwell. Such a belief (the antithetical corollary to the conspiracy theory that Marvell himself promoted in the *Account*) has obvious bearing on the cancellation of the 'Cromwell' poems from Marvell's *Miscellaneous Poems* in 1681, by which time his *Account* had been republished under his name. It also involves a theory of the posthumous work as a special problem for the censor. As L'Estrange put it in another violent published attack, he was obliged to reprint his reply, 'the *other side* having reviv'd the occasion of it, since the death of *Andrew Marvell*, by a *Posthumous Impression*, with his name at length to it.' And among the motives he listed for this second edition of the *Account*, which included capitalizing on the emergence of the Popish Plot, L'Estrange suggested bitterly that his friends intended 'to *Canonize* Mr. *Marvell* (now in his grave) if not for a *Saint*, yet for a *Prophet*, that foretold the *Growth of Fanaticism*, as well as he did the *Growth of Popery*'.[17]

L'Estrange's wrestling with the ghost of Marvell makes it clear that anything that appeared, with the new immunity of the posthumous, under his name would have carried an ideological freight. But, in addition, the consistently Parliamentary emphasis of these documents serves as a complex gloss on the title-page of the *Miscellaneous Poems* and the date at which Mary 'Marvell' affirmed her 'late dear Husband' as their author. For on 21 October, just under a week after the date she specified, that same 'Honourable House of Commons' was due to be recalled for the first time since mid-May 1679. Since one of Marvell's arguments in the *Account* was that Charles had been using the device of prorogation to *de facto* nullify the constitution, it was much to the point that the October Parliament followed the frustration of more than a year's recess; that on January 18, 1681 Charles again dissolved it, and summoned a new (and presumably more tractable) Parliament to meet at Oxford on March 21; and that on March 28 this too was dissolved. As H.T. Swedenberg put it, recounting these events as the context of Dryden's *Absalom and Achitophel*, 'there would be no further meeting during the reign of Charles II'.[18] It is also to the point that Marvell's *Miscellaneous Poems* were advertised for sale in January 1681 and that a copy owned by Narcissus Luttrell is dated January 18, the very day of the London Parliament's dissolution.

The context of Marvell's volume was, then, the same as that of *Absalom and Achitophel*; that is to say, the Popish Plot and its aftermath, in which the Whigs in Parliament, led by Shaftesbury, attempted to exclude the Roman Catholic James, Duke of York, from the succession. Confused rumours of the Plot were already circulating in the week that Marvell died, in August 1678, and the affair reached some kind of conclusion in July 1681, when the Whigs had definitively lost the battle in the Oxford Parliament, and Shaftesbury was arrested on a charge of treason. We can get some sense of how intricate was this context by noting that, on the very same page of the *London Gazette* for March 21–15, 1678 which carried L'Estrange's advertisement for information about those responsible for Marvell's *Account*, there appeared another, for *All for Love: Or, the World well Lost. A Tragedy, as it is Acted at the Theatre Royal . . . By John Dryden, Servant to His Majesty.* Dedicated to the Earl of Danby, Charles's chief minister, the published text of the play used the occasion to inveigh against republicanism, past and present:

> Both my Nature, as I am an Englishman, and my Reason, as I am a Man, have bred in me a loathing to that specious Name of a Republick: that mock-appearance of a Liberty, where all who have not part in the Government, are Slaves: and Slaves they are of a viler note than such as are Subjects to an absolute Dominion. For no Christian Monarchy is so absolute, but 'tis circumscrib'd with Laws: But when the Executive Power is in the Law-makers, there is no farther check upon them.

Citing Satan as the source of all rebellion, and clearly alluding to Shaftesbury as 'He who has often chang'd his Party' and so 'gives little evidence of his sincerity for the Publick Good', Dryden also looked backwards, as many would do during the Exclusion crisis, to the revolutionary period of the 1640s and 50s:

> they who trouble the Waters first, have seldom the benefit of the Fishing: As they who began the late Rebellion, enjoy'd not the fruit of their undertaking, but were crush'd themselves by the Usurpation of their own Instrument. Neither is it enough for them to answer that they only intend a Reformation of the Government, but not the Subversion of it: On such pretences all Insurrections have been founded.[19]

The sweep of his allusions therefore included not only Cromwell, the Usurping Instrument of the Long Parliament; not only, in all probability, John Milton, whose epic on the first great rebel, Satan, had been republished in 1674 with a commendatory poem by Marvell; but also Marvell himself, whose 'First Anniversary' of Cromwell's government, and specifically of the parliamentary legislation of the 'Instrument of Government', had been published in January 1655. It was surely no coincidence that Dryden, who had struggled with Marvell for control of the media in the years of the Great Fire and the second Dutch war,[20] referred to republican leaders as 'they who trouble the waters first'. For Marvell's 'First Anniversary' had concluded with these lines of praise for Cromwell:

> ... thou thy venerable Head dost raise
> As far above their Malice as my Praise.
> And as the Angel of our Commonweal,
> Troubling the Waters, yearly mak'st them heal.
>
> (p. 129)

These last years of Charles II's regime, in other words, exhibit a culture marked by intense political friction, in which texts supposedly separated by the literary-extraliterary divide in fact spoke to each other in debate, and contested with each other, again, the major issues of political theory and value that had first been articulated in fully partisan terms forty years earlier, and were now perceived as returned from the grave to haunt the Restoration government.

This being so, we may infer that it would have been impossible for Marvell's *Miscellaneous Poems* to appear when they did, with precisely those preliminaries, without exciting the political imagination. And there is some evidence to suggest that those who carried it to the printer knew this. In the business dealings uncovered by Tupper, it appears that both Thompson and Nelthorpe, the bankrupt bankers whom Marvell, with the assistance of Mary Marvell, concealed in secret lodgings in the spring of 1678, were connected to political activists on the side of Shaftesbury;[21] Tupper observed that 'Thompson's brother-in-law, 'reputed to be a great fanatick', put him more intimately into the group of anti-Royalist plotters than we had realized'; while Robert Boulter, who printed the *Miscellaneous Poems*, was actually arrested in July 1681 for seditious talk, saying that 'he did not question to see the monarchy reduced into a commonwealth and very speedily'.[22] It is most unlikely, therefore, that Mary Palmer's motives were purely (or impurely) mercenary; most probably she collaborated with Thompson and Boulter in a decision to publish Marvell's poems at a moment calculated to assist the cause to which he had devoted the last ten years of his life. Certainly the volume was of particular interest to a particular group: as Anthony à Wood reported, Marvell was already 'a celebrated wit among the fanatics', and his poems, when published, 'were taken into the hands of many persons *of his persuasion*, and by them cried up as excellent'.[23]

It ought to be registered here, however, that Marvell's 'persuasion', though clear, was not as narrowly defined as L'Estrange, Dryden and Wood assume. It seems to have included a certain brand of imaginative sympathy for Charles I, classical republicanism, strong support for Cromwell's authoritarian Protectorate, an equally strong aversion to the Restoration, and a more less continuous identification with Puritan or Nonconformist thought, *provided that* its bearers were not in a position of strength. This latitudinarianism, and its theoretical relation both to historical understanding and polemic, had been carefully if somewhat disingenuously expressed in the first part of the *Rehearsal Transpros'd*, where Marvell accused Samuel Parker of distorting the historical record of the 1640s in order 'to prove that the late War was wholly upon a Fanatical Cause, and the dissenting party do still goe big with the same Monster'. In response, Marvell claims to have 'hereupon' begun his own instruction in that history, in order to speak objectively:

> I grew hereupon much displeased with my own ignorance of the occasion of those Troubles so near our own times, and betook my self to get the best Information concerning them, to the end that I might, if it appear'd so, decline the dangerous acquaintance of the Nonconformists, some of whom I had taken for honest men, nor therefore avoided their Company. But I took care nevertheless, not to receive Impressions from any of their party; but to gather my lights from the most impartial Authorities that I could meet with.[24]

It is worth noticing that Mary 'Marvell' addressed herself not to a particular group, whether Whigs or Nonconformists, but to

198 The Political Identity of Andrew Marvell

'every Ingenious Reader'. This word was of peculiar significance in Marvell's personal lexicon. For him it meant a complex of values derived from the classical *ingenium*, and perhaps particularly associated with Cicero: natural talent, verbal wit, genius, political intelligence. These qualities were capable of crossing political or other boundaries. In 1676 Marvell defended Bishop Herbert Croft, author of *The Naked Truth*, against his detractors, and in the course of that defence had defined the religious polemicist as one 'to whom the bishop shall commit *omne et omnimodum suum ingenium*' (absolutely all his wit).[25] A true 'fanatic', we might say, would have had nothing to do with bishops. Likewise, at the beginning of his career as a writer Marvell had defended Richard Lovelace's *Lucasta* against *its* detractors, and in the process equated being ingenious with cultural toleration. Intolerance, Marvell's commendatory poem asserted, was a most unfortunate product of the Civil War:

Our times are much degenerate from those
Which your sweet Muse which your fair Fortune chose,
And as complexions alter with the Climes,
Our wits have drawne th'infection of our times.
That candid Age no other way could tell
To be ingenious, but by speaking well.
Who best could prayse, had then the greatest prayse.
'Twas more esteemd to give, then weare the Bayes:

These vertues now are banisht out of Towne,
Our Civill Wars have lost the Civicke crowne.

The barbed Censurers begin to looke
Like the grim consistory on thy Booke;
And on each line cast a reforming eye,
Severer than the yong Presbytery.

Some reading your *Lucasta* will alledge
You wong'd in her the Houses Priviledge.
Some that you under sequestration are,
Because you write when going to the Warr,
And one the Book prohibits, because *Kent*
Their first Petition by the Authour sent.[26]

So Marvell in 1649 had played with the notion that a collection of lyric poems ought to be immune from political censorship, a neutral event to be read independently of its author's political reputation, and identified those who thought otherwise (by analogy) with the most intolerant aspects of Presbyterianism. When Mary 'Marvell' addressed herself to 'every ingenious Reader', then, she may have been appealing to the same principles; if so, we must read the failure of this appeal in the fact that the 'Cromwell' poems were, after all, banished from the volume.

We shall probably never know to what extent this was an act of self-censorship. Neil Keeble has documented the way in which L'Estrange could intimidate a bookseller. At the time of the controversy involving bishop John Bramhall, the Nonconformist John Owen, Samuel Parker and Marvell himself, Baxter had thought to contribute yet another phase to the dispute:

> But Mr. [Nevill] Simmons, my Bookseller, came to me, and told me, That Roger Lestrange, the Over-seer of the Printers, sent for him, and told him, That he heard I was Answering Bishop Bromhall, and Swore to him most vehemently, that if I did it, he would ruin him and me, and perhaps my Life should be brought in question: And I perceivd the Bookseller durst not Print it, and so I was fain to cast it by.[27]

According to Pierre Legouis, it was the defeat of the Whigs over the second Exclusion Bill, and the parliamentary dissolution on January 18, that probably led the printer of the *Miscellaneous Poems* to lose his nerve and cancel the 'Cromwell' poems; and the result was a volume in which, 'sous le titre sans pretention', the public received all of Marvell's work that 'la censure la plus soupçonneuse devait déclarer inoffensifs'.[28] Perhaps. I am not so sure that the remaining contents of the volume were quite so inoffensive; the original order of the poems both speaks to the fear of censorship and survives it. In what remains, the ordering of the items permits messages to emerge that would have been highly acceptable, possibly even helpful, to the temporarily frustrated Opposition.

As in the case of Donne's 1633 *Poems*, the most dangerous material was, or was to have been, placed at the back of the volume; and right up front, (again like Donne's 1633 volume) was a group of eight devotional poems: the most unequivocally inoffensive category of lyric at any time, one might suppose, although the recent paranoia about 'popery' had rendered the *style* of devotion problematic. It was characteristic of Marvell, but it was also wise of the volume's promoters, to confuse initially the question of where the author stood on the definition of the religious life. Several of these poems have apparently Roman Catholic texts or genres as models or analogues: 'On a Drop of Dew' derives from Henry Hawkins's *Partheneia Sacra*, 'A Dialogue between the Soul and Body' from a Jesuit emblem book,[29] 'Eyes and Tears' recalls the Counter-Reformation 'poetry of tears', with its focus on the Magdalene. Yet 'Bermudas' celebrates the escape from 'Prelat's rage' of Puritan settlers in the New World, a theme more obviously appropriate to Marvell's Nonconformist connections. Very close readings may determine that these poems rewrite or modify the positions from which they seem to start, creating a delicate structure of objectivity, if not of non-alignment; and the cursory reader would certainly find nothing he must approve or disapprove, nothing to alarm him.

It is quite startling, however, to see what happens to this group of devotional lyrics in Margoliouth's edition. For after 'Clorinda and Damon', clearly a spiritualized eclogue, a mini-drama of conversion, Margoliouth inserted 'A Dialogue between Thyrsis and Dorinda' on the grounds that it was 'misplaced' in the folio and belonged with 'the other poems of its kind' (1:247). A preliminary distinction between spiritual and secular pastoral is thus destroyed but not, however, for the sake of another kind of consistency, since another pastoral dialogue, 'Ametas and Thestylis making Hay-Ropes', was left in its original place.

That place is within the second obvious grouping, a set of twenty poems, all of which (with one major exception) deal in some form with attraction (usually sexual) to the things of this world (predominantly female). The effect of the group is complicated by the opening and closing poems, 'The Nymph complaining for the death of her Faun' and the two versions of 'The Garden', English and Latin; for the nymph's language always trembles on the brink of spiritual or church-historical allegory, the speaker in the garden is poised for longer flight, and both poems powerfully suggest the liminality of categories of experience, the difficulty of impermeable categorization. Yet the overall effect of the group is of a blend of 'metaphysical' and 'cavalier' modes of poetry, perfectly acceptable to a Restoration audience, and, from a Modernist perspective, revealing Marvell at his best.

As already mentioned, however, this group contains one seeming anomaly, 'Tom May's Death'. The subject of this poem is, in a sense, the posthumous: either the actual death of the poet-historian Thomas May in 1650, or the exhumation of his remains from Westminster Abbey in September 1661, a possibility that would explain these lines:

> If that can be thy home where Spencer lyes
> And reverend Chaucer, but their dust does rise
> Against thee, and expels thee from their side.

> (p. 37)

The poem focuses on May's imagined descent into the underworld, where he is condemned by the ghost of Ben Jonson as a 'servil' wit, and Mercenary Pen', who destroyed his credibility as a writer by turning 'Chronicler to Spartacus', that is to say, the Puritan revolutionaries. Jonson's ghost is cited as singing his own song in the underworld:

> Sounding of ancient Heroes, such as were
> The Subjects Safety, and the Rebel's Fear.
> But how a double headed Vulture Eats,
> Brutus and Cassius the Peoples cheats.

In other words, 'Tom May's Death' uses the ghost of Jonson as a spokesman for the position of L'Estrange and Dryden to renounce all supporters of the Commonwealth; an anomalous poem indeed not merely in this group of amorous lyrics but in Marvell's canon, provided we take the poem at its face value, and assume that 'Jonson' actually spoke for Marvell. If so, the clash between 'Tom May's Death' is evidently less if we posit its composition in 1650, when, to judge from the 'Horatian Ode', Marvell was only preparing himself intellectually for Cromwell's dominance; whereas in 1661 we must also deal with the chronological pre-existence of the 'First Anniversary' and the evidently personalized lament for Cromwell in 1658.

Two escape routes have so far been taken by those whom this poem disturbs. The first (an earlier position of my own) is to read the poem ironically, noting that Marvell himself indulged in precisely the same activity for which 'Jonson's' ghost blames May: drawing historical parallels between contemporary England and republican Rome:

> Go seek the novice Statesmen, and obtrude
> On them some Romane cast similitude,
> Tell them of Liberty, the Stories fine,
> Until you all grow Consuls in your wine.
>
> Transferring old Rome hither in your talk,
>
> Foul Architect that hadst not Eye to see
> How ill the measures of these States agree.

For such a critique to consist, if not with Marvell's *sympathies* in the 'Horatian Ode', at least with his allusive practice, it is necessary to assume that the poem deliberately adopts a reactionary stance, one that was both dramatically appropriate to Jonson as himself a 'Mercenary Pen' to both the earlier Stuarts, and inappropriate to him as the author of the Roman tragedies, *Sejanus* and *Catiline*. If Marvell wrote this poem, so the argument for irony goes, he was not so much contradicting himself as continuing the practice of historical analogy (and implying its inevitability) under the guise of inveighing against it. And at the heart of its message, then, we can place not the dismissal of May to everlasting torment, but 'Jonson's' definition of the true historian, who 'Sings still of ancient Rights and better Times': a phrase that was already ambiguous in 1650, when the 'Horatian Ode' could imagine Justice pleading 'the ancient Rights in vain'. Ancient rights or liberties had most often been asserted by parliamentarians as an appeal to law against prerogative and an utopian rhetorical strategy,[30] and by 1681 the phrase had also acquired a currency in the literature of Nonconformity.[31]

The second escape route is to assume that the poem is not Marvell's; and indeed its canonical status has been thrown into question by the discovery that it was carefully excised from the 'Popple' manuscript of Marvell's poems, a manuscript that almost certainly derives from the family of Marvell's beloved nephew William Popple, and appears to be a copy of the *Miscellaneous Poems* amended in preparation for a new edition.[32] Yet the central editorial tradition has retained the poem as Marvell's, while moving it, following Margoliouth, to a new group of 'satirical, commendatory and political poems' for which some date could be ascertained or conjectured. The effect of such a move is to increase the apparent conflict with the 'Horatian Ode', which thereby precedes it in the reader's experience. But there remains a third, compromise hypothesis. Let us suppose that 'Tom May's Death' appeared in the *Miscellaneous Poems* in 1681 as a form of insurance, and was placed among the other 'Cavalier' poems as a sign (to the cursory and unsophisticated reader) of the volume's political intentions; it might then have been removed from the 'Popple' text, early in the eighteenth century, as a precautionary device no longer needed, all too capable, as its subsequent critical history has shown, of distorting Marvell's then-growing reputation as the patriotic Whig historian.

After the 'Cavalier' poems, the 1681 volume offered its readers a group of poems that were obviously difficult to categorize by theme or mode of experience, yet that share the premise of *literary* occasion:[33] the Latin response to the graphologist Joseph de Maniban, who had analysed Marvell's handwriting; the satire on Richard Fleckno, author of 'hideous verse' inflicted on Marvell during a visit to Rome: the Latin and English compliments to Dr. Robert Witty on his translation of the *Popular Errors* in medical thought, the wonderful poem 'On Mr. *Milton's* Paradise Lost'; and a handful of occasional Latin epigrams. Again, it would be difficult for a reader to determine with any certainty what Marvell's 'persuasion' was by attempting an ideological analysis. The connection with Milton, and the implied attack on Dryden as 'the Town-Bays' who intends to 'tag' Milton's lines with rhyme, pull in one direction; the series of epigrams written to commemorate the building of the Louvre by Louis XIV pulls in another. And there is certainly an implied caution against too early or too simple interpretation of authorial character and motive in the first item of this group, the epistle to Maniban, whose English title read: 'To a Gentleman that only upon the sight of the Author's writing, had given a Character of his Person and Judgement of his Fortune', (p. 53). 'Who after this would commit his thoughts to babbling paper', Marvell had jocularly written, in what was essentially a hyperbolic compliment to Maniban:

> If he thought that his fate would be exposed by his pen?
> And if the guilty handwriting might proclaim the fortune
>   of the writer,
> What thing in life would he more wish to have hidden?
> Nevertheless, in the turnings of the reed-pen all things are
>   read spontaneously.

> What the words do not signify, the shape makes
> known.[34]

And if this group opens with an ironic reclusiveness, it also ends with a wish for a life-long anonymity, a translation of a famous chorus from Seneca's *Thyestes* (act 2, end). Its rejection of the 'publick Stage' is, as with Jonson, part classical Stoicism, part pose, part ruse: at the very least a wish that Marvell's real career denied:[35]

> In calm Leisure let me rest;
> And far of the publick Stage
> Pass away my silent Age.
> Thus when without noise, unknown,
> I have liv'd out all my span,
> I shall dye, without a groan,
> An old honest Country man.
> Who expos'd to others Ey's,
> Into his own Heart ne'r pry's,
> Death to him's a Strange surprise.
>
> (p. 64)

The ethos of this poem also serves as a transition to the next grouping in the *Miscellaneous Poems*: a series of epitaphs, in prose and verse, to members of Puritan families and the letter consoling Sir John Trott for the death of one of his sons. These six pieces, all completely dispersed in Margoliouth's edition, supply the credo that was only barely discernible in the opening devotional section. They are all, of course, tributes to Puritan virtues and values: Jane Oxenbridge's '*antiqua modestia*', the '*Honesta Disciplina*' that Edmund Trott acquired from his parents, the unnamed young man who was 'Chearful without Gall, Sober without Formality, Prudent with Stratagem; and Religious without Affectation'; and the unnamed young woman whose life was a reproach to 'this Age loose and al unlac't.' All these make explicit (even if in Latin) what was only implicit in 'Bermudas' but fully developed in Marvell's prose pamphlets of the 1670s, especially *The Rehearsal Transpros'd*: that the Nonconformists were not narrow-minded zealots, but culturally worthy of respect. It is interesting to note, too, that the young John Trott is described as having been 'Ingeniosus supra Fidem', enhancing faith with wit.

And if we wonder why the letter to his bereaved father appears here in such splendid *formal* isolation[36] (made more splendid by the hugely bold type that introduces it), the answer may lie in a peculiarly ingenious form of topicality. When Marvell originally wrote the letter in 1667, he was obsessed, as we know from his satires, by the debacle of the Second Dutch War and the role in that disaster of Edward Hyde, then Chancellor, later Earl of Clarendon. It was that preoccupation that no doubt explained his peculiar illustration of bereavement by the story of Eli who 'had been Chancellor, and in effect King of Israel, for so many years':

> he heard that Israel was overcome, that his two Sons Hophni and Phineas were slain in one day, and saw himself without hope of Issue, and which imbittered it further without succession to the Government, yet he fell not till the News that the Ark of God was taken. I pray that we may never have the same paralel perfected in our publick concernments.

> (p. 68)

One has to wonder what consolation Sir John was supposed to derive from this dubious 'paralel' to his own situation. But when the letter was published in 1681, the nature of the parallel had significantly altered. The King was without legal issue, the problem of the succession was foremost in everyone's mind, and the reference to 'publick concernments' would have leaped from the page, in a context of sternly Puritan idealism.

It is not without preparation, then, that the volume proceeds to the character and contributions of another Puritan family – Thomas Lord Fairfax and his wife and daughter, to whom Marvell acted as tutor in 1651–53. The three Fairfax poems retained their natural connection to each other in Margoliouth's edition, excluded for want of confident dating from his chronological reorganization, but not in Lord's, where the 'Epigramma in Duos montes' had to be removed to the section reserved for Latin poems. What they offered, in the original grouping, was a gradually more complex analysis of the competing ideals of the quiet life and of political responsibility, as exemplified by a family that had had singular opportunity to explore them both. 'Upon Appleton House', in particular, can be read as a long apology both for the revolutionary leader who abandoned 'publick concernments' for the pleasure of retirement on his country estate, and for the poet-tutor whose opportunity to share that retirement temporarily made the writing of these poems possible.

But the point of the 'Fairfax poems' is made still clearer when we come to the last section of the *Miscellaneous Poems*, where a political imperative is massively reinstated; or rather, was to have been massively reinstated, until (in all but two surviving copies) the 'Horatian Ode', the 'First Anniversary' and the elegy for Cromwell's death were excised, and replaced by two single leaves, which reprinted what the Scolar Press facsimile referred to as 'the non-Cromwellian parts of the cancelled leaves'.

It would have been more accurate to observe, however, that this last section originally contained, with one exception,[37] poems devoted to the praise of English republicanism, with Cromwell as its presiding genius, or to Cromwell's character as patriarch. The group, as originally represented, begins with naval imperialism, in 'On the Victory obtained by Blake over the Spaniards. . . . 1657', and 'The Character of Holland', probably written early in 1653 as propaganda for the First Dutch War; it proceeds to the 'Horatian Ode' and the 'First Anniversary', telling the story of Cromwell's rise from parliamentary general to Protector. International diplomacy is represented by the poem on Oliver St. John's embassy to the United Provinces, the Latin 'Letter to Doctor Ingelo, then with my Lord Whitlock, Ambassador from the Protector to the Queen of Sweden', and two Latin epigrams on the portrait of himself that Cromwell sent to Queen Christina. The role of Cromwell as the possible founder of a dynasty is then suggested in the 'Two Songs at the Marriage of the Lord Fauconberg and the Lady Mary Cromwell', pastoral dialogues carefully segregated by the location from their *formal* analogues in the first and second sections of the volume. And the series would have ended, appropriately, with 'A Poem upon the Death of O.C.', whose last lines celebrated, however in the event abortively, the succession of 'Richard to Oliver'.

When the major 'Cromwell' poems were excised, the epithalamic songs became the volume's conclusion. Yet their representation of Cromwell as the shepherd Menalca[s] was no less ideological, given what preceded it, than the final elegy would have been. Indeed, in 1681 some of the lesser poems in this group might have been even more significant, at least in terms of topical rereading in the light of later events. The two poems on Anglo-

Dutch relations acquire a certain irony in the knowledge that the First Dutch War had been followed by the Second, in 1664–68, and by the Third in the 1670s; in the knowledge that Marvell had come to take a very different position toward the Dutch, both in his *Last Instructions to a Painter* in 1667, and especially in the *Account* by which time he had become convinced that the Third Dutch War was merely a ploy to conceal the sinister dealings between Charles II and Louis XIV of France. Similarly, the epic alliance that Marvell had envisaged in 1653 between Cromwell and Queen Christina was to have had as its objective an anti-Catholic campaign in Europe. The difference between those hopes and the facts of 1681 was, from the perspective of a 'Member of the Honourable House of Commons', all too apparent.

It is worth noticing, finally, that the Latin epigram on Oliver St. John's mission to the Dutch reintroduces Mary 'Marvell's' mode of address to the reader. 'Ingeniosa Viris contingunt Nomina magnis', Marvell had written in 1651, intending to play ingeniously on the ambassador's name, especially its fortuitous connection with Oliver Cromwell. But the epigram also assumes a principle of encoding. 'Chance', Marvell continued, 'covers truth under a prophetic name'; and since the republic has entrusted its diplomacy to a man so mysterious named,

> Non opus Arcanos Chartis committere Sensus,
> Et varia licitos condere Fraude Dolos.
> Tu quoque si taceas tamen est Legatio Nomen
> Et velut in Scytale publica verba refert.

> (p. 130)

> [It is not necessary to commit arcane meanings to paper, and conceal licit stratagems with multiple deceit. Even if you say nothing, your name is an embassy; and just as in Scytale it carries public significance.]

I think we could probably say the same for the naming that appeared on the title page of the 1681 folio; and as in the art of Scytale, an ancient Spartan form of code, the message could only be read when wound on a staff of a particular shape and size, so the meaning of the 1681 folio depends in part on its structure. 'What the words do not signify, the shape makes known'. In fact, as the relationship between *respublica* and *publica verba* is an extraordinarily complex one, not only in English political history, but also in language theory and ideas of representation, one might venture the larger statement, however rhetorically crude, that the original shape of the volume *was* its meaning in 1681.

In it, a peculiar relation is asserted between poems of a certain kind or 'persuasion', and historical time or chronology; or perhaps more strictly, a relation between different 'times' and cultural formations. The republican poems put prudently at the back of the volume constitute the only grouping that draws attention to the need for historical analysis, and does so with the insistence of Jonson's *Under-wood*. Between Mary 'Marvell's' opening insistence on October 15, 1680 and the poem on Blake's victory, firmly dated 1657, there is only one date in the entire volume, hidden in the prose elegy for Jane Oxenbridge, who happened to die in the same year as Cromwell (p. 65). But the 'Horatian Ode upon Cromwell's Return from Ireland' and 'The First Anniversary of the Government under O.C.' carry their dates implicitly in their titles and insist on the theme of historical time and change in their opening lines; and 'A Letter to Doctor Ingelo, *then* with my Lord Whitlock, Ambassador from the Protector to the Queen of Sweden' explicitly, in its 'then', invokes that same look backward, that sense of the continuity in the republican tradition, that those of Marvell's 'persuasion' and those who feared them were constantly evoking. It bears obvious relation to the 'poet's time', the phrase that appeared in 'Tom May's Death' at the heart of a positive definition of historicist activity.

It is not, evidently, the same as a literary-historical chronology. This is not to devalue Margoliouth's edition, the object of which was to show as far as possible the shape of Marvell's career as a poet and hence the importance of compositional order, when determinable. It is to revalue the *Miscellaneous Poems* as a legitimate source of information about Marvell, a source whose interest involves both reception history and a flexible theory of intention. If Marvell did not himself arrange his poems in the way we find them in the *Miscellaneous Poems*, leading his readers from an innocuous and catholic devotion to worldliness, and from there through private versions of puritanism to the more unstable model of Fairfaxian politics in retreat, until they arrived at active republicanism, it was done by someone who knew his work and its import extremely well.

Notes

1. I refer to the opening sentence of Stephen Greenblatt's *Shakespearean Negotiations: The Circulation of Social Energy in Renaissance England*, Berkeley and Los Angeles: University of California Press, 1988, p. 1.
2. See John T. Shawcross, 'The Arrangement and Order of John Donne's Poems', in *Poems in their Place*, ed. Neil Fraistat, Chapel Hill: University of North Carolina Press, 1986, pp. 119–63, especially pp. 141–42.
3. Arthur Marotti, 'John Donne, Author', *Journal of Medieval and Renaissance Studies* 19 (1989), p. 71.
4. Ben Jonson, *Works*, ed. C.H. Herford and Percy and Evelyn Simpson, Oxford: Clarendon Press, 1947, 8:16. For Jonson's editors' view that this statement implied Jonson's own preparation of the *Under-wood*, see *Works*, 11:47–48.
5. Thomas Cooke, *The Works of Andrew Marvell Esq.*, London, 1726, 1:36.
6. Fred S. Tupper, 'Mary Palmer, alias Mrs. Andrew Marvell', *PMLA* 53 (1938), 367–92.
7. H.M. Margoliouth, ed., *The Poems and Letters of Andrew Marvell*, 1927: revised Pierre Legouis, Oxford: Clarendon Press, 1971, 1:242.
8. See Hilton Kelliher, *Andrew Marvell, Poet and Politician*, London: The British Library, 1978, p. 115, who himself notes more circumspectly that 'unfortunately the church register that might have substantiated her claim is now missing'.
9. *Poems and Letters*, 1:225. Subsequently George de F. Lord, ed., *Andrew Marvell: Complete Poetry*, New York: Modern Library, 1968, opted for a more rigorous generic arrangement, and Elizabeth Story Donno for 'chronological order in so far as this can be ascertained'; see *Andrew Marvell: The Complete Poems*, Harmondsworth, Middlesex: Penguin Books, 1972, p. 11. In 1969 Scolar Press published a facsimile of the 1681 edition, from which, for the special purposes of this argument, all quotations of Marvell's poetry will be cited.
10. For Marvell's *Account* as a story of how parliamentary government in England had been undermined by Charles and his ministers, see my *Marvell and the Civic Crown*, Princeton: Princeton University Press, 1978, pp. 221–52.
11. *Poems and Letters*, 2:357.
12. *The Rehearsal Transpros'd; and The Rehearsal Transpros'd. The Second Part*, ed. D.I.B. Smith, Oxford: Clarendon Press, 1971, p. 223 (italics original).

13. For the activities of L'Estrange and their relation to Marvell, see N.H. Keeble, *The Literary Culture of Nonconformity in Later Seventeenth-Century England*, Athens, Ga.: University of Georgia Press, 1987, pp. 102–119. Keeble also describes the effects of the 'Clarendon Code' against dissenters, (pp. 46–47) and the various strategies for evading censorship (manuscript circulation, anonymous publication, false foreign imprints, clandestine presses, and 'plurisignation', or ambiguously referential writing, pp. 110–20). For my own discussion of functional ambiguity throughout the seventeenth century, see *Censorship and Interpretation*, Madison, Wis.: University of Wisconsin Press, 1984.

14. See Keeble, p. 114; and D.I.B. Smith, ed., *The Rehearsal Transpros'd*, xx-xxv. The *Second Part* was published with no difficulty over Marvell's name.

15. Sir Roger L'Estrange, *An Account of the Growth of Knavery*, London, 1678, p. 3. Likewise *A Letter from Amsterdam*, dated '18 April 1678', indicated that Marvell's authorship was known: 'I am sorry we have lost the *Prime* Pen; therefore make sure of Andrew . . . 'Tis well he is now Transprosed into Politicks', (p. 5).

16. Cited in Kelliher, *Andrew Marvell*, p. 113, from Public Record Office, SP 29/406, f. 49.

17. L'Estrange, *The Parallel or, An Account of the Growth of Knavery*, London, 1679, 'Address to the Reader'. For an account of the Popish Plot that indeed begins with a quotation from Marvell but discounts his theory that Catholicism was a serious threat, see John Kenyon, *The Popish Plot*, London: Heinemann, 1972, pp. 1, 21. In an essay like mine it is impossible not to work within Marvell's own assumptions; but Kenyon's work helps to provide balance, not least in its view of the House of Commons as second only to Titus Oates and his accomplices in irresponsible malice against Catholics.

18. H.T. Swedenberg, Jr., ed., *The Works of John Dryden: Poems 1681–1684*, Berkeley and Los Angeles: University of California Press, 1972, Vol. 2 of *Works*, p. 224.

19. Dryden, *All for Love, Oedipus, Troilus and Cressida*, eds. Maximilian E. Novak and George E. Guffey, Berkeley and Los Angeles: University of California Press, 1984, Vol. 13 of *Works*, pp. 6–7.

20. Dryden's hatred of Marvell is well-attested, and full of the signs of a conspiracy theory involving a continuous opposition. In his 'Epistle to the Whigs' prefatory to *The Medal*, 1682, Dryden remarked that much of the recent *No-Protestant Plot* 'is stolen, from your dead Authour's Pamphlet call'd, the *Growth of Popery*'; and in the preface to *Religio Laici*, 1682, Dryden extended the retroactive history of party back to the 1580s, referring to 'Martin Mar-Prelate (the Marvel of those times)' as 'the first Presbyterian Scribler, who

sanctify'd Libels and Scurrility to the use of the Good Old Cause',
(b1).

21. Tupper, 'Mary Palmer', pp. 368, 372 n.
22. See *Poems and Letters*, 1:241. cited from *Calendar of State Papers
Domestic*, 1680/1, pp. 382, 385–86.
23. Anthony à Wood, *Athenae Oxonienses*, ed. Philip Bliss, London:
F.C. and J. Rivington, 1813–20, 4:239; italics added.
24. *Rehearsal Transpros'd*, p. 125.
25. *Mr. Smirke: Or, The Divine in Mode*, London, 1676, in *Complete
Works*, ed. A.B. Grosart, London: Robson and Sons, 1875, 4:8–9.
26. The poem, not included in the *Miscellaneous Poems*, is cited from
Poems and Letters, 1:2–3. It refers to the sequestration of Lovelace's
estate by the Long Parliament as punishment for his part in the
royalist military campaign, and to his involvement in the first Kent-
ish Petition on behalf of the king. *Lucasta* was granted a licence on
February 4, 1648, but not registered for actual publication until
mid-May 1649. The delay was obviously caused by his arrest in
April 1648 by the parliamentary forces led by Fairfax. He was
finally released on April 10, 1649, and the sequestration of his estate
remitted by the House of Commons on May 5.
27. Keeble, *The Literary Culture of Nonconformity*, p. 105. On self-
censorship, see also Christopher Hill, 'Censorship and English
Literature', in *Writing and Revolution in Seventeenth-Century
England: The Collected Essays of Christopher Hill*, Vol. 1, Amherst,
Mass.: University of Massachusetts Press, 1985, pp. 32–71.
28. Pierre Legouis, *André Marvell: poète, puritain, patriote, 1621–1678*,
Paris: Henri Didier, and London: Oxford University Press, 1928,
p. 428.
29. For the relationship between Marvell's dewdrop and one of the
sacred emblems in *Partheneia Sacra*, Rouen, 1633, see Rosalie M.
Colie, *'My Ecchoing Song': Andrew Marvell's Poetry of Criticism*,
Princeton: Princeton University Press, 1970, pp. 115–17; for the
'source' of his soul-body debate in Hermann Hugo, *Pia Desideria*,
Antwerp, 1614, another Jesuit emblem book, see Kitty Scoular
Datta, 'New Light on Marvell's "Dialogue between the Soul and
Body" ', *Renaissance Quarterly* 22 (1969), 242–55.
30. See, for instance, the speech of Thomas Hedley in the 1610 Parliament, which ended by appealing to 'the ancient freedom and liberty
of the subject of England, which appeareth and is confirmed by the
great Charter of the liberties of England', in *Proceedings in Parliament, 1610*, ed. Elizabeth Read Foster, 2 vols., New Haven: Yale
University Press, 1966, 2:190.
31. John Howe called the Second Conventicle Act of 1670 an attack on
Magna Carta; another pamphlet of 1670 was entitled *The Peoples*

Antient and Just Liberties Asserted; see Keeble, pp. 47, 87. Marvell himself, in *The Rehearsal Transpros'd*, asserted that the 'Episcopal Cavalier party' was attempting to subvert 'the great Charter of Christian Liberty', (p. 246), a clear transfer of parliamentary appeal to Magna Carta to the issues of religious toleration; and we might additionally note Milton's assertion, in the preliminaries to the 1674 edition of *Paradise Lost*, of the 'ancient liberty recover'd to Heroic Poem from the troublesom and modern bondage of Rimeing'.

32. The status of the Bodleian manuscript, Eng. poet. d. 49, remains a matter of debate. For the most recent discussion, see Warren L. Chernaik, *The Poet's Time: Politics and Religion in the Work of Andrew Marvell*, Cambridge: Cambridge University Press, 1983, pp. 206–9.

33. This may have inspired George de F. Lord to create a category of poems on 'Poets and Heroes', which are, however, separated from 'Poems in Latin and Greek', thereby breaking down the initial cluster.

34. The translation is by William A. McQueen and Kiffin A. Rockwell, *The Latin Poetry of Andrew Marvell*, Chapel Hill: University of North Carolina Press, 1964, p. 31.

35. For Marvell's continual struggle between the imperatives of self-concealment and political commitment, see *Marvell and the Civic Crown*, especially pp. 10–12, 195.

36. In Margoliouth's edition it was removed to the second volume of correspondence.

37. The exception is 'Thyrsis and Dorinda'. This poem was, however, excised from the Popple manuscript, and recent scholarship has discovered manuscript versions of it too early for Marvell's authorship. See Chernaik, *The Poet's Time*, p. 207.

Index

The index to a collection such as this raises the problem of terminology control in a particularly acute form. The reader should therefore note that standardization has been imposed and on occasion the term in the index may not be exactly that on the page.

Although notes appear as endnotes, they have been indexed as though they were footnotes. That is, where an index entry directs the reader to that part of the text where the note number occurs, the note is not separately indexed unless it contains substantial additional material.

The individual works of Andrew Marvell appear under their own titles to allow for subheadings under those extensively discussed.

Modern authors are shown with initials only to distinguish them from earlier writers whose names are given in full. Those with titles appear under that name by which they are most generally known.

Averil Condren

218   Index